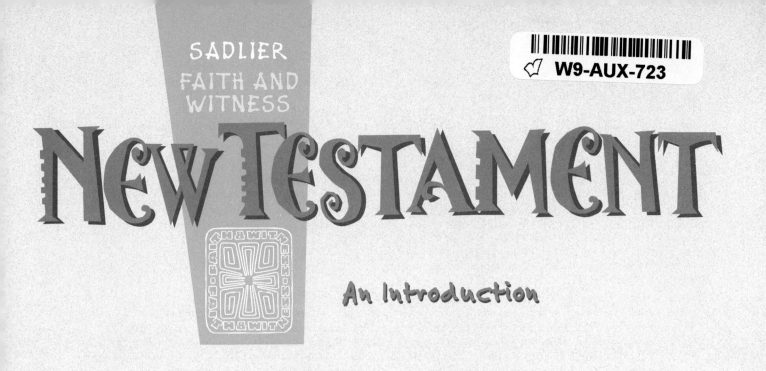

SADLIER
FAITH AND
WITNESS

New Testament

An Introduction

Annotated Edition

Guide Writer

Gloria Hutchinson

Text Authors

Norman F. Josaitis, S.T.D.

Rev. Michael J. Lanning, O.F.M.

Special Consultant

Mary Ann Getty, S.T.D.

William H. Sadlier, Inc.
9 Pine Street
New York, New York 10005-1002
http://www.sadlier.com

Acknowledgments

Scripture excerpts are taken from the *New American Bible with Revised New Testament and Psalms* Copyright ©1991, 1986, 1970 Confraternity of Christian Doctrine, Inc., Washington, D.C. Reprinted with permission. All rights reserved. No part of the *New American Bible* may be reproduced by any means without permission in writing from the copyright owner.

Excerpts from the English translation of the *Catechism of the Catholic Church* for use in the United States of America, copyright ©1994, United States Catholic Conference, Inc.—Libreria Editrice Vaticana.

Excerpts from the English translation of *Rite of Baptism for Children* ©1969, International Committee on English in the Liturgy, Inc. (ICEL); excerpts from the English translation of *The Roman Missal* ©1973, ICEL; excerpts from the English translation of *The Liturgy of the Hours* ©1974, ICEL; excerpts from the English translation of *A Book of Prayers* ©1982, ICEL; excerpts from the English translation of *Book of Blessings* ©1988, ICEL. All rights reserved.

Excerpts from *Catholic Household Blessings and Prayers* Copyright ©1988 United States Catholic Conference, Inc., Washington, D.C. Used with permission. All rights reserved. Neither this work nor any part of it may be reproduced by any means without permission in writing from the copyright owner.

Excerpts from the Dogmatic Constitution on Divine Revelation, *The Documents of Vatican II,* Walter M. Abbott, S.J., General Editor, ©1966 by America Press, Inc., 106 West 56th Street, New York, N.Y. 10019.

Excerpts from *How to Read the Church Fathers* by Alfred Hammon. New York: Crossroads, 1993.

Excerpt from *Daily Readings with St. Augustine* by Dame Maura See, O.S.B., ed. Springfield, IL: Templegate Publishers, 1986.

"Desert Places" from **THE POETRY OF ROBERT FROST, edited by Edward Connery Lathem,** Copyright 1936 by Robert Frost. ©1964 by Lesley Frost Ballantine. ©1969 by Henry Holt & Company. Reprinted by permission of Henry Holt and Company, Inc.

"A word is dead" by Emily Dickinson, from *Final Harvest: Emily Dickinson's Poems*. Selected and introduced by Thomas H. Johnson. Boston: Little, Brown, and Company, 1961.

Cover illustrator: David Diaz
Map illustrator: Mapping Specialists, Ltd.

Photo Credits

Adventure Photo and Film/ Brian Bailey: 84.

Ancient Art and Architecture: 24, 64.

Art Resource/ 96; Alinari: 10; Victoria and Albert Museum, London: 16; The Pierpont Morgan Library: 6A, 18; Nicolo Orsi Battaglini: 32; Murillo: 78A; D.Y.: 97 right, 98 bottom, 99top, 100 top; Scala: 102 bottom, 103 right center, 103 left top, 120 top, 122, 123 left, 123 bottom; Giraudon: 103 left center; Bildarchive Foto Marburg: 103 bottom; Erich Lessing: 102A, 114A, 118 bottom, 121 bottom right; Tate Gallery, London: 119 top left 126A.

Scott Barrow: 6-7 hands.

Boltin Picture Library: 118 top.

John Brandi, Jr: 106.

Bridgeman Art Library, London/New York: HGM81129 Christ, c. 1656 (panel) by Harmensz van Rijn Rembrandt (1606-69) Haags Gemeentemuseum, Netherlands; Guildhall Art Gallery, Corporation of London: 82; Birmingham Museum and Art Gallery: 120 bottom, 174A; National Gallery of Scotland, Edinburgh: 121 center.

Bridge Building Images: 119 top right.

Catholic News Service/ Charles Schisla: G21; Joe Rimkus, Jr.: G24; Nancy Wiechec: G25.

Crosiers/ Gene Plaisted, OSC: 66A, 90A, 102 right-103, 107.

FPG/ John Terrance Turner: G12-13; Stephen Simpson 6C, 9; Richard Laird: 91; Telegraph Colour Library: 114C;

Granger Collection: 12, 51, 76 left, 76 right.

Image Bank/ 78C; Will Crocker: 26; Petrified Collection: 59.

Ken Karp: 60.

Liaison International/ Baitel-Kires: 75; Annie Assouline: 83; Quidu: 86-87.

The Metropolitan Museum of Art/ H.O. Havemeyer Collection, Bequest of Mrs. H.O. Havemeyer, 1929(29.107.7): 119 bottom; Bequest of Benjamin Altman, 1913 (14.40.631): 123 top.

Museum der Bildenden Kunste: 121 top.

Natural Exposures/ daniel Cox: 40-41.

Richard T. Nowitz: 42A, 67, 72-73, 76 center, 80 background, 81, 104.

Panoramic Images/ Naoya Nishida: 30-31, 94-95.

Photonica/ K.Nagasawa: 38-39; Allen Wallace: 138A.

Photo Researchers/ Allen Morton and Dennis Milon: 48; John Foster: 49; Mike Agliolo: 70-71.

Picture Cube: G18.

Picturesque/ Alex Bee: 31.

Greg Probst: 14-15.

Questar: 54A, 80 foreground.

Sisters of the Mississippi Abbey: 65.

Stock Boston/ David Ulmer: G21.

Stock Imagery/ Powers: 22-23, 112; Katz 32-33; Evenson: 58; Stacks: 115 sky; Share: 115 prayer.

Stock Market/ Brent Peterson: 68; Jose Fuste Raga: 110-111.

Superstock: 8, 10-11, 88, 90C, 97 left, 98 top, 99 bottom, 100 bottom, 113.

Tony Stone Images/ Mike Magnuson: 6-7 clouds; Lawrence Migdale: G12-13; Mary Kate Denney: G19;Zigy Kaluzny: 19; Jonathan Morgan: 28 man; Glen Allison: 28 volcano; Stephen Johnson: 18C, 27; Earth Imaging: detail 34,35; Wayne Eastep: 30A, 42; David Young-Wolff: 30C, 43; Darryl Torckler: 46-47; I. Burgam/P. Boorman; 42C, 52 background; Will and Deni McIntyre: 52 foreground; David Austen: 54-55; Robert E. Daemmrich: 62-63; Rohan: 74; Joe Cornish: 78-79; Camille Torkerud: 90; Bob Schlowsky: 126C; Simon Norfolk: 162C.

Viesti Associates/ Richard Holden: G10.

Westlight/ Digital Art: 89.

Bill Wittman: 18A, 36, 150A.

General Consultant for Texts
Rev. Joseph A. Komonchak, Ph.D.

**Official Theological Consultant
for Texts**
Most Rev. Edward K. Braxton, Ph.D., S.T.D.
Auxiliary Bishop of St. Louis

Publisher
Gerard F. Baumbach, Ed.D.

Editor in Chief
Moya Gullage

Pastoral Consultant
Rev. Msgr. John F. Barry

Scriptural Consultant
Rev. Donald Senior, C.P., Ph.D., S.T.D.

General Editors
Norman F. Josaitis, S.T.D.
Rev. Michael J. Lanning, O.F.M.

Catechetical and Liturgical Consultants
William Sadlier Dinger
Eleanor Ann Brownell, D. Min.
Joseph F. Sweeney
Helen Hemmer, I.H.M.
Mary Frances Hession
Maureen Sullivan, O.P., Ph.D.
Don Boyd

"The Ad Hoc Committee to Oversee the Use of the Catechism,
National Conference of Catholic Bishops,
has found the doctrinal content of this teacher's manual to
be in conformity with the *Catechism of the Catholic Church*."

Nihil Obstat
✠ Most Reverend George O. Wirz
Censor Librorum

Imprimatur
✠ Most Reverend William H. Bullock
Bishop of Madison
July 16, 1998

The *Nihil Obstat* and *Imprimatur* are official
declarations that a book or pamphlet is free of
doctrinal or moral error. No implication is contained
therein that those who have granted the *Nihil Obstat*
and *Imprimatur* agree with the contents, opinions,
or statements expressed.

Printed in the United States of America.

S® is a registered trademark of William H. Sadlier, Inc.

Home Office:
9 Pine Street
New York, NY 10005–1002

ISBN: 0–8215–5661-4
23456789/02 01 00

New Testament: An Introduction

This section can be used at any time during the course, e.g., during retreat day, as a "break" week or in a holiday-shortened week. It needs to be scheduled and prepared well in advance.

Sadlier's new FAITH AND WITNESS PROGRAM is a creative response to the needs of adolescents in the Catholic Church. It is rooted in a desire to serve effectively these young people, as well as those adults who teach, guide, and parent them on their faith journey.

It is shaped by an awareness of the multiple challenges and rewards of working with this vulnerable age group, which has been described as having one foot in childhood and the other groping toward adulthood.

At the heart of **Faith and Witness** is "a Person, the Person of Jesus of Nazareth, the only Son from the Father." And its aim is to draw adolescents into "communion with Jesus Christ." *(Catechism of the Catholic Church,* 426)

Just as Jesus himself related to and communicated with people "on their own level," so this program respects and responds to the adolescent's urgent questions: Who am I? Where am I going? What is my purpose in life?

Research done by the Carnegie Council on Adolescent Behavior verifies that many adolescents in our society have not been receiving the kind of guidance and support they need to thrive during this difficult period of metamorphosis. The Council's report warns that youth between ten and fourteen have become "a neglected generation." It notes alarming increases in adolescent suicide, firearm use, smoking, drug and alcohol addiction, pregnancy, and poor grades. Its recommendations stress that schools should create programs better suited to adolescents' developmental needs, and parents should be

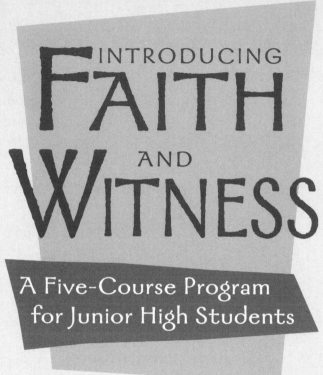

INTRODUCING
FAITH
AND
WITNESS

A Five-Course Program
for Junior High Students

encouraged to become more involved in their young people's lives.

Sadlier's new **Faith and Witness Program** endeavors to meet these goals through an integration of the specific social, intellectual, religious, and spiritual needs of youth. It addresses "the desire for God [that] is written in the human heart" *(Catechism,* 27) as well as the Church's pastoral mission. Particular attention is paid to the following aspects of that mission: examining the reasons for belief, celebrating the sacraments, being integrated into the faith community, providing and calling forth gospel witness *(Catechism,* 6).

The semester courses that together comprise the program draw young people into relationship with Jesus and the New Testament, Liturgy and Worship, Church History, Morality, and the Creed. Each course invites young people to venture further into the mystery of faith and the challenge of discipleship. Through shared study, reflection, prayer, and action in response to God's word, young people experience themselves as a small faith community within the larger community of the parish and the Church itself.

We asked the writers of the courses to share with you, in a few sentences, their response to the following question:

What hopes do you have for the young people who will use your book?

Creed

"We know what a privilege and a challenge it is to share with young people the dynamic teachings of our Catholic faith. Moreover it is important to share that faith in a clear and meaningful way with the next generation of believers. We do this in two parts: Creed Part I, covering faith and revelation; Creed Part II, covering the Church and the Holy Spirit. Our hope is that young people will come to love Jesus and his Church ever more and take their place in society as committed evangelizers."

**Dr. Norman F. Josaitis, S.T.D., and
Rev. Michael J. Lanning, O.F.M., authors**

Liturgy and Worship

"We all know that it takes a lot more knowledge and skill to do something than to watch something. I hope that this book will provide the students—the next generation of young Catholics—with the help they need to celebrate the sacraments intelligently, joyfully, and fruitfully."

**Rev. Thomas Richstatter, O.F.M., S.T.D.,
author**

New Testament

"The purpose of this book is to provide an introduction to the New Testament that will offer young people a mature appreciation of their faith. Knowing all about the good news of Jesus Christ is more than the work of one lifetime. But it is our hope that this book will help young people to become more committed disciples of Jesus and stronger members of his Church."

**Dr. Norman F. Josaitis, S.T.D., and
Rev. Michael J. Lanning, O.F.M., authors**

"This introduction, I hope, will make accessible to young people twenty centuries of Christian reflection on the New Testament."

**Dr. Mary Ann Getty, S.T.D.,
special consultant**

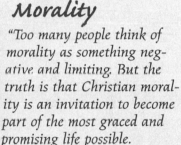

Morality

"Too many people think of morality as something negative and limiting. But the truth is that Christian morality is an invitation to become part of the most graced and promising life possible. Morality is all about authentic happiness and rich, lasting loves. My hope with this book is that students will discover that God loves them and wants the best for them, and that people who care for them will always challenge them to be good."

Rev. Paul J. Wadell, Ph.D., C.P., author

Church History

"I love Church history and agree with Cicero who said: 'To know nothing of what happened before you were born is to remain ever a child.' The same is true of Catholics who are unaware of our own religious heritage. The history of the Catholic Church is a marvelous story of saints and sinners, successes and failures, hopes and disappointments. For a person of faith, it is not only a human story but also a divine drama of God's grace at work in our world."

Rev. Thomas J. Shelley, Ph.D., author

You Are a Catechist

Grace and peace to you! You have been called to be a catechist, a faith-filled minister of the word to adolescents. The aim of your ministry is to bring young people into intimate communion with Jesus Christ, and to draw them more deeply into the faith life of the Church. Think for a moment:

◆ Why do you think you were invited to do this work with young people?
◆ What gifts, talents or experiences do you bring to this ministry?

Ministry to the Needs of Youth

Ministry to young people has two main goals:

• to contribute to the personal and spiritual growth of each young person in your care;

• to invite young people into responsible participation in the life, mission, and work of the faith community. The components of your ministry include:

Evangelization—reaching out to young people who are uninvolved in the life of the Church and inviting them into a relationship with Jesus and the Catholic community.

Catechesis—promoting a young person's growth in the Catholic faith through a teaching process that emphasizes understanding, reflection, and conversation.

Prayer and Worship—guiding young people in developing their relationship with Jesus through personal prayer; drawing them more deeply into the sacramental life of the Church; involving them in a variety of prayer and worship experiences to celebrate their friendship with Jesus in a faith community of their peers.

Community Life—forming young people into the Christian community through programs and relationships that promote openness, trust, respect, cooperation, honesty, responsibility, and willingness to serve; creating a climate where young people can grow and share their struggles, questions, and joys with other young people and feel they are valued members of the Church.

Justice, Peace, and Service—giving direction to young people as they develop a Christian social consciousness and a commitment to a life of justice and peace by providing opportunities for service.

The Catechetical Environment

A catechetical environment is created when young people are able to experience Christian community in their families, their parish, and their cultures. Such a community is formed through study, prayer, worship, sharing of food and recreation, and telling our stories about the ways God has been present in our lives. Here are important components that go into building such a community.

Knowing the Young People

The environment and practices in the home and neighborhood have had, and continue to have, a powerful influence on the faith development of the young people in your group. It is important to be aware of the world the young people inhabit. Here are ways to develop that awareness.

◆ Be sure that your consistency, dependability, and fairness are such to win their confidence.

◆ Review the information you have been given regarding each young person.

◆ Become familiar with where and with whom each young person lives and who has legal custody.

◆ Make sure you are aware of young people who may be neglected or who come from homes that appear to be unhappy.

◆ Be available for private conferences with parents or family members, even if it means rearranging your schedule to meet their employment or family obligations.

◆ Be mindful of and sensitive to the language spoken in the home and the religious affiliation of parent(s) or guardians.

◆ Be alert to the general health and well-being of the young person.

Getting Families Involved

The mission of Catholic education is to support, develop, enhance, and encourage the positive learning that takes place within the home. It is essential, therefore, to involve the family in the catechetical process. Encourage them to participate fully in ongoing religious development of the young person. Regular family conversations about God and religion have a tremendous positive effect on a young person's faith attitudes and practices.

◆ Welcome the families when the program begins. Explain the catechetical program and invite their participation.

◆ Introduce them to the courses. The table of contents for each course provides an excellent overview of what the young people will be expected to learn about our Catholic faith during the program.

◆ Encourage a conversation about ways they can share with their son or daughter the *You Are My Witnesses* page. Duplicate and send home *Highlights for Home* from each chapter of the guide.

◆ Make positive telephone calls to parents. Conversations can be barrier-breakers, and from them catechists can gain great parental support and insight.

◆ Make a "Parents' Day" part of your yearly tradition so that the parents are given the opportunity to share their hopes and dreams for their daughters and sons.

Knowing the Neighborhood

◆ Become aware of the out-of-school activities both of the young people and of those with whom they frequently associate. If possible, attend some of their athletic or musical events.

◆ Be available and willing to listen to the young people without suggesting cures. When necessary, suggest that they seek professional advice as to how to deal with any unhealthy behaviors. Discuss these with the parents as well as any neighborhood influences and/or friends who are adversely affecting the young people's social, emotional, and spiritual development.

◆ Invite professionals to help the young people learn ways to cope with social pressures and problems such as alcohol, drugs, and peer pressure.

Sadlier's **Faith and Witness Program** is designed to nurture in young people a wholesome sense of self and a secure relationship with God in the context of the faith community. By integrating the teaching of Jesus and of the Church with the realities of their lives, they will be better prepared to minister to a world in which secular values often oppose the good news.

Making Discipline Positive

Positive discipline entails creating a climate in which young people feel secure, accepted, and supported. Here are suggestions for establishing and maintaining positive discipline in the group setting.

◆ Establish a sense of order immediately. Clearly and briefly explain to the young people what is expected of them. Rules should be few and easy to remember.

◆ Use affirmation; acknowledge the young people and remember to praise and affirm good behavior.

◆ Provide activities that build healthy self-esteem.

◆ Respect their thoughts and ideas, and expect them to do the same with you and their peers.

◆ Provide activities that challenge them to cooperate with one another.

◆ Deal with those who act inappropriately in a way that will calm them; set aside a space where they can think quietly about their actions and the consequences of them. If correcting is necessary, do it one-to-one, never publicly.

Developing Multicultural Awareness

True Christian community takes place within the context of the cultural heritage and the identity of the young people we teach.

◆ Be aware of and sensitive to ethnic and cultural diversity.

◆ Encourage the young people to express their cultural uniqueness through art, music, dance, food, and dress.

◆ Send communications home in the languages of the families, if possible.

◆ Invite families to share their cultural symbols and food at celebrations.

◆ Be aware of possible conflicts because of ethnic or cultural diversity among young people.

Youth With Special Needs

In recent years, the bishops of the United States have encouraged religious educators to pay particular attention to those young people who have special needs and to integrate these young people, when possible, into regular programs of religious education.

There are many different kinds of special needs. Some young people have *physical* needs that must be taken into consideration. Physical needs may involve any of the five senses, as well as special motor needs. Some have *emotional* needs that require our recognition, attention, and consideration. Still others have *special learning* needs. Learn about the special needs of these young people from the trained professionals who have dealt with them and their families.

Try to ascertain what adjustments or adaptations need to be made for your group. Be aware also of any adaptations necessary to enable the young people to profit from their religion materials. Plan the seating arrangement so that each person feels part of the group. Be sure that the group is aware of and sensitive to the special needs of all.

Recognize how all of us need to receive from as well as give to those who are disabled or challenged in any way. Jean Vanier, founder of the L'Arche communities in which people with disabilities and their caregivers live together, observes that those who are "broken" can reveal to us our own spiritual or psychological "brokenness." By this mutuality, we are strengthened, reconciled, and healed.

Understanding the Adolescent

Adolescence—the period that normally covers the years between eleven and fifteen—is a time of major change, development, and sometimes upheaval in the young person's life. To the young person everything seems to be in flux, in motion—physical development, emotions, ideas, relationships. It is a time of challenge and enormous potential for growth; it can also be a time of frustration and confusion both for the adolescents and for the adults—parents and catechists— who care for them.

Social Development

As young people move into adolescence, their interests begin to extend beyond family and school to wider horizons. As these new interests develop, relationships that had been of primary importance, especially those with family, sometimes seem to recede. Although there is still an essential need for the security and support of family and other adults, it is a time when old ties and the excitement of an enlarging world can conflict. The growing desire of the young people for greater freedom and their continuing need for support and security offer a real challenge to parents and catechists, who must find ways to facilitate this process of progressive emancipation. The sociability of the teenagers should be utilized and their energies channeled into common pursuits. It is the right age for such educational techniques as small-group projects or discussions, debates, panel presentations, retreat days, youth days, and service projects.

Intellectual Development

Young adolescents are increasingly capable of all the intellectual operations. There is specific growth in the ability to deal with abstract ideas and judgments in those young people who have matured beyond the egocentrism of an earlier stage. As they come more and more into contact with the judgments and opinions of others, they will need to be helped and challenged to think more accurately, perceptively, and critically. The broadening intellectual and social world of the young people stimulates a questioning and critical spirit. We can foster a *positive* questioning and critical attitude in the young people by challenging them to explore, probe, and reflect.

Also on a positive level, God's relationship with the young people is often expressed in a more "spiritual" way than before. Prayers become more other-oriented and less egocentric. The Church can be more readily understood as a community of believers, and worship is seen as a natural expression of belief and a way to become a better person.

The catechist should be aware that as real religious insights such as these occur, there can also be a tendency for negative attitudes to develop. This is often especially true for less mature young people, who, when faced with the struggle to move from an egocentric to a more mature religious belief, find it difficult to wrestle with the problems this involves and retreat into indifference or hostility. The challenge to the catechist is great. The first challenge is to recognize some very basic needs of adolescents.

Some Basic Needs

1. *Affirmation and Approval.* Young people must consistently be affirmed by their parents, catechists, and peers. Most have a precarious sense of self-esteem. They suffer anxiety about their physical appearance, their popularity, their skills and talents. They need to be told and shown that they are accepted, appreciated, and approved for who they are right now.

2. *Security and Success.* Because intellectual and other abilities vary so broadly among adolescents, they need multiple opportunities to succeed. An effective catechist discerns and draws out the particular skills of each young person. When a relationship of trust is nurtured between catechist and young person, the young person feels secure enough to do his or her best.

3. *Freedom and Structure.* Like fledgling pilots, adolescents love to fly but they depend heavily on the voice from the control tower. They want freedom to experiment and explore yet they require a reliable home base to return to as needed. Catechists who come to the group well-prepared, who require young people to abide by simple rules, and who consistently offer opportunities for choice and self-expression will do well with this age group. Giving clear directions and guiding young people step-by-step through a new process or ritual reinforces awareness of structure.

4. *Idealism and Self-Definition.* Youth have a great capacity for energetic idealism which can be effectively harnessed in the causes of justice, equality, and peacemaking. When motivated and well directed, they will unselfishly participate in the works of mercy—particularly in one-on-one situations. However, if their idealism and altruism are not channeled by catechists and adult mentors, youth readily take refuge in cynicism and hostility. Their need for self-definition must be met through individual attention from adults and by enlisting their particular abilities in ways that serve others.

5. *Physical Activity and Social Interaction.* Driven by hormonal changes and uncontrollable growth spurts, adolescents literally "cannot sit still" for extended lectures. They need to move from place to place, activity to activity, individual to partnered or group pursuits. Their hunger for interaction with peers can be met in diverse ways (discussions, debates, art or craft projects, sharing food and music, games, dancing, human sculptures).

Thinking Skills for Discipleship

More and more often, a complex and technological society demands critical thinkers. Critical thinkers see beneath surface impressions to the root of an issue or event. They are able to discern causes rather than symptoms, and they are able to project consequences rather than to be satisfied with quick solutions. Above all, critical thinkers are capable of reflection—not only on issues outside themselves, but capable of their own responses and reactions as well. How can we help our young people develop critical thinking skills? And how can we encourage them to use these skills as disciples of Christ?

The ability to think critically can be developed in young adolescents through questions and activities that involve the following:

- solving problems
- making decisions
- imagining outcomes
- setting up criteria
- finding reasons
- reflecting/meditating
- choosing applications to life

"Who do you say I am?" Jesus asked his disciples. It was a question that demanded the disciples to go beneath surface impressions to the heart of the matter. Instead, the disciples responded by repeating what *others* had said— "Some say John the Baptist; others Elijah; still others responded Jeremiah or one of the prophets." Jesus refused to accept the superficial, unreflective answer. He probed further. "But who do you say that I am?"

This is the basic question of our faith. This is the question that we want our young disciples to answer with personal conviction, commitment, and hope.

"You are the Messiah, the Son of the living God" (Matthew 16:13–16).

Prayer and the Young Person

A well-known youth minister was asked what advice he would give to religion catechists. "Be bold about the spiritual," he said. "These kids want and need religious experience. They need help with prayer."

Forms of Prayer

Many young people have experienced prayer as "talking to God" and reciting prayers. They are ready to explore new ways of expressing their relationship with God. In addition to liturgical prayer, the official prayer of the Church, they can enrich their prayer life by using prayer forms like the following:

- **The Breath Prayer**
  Seated with back straight and eyes closed, the person focuses on the flow of breath in and out of the body. As breath is exhaled, one can "breathe" a simple word or phrase like "Jesus" or "Here I am, Lord."

- **Prayer with Scripture**
  Herein lie unlimited riches. Try gospel meditations using imagination, i.e., "place yourself in the scene . . ."; read the psalms in choral fashion; learn personally chosen passages by heart; and practice proclaiming the word of God.

- **The Symbol Prayer**
  Potent symbols from the Bible and the liturgy (water, wind, oil, fire, light, incense) may speak more powerfully to meditating youth than would many words or explanations.

- **The Prayer of Music**
  This native tongue of youth speaks to them of God as they reflect on, participate in, and respond to music (religious, classical, contemporary).

- **The Prayer of Journaling**
  Prayers, Scripture responses, poems, dreams, doubts, questions, dialogues with Jesus and the saints are recorded in words and/or art in the young person's book of life. He or she comes to know God and self more intimately.

- **Traditional Vocal Prayer**
  Traditional prayers—prayers of the Catholic community—are the most used and taken-for-granted form of prayer. When they are prayed slowly and thoughtfully, instead of rattled off, they can be a source of comfort, rootedness, and connectedness for young people. One way to make traditional prayers take on new meaning is to pray them against a background of beautiful music or visual images.

Young people should be invited to help choose and prepare for these and other prayer experiences. Suggestions for these prayer experiences (about 10 minutes) are provided in the *Introduction* and *Conclusion* of each session. However, brief opening and closing prayers (a minute or two) may be used to frame the session itself as an extended prayer. Sources for these include: a line or two from traditional prayers, the Mass, the psalms, inspired songs, prayers of the saints, collections of prayers by teenagers, and the words of Jesus.

Do not assume that young people reject prayer. They are hungry for the spiritual, for relationship with God. Prayer is a way for them to touch the living God who is with them and in them.

Some resources that might be helpful:

Hokowski, Maryann. *Pathways to Praying with Jesus.* Winona, MN: Saint Mary's Press, 1993.

Koch, Carl, FSC. *More Dreams Alive: Prayers by Teenagers.* Winona, MN: Saint Mary's Press, 1995.

Bolton, Martha. *If the Pasta Wiggles, Don't Eat It. . . .* Ann Arbor, MI: Servant Publications, 1995.

Morris, Thomas H. *Prayer Celebrations for the Liturgical Year.* New York, NY: William H. Sadlier, 1998.

Questions That Matter

Questions have to be carefully prepared if they are to be truly effective. Part of preparation for teaching each lesson should be the formulation of questions that stimulate, challenge, and engender deeper thought. Besides simple recall, questions should motivate and stimulate emotion, evaluative thinking, imagination, and creative problem solving. Vary your techniques; allow time for responses (research shows that most teachers wait less than 4 seconds); above all, *listen* to the answers! Here are some sample questioning techniques.

Recall

- List the types of evidence for believing in God. Other "recall" words: name; define; outline; describe.

React

- Imagine a friend tells you that he no longer believes in God. List four questions you would ask your friend about his reasons for not believing.

Compare

- In what ways are the early Church (A.D. 33–300) and today's Church alike?

Contrast

- In what ways are they different?

Preference

- Which would you rather be—a stained glass window or a church bell?
- Which helps you to pray—silence or music?

Personification

- What questions would you like to ask Francis of Assisi (or Mary, or...)?
- What would Jesus think or say about this issue? How might he say it?

Creative Thinking

- What if there had been television in Jesus' time?
- What if you could trade places with Saint Paul (or Catherine of Siena...)?
- Suppose that Jesus had not come. What would the consequences be?

Application

- Give Luther a list of alternatives to leaving the Church.
- Ask several "when" questions about the Church.
- Ask five "why" questions about faith.

Research Skills

- Would it have been possible for Pope John Paul II to meet Hitler?
- Would it have been possible for Catherine of Siena to have dinner with Ignatius Loyola?

Synthesis

- What might be some of the moral consequences of violent or sexual content in some contemporary music?
- The answer is "life." What is the question?

Ways of Learning

In his book *Frames of Mind*, Dr. Howard Gardner identified seven types of intelligence of which educators need to be aware among their students.

Because young people vary so widely in their intellectual abilities, it is especially important that catechists recognize these multiple intelligences.

The following list describes seven intelligence types and suggests appropriate teaching strategies within the context of the FAITH AND WITNESS PROGRAM.

1. Linguistic Intelligence

Exhibits sensitivity to the meaning and order of words

- *Storytelling:* scriptural, traditional, contemporary and imaginary stories to be told, re-told, or written
- *Brainstorming:* unleashing a torrent of ideas on a specific issue or question, i.e., How would we describe Jesus to teen aliens who had never heard of him?
- *Speaking a New Language:* learning a prayer in Aramaic, Spanish, Latin, or American Sign Language
- *Publishing:* collecting and publishing a semester's worth of young people's reflections, prayers, responses

2. Logical-Mathematical Intelligence

Shows ability to discern patterns of reasoning and order; dexterity with numbers

- *Classification:* organizing information (on Church history, Creed, or New Testament) on attribute webs (listing attributes of a person, place or thing as spokes around the subject)
- *Devising Strategies:* for computer or board games on history or Scripture
- *Socratic Questioning:* catechist or leader questions young people's views to sharpen critical thinking skills (e.g., "Do you think human beings will eventually have the power to understand the mysteries of life?")

3. Spatial Intelligence

Demonstrates ability to grasp how things orient to each other in space

- *Making Maps and Architectural Models:* recreating scenes or places from Scripture and Church history
- *Making Timelines and Murals:* visualizing historical, liturgical and creedal developments

4. Bodily-Kinesthetic Intelligence

Using the body skillfully and handling objects with unusual aptitude

- *Drama and Dance:* role-playing moral decision-making; acting out stories from Scripture and history; ritual prayer in which dance or choreographed movement is integrated
- *Human Sculptures and Relays:* small groups form "sculptures" of faith concepts or objects (community, steeple, fishermen's boat) using only their bodies; teams perform physical "feats" and respond to faith questions on relay "batons."
- *Crafts:* using clay, pipe cleaners, papier-maché, looms, wood, beads to make faith-related objects (from Scripture, Church history, prayer traditions)

5. Musical Intelligence

Using sensitivity to sound, melody, instrumentation and musical mood

- *Rhythms, Songs, Chants, Raps:* employing these as aids to internalization and memorization (composing songs on moral issues or chants of favorite prayer lines)

- *Producing Audio and Video Tapes:* singing and playing instruments (drums, guitars, tambourines, piano, bells) for taped prayer, gospel productions, historical skits

- *Collecting Disks:* resource of religious, classical and contemporary music to illustrate, amplify or embody content themes ("Godspell," "Messiah," "Tears In Heaven," plus nature recordings)

6. Interpersonal Intelligence

Showing relationship skills, understanding and empathy

- *Peer Sharing:* interacting with partners or small groups to explore content questions and personal responses; peer tutoring and mentoring by older youth or adults

- *Doing Simulations:* groups participate in "as-if" environments (e.g., "You have just heard Jesus' Sermon on the Mount and are now on the road home. What are you feeling, thinking, planning to do?")

- *Making Murals, Puzzles, Banners:* working cooperatively to produce an art project illustrating a faith theme

- *Peacemaking Strategies:* role-playing ways of reconciliation practiced by Jesus, saints, Gandhi, Martin Luther King, Jr., youth

- *Culture Sharing:* putting together prayer and worship experiences enriched by African-American, Hispanic, Asian, Native American and other cultural expressions within the Church

7. Intrapersonal Intelligence

Showing self-knowledge and self-discipline; awareness of one's inner life

- *Doing One-Minute Reflections:* taking "time out" in the midst of interactive learning for reflection or deep thinking (no talking; occasional background music)

- *Praying, Journaling, Retreats:* responding to youth's hunger for God and need for self-awareness

- *Offering Choices:* enhancing self-discipline and self-expression by offering choices on projects, methods, ways of responding to content

- *Expressing Feelings:* calling forth expressions of wonder, surprise, anger, joy, caring, humor, sadness in response to faith experiences (through stories, poems, videos, photos, music, personal witness, prayer)

The Learning / Teaching Process

Adolescents need to feel some ownership of the learning situation. They do not respond positively to being "talked at" or "talked down to." They need to participate as much as possible in the planning, presentation, and carrying out of the program. Above all, they need to be challenged to take responsibility for their learning.

The courses in SADLIER'S FAITH AND WITNESS PROGRAM are designed with these realities in mind. The process suggested is simple yet comprehensive. Each lesson consists of three steps:

1. Introduction

The lesson begins with an *opening prayer*—preferably led by one or more of the young people. (See page G21.)

• The opening prayer is followed by the *forum* (see page G20) in which the young people present their responses, reflections, or reactions to the assigned reading and activity.

2. Presentation

• The catechist clarifies the material the young people have read. This can be done through a variety of techniques including questions, activities, dialogue, highlighting, guest speakers, and so on.

3. Conclusion

• Young people and/or catechist give a brief summary of the work of the lesson.

• Catechist gives forum assignment for the next lesson.

• Session closes with a brief prayer or song.

This guide will suggest a variety of techniques, activities, questions to facilitate this process. The key with young people is to have a balance of consistency and variety so that every lesson is solid but not predictable.

Preparing a Lesson

If we truly believe that our catechetical work with young people is the most important teaching we can do, it is essential that we go to them prepared. Preparation for religion class is absolutely essential.

Here are a few suggestions for preparing to teach this course. The suggestions are especially intended for those who may be new—either to teaching religion or to teaching adolescents.

Remote Preparation

- Read the whole text carefully. This will give you an understanding of the scope of the whole course and the sequence of ideas throughout.

- As you read make marginal notes about any ideas you have regarding the material and how to present it.

- Look at the list of resources and try to familiarize yourself with at least one of them.

  - Check the references given throughout to the *Catechism of the Catholic Church*. Read over the cited paragraphs and make them your own.

Immediate Preparation

- Read the chapter for the session.

- As you read highlight what you consider to be the main points of each lesson. The highlighted statements on the reduced pupil pages will help you.

- List these main points for yourself. It will help to clarify and to focus your objectives.

- Write out the questions you feel will help direct the group's understanding of the material. (See the suggestions for questioning on page G15.)

- Plan the activities you wish to use during the lesson. Make sure you know exactly what you wish the group to do. Assemble any materials you will need.

- Plan the *forum* assignment you will give the young people for the following lesson. Make the assignment clear and simple, but be creative.

- Immediately before the lesson begins, talk to those who are responsible for leading the opening prayer to make sure they have what they need.

- Take a minute for quiet reflection. Ask the Holy Spirit to be in your mind, heart, and mouth as you share the faith with your group.

Youth Interaction

Youth interaction is essential to the success of this program. Their participation in and ownership of the learning process provides stimulus, enthusiasm, and energy to the whole program.

The **Faith and Witness Program** is organized on the principle of youth involvement and responsibility. The two most important elements in the program are, therefore, the youth-directed prayer, and the youth-led *Forum*.

Forum

The purpose of the *forum* is to involve the young people immediately and interactively in each session. We want them to become not simply passive receivers of information, but active partners and participants in the learning process.

It is essential, therefore, that the young people assume responsibility for the *forum* and for the preparation necessary to take part in it. If this is not done, the religion lesson will become a reading exercise or a lecture. These are not acceptable alternatives.

How Does the Forum Work?
◆ At the end of each lesson ask the young people to prepare for the next *forum* by doing two things:

• Read carefully the text pages assigned, and underline key ideas.

• Prepare a written or oral response to the question, reflection, or activity assigned.

◆ Following the opening prayer, each lesson begins with the *forum* in which the young people share both the results of their reading and their responses to the *forum* assignment.

The *forum* should take approximately 15 to 20% of the total class time. if the above process is not possible in your situation, see page G26.

Ideas for Forum Assignments
Each *forum* assignment should act as an interesting and creative "doorway" for the young people into the work of the lesson. Their responses and reactions at the outset of the lesson should provide an initial dialogue that helps them enter enthusiastically into the ideas and content of the lesson. Some ideas:

◆ Always the first part of the assignment is to read the pages of the lesson. Encourage the young people to underline in pencil sentences that they feel are key ideas on these pages.

◆ Some of the suggestions on *Questions That Matter* are excellent ideas for *forum* assignments—especially those under *Recall, React, Personification, Creative Thinking, Application,* and *Synthesis.* (See page G15.)

◆ *Journaling* could occasionally be the *forum* assignment. Be careful not to require a response that would be too personal or too revealing for a young person to share with the group.

◆ *Simple Research* to discover more information about an idea is helpful if the young people have access to computer on-line services.

Journaling

The young people keep a journal throughout the course. Journal suggestions appear in each chapter. There is a *Sadlier Journal* for *Creed, Morality, Liturgy and Worship,* and *New Testament.*

Purpose:
It provides an outlet for private, ungraded, uncensored expressions of the young people's thoughts, reflections, imaginations, feelings.

Outcomes:
• young people become more in touch with themselves, their feelings, their personal questions;

• young people become better writers;

• young people have something to look back on that will give them insights into their own change and growth.

Youth-Led Prayer

Purpose:
- provides immediate responsibility for and involvement by the young people in the spiritual dimensions of their learning;
- gives them the opportunity to express their own spiritual concerns and to lead others in prayer.

Outcomes:
- young people are enabled to be less self-conscious about their faith;
- they are given the freedom to express their relationship with God and their concerns in personal and creative ways;
- the experience can draw them deeper into their personal life of prayer with God.

Needs:
- especially in the beginning: the catechist's help, support, and suggestions;
- scriptural and other resources (see *Teaching Resources* chart for each chapter);
- partners! Sometimes it is easier with a friend.

How to:
- at the end of each session meet with the young people who will be leading prayer during the next session;
- if they request help, make resources available;
- encourage them—prayer does not have to be perfect; it only has to be sincere.

Faith in Action

*I*nvolvement in active service for others is an integral part of the FAITH AND WITNESS PROGRAM.

Purpose:
Young people have so much to give—energy, generosity, enthusiasm, idealism, compassion. It is essential that we help them find practical and immediate ways to share these gifts.

Outcomes:
They will find that they receive far more than they give—a humbling and joyful discovery. They will begin to develop and to live the values of God's kingdom in very real, practical, and sometimes demanding ways.

Needs:
Ideas and suggestions from the parish and communities concerning needs and opportunities the young people can address.

How to:
From the beginning, make it clear to the young people that an essential component of the program is their willingness to serve. A list of suggestions for projects is supplied on page G25, but you might find other ideas more appropriate for your particular situation. Set aside time during and at the end of a service project to help the young people evaluate their service, their attitudes, and their reflections.

FAITH AND WITNESS Program

Morality A Course on Catholic Living

We were made for happiness, a happiness that God alone can provide. Modeling our lives on Christ, we know that the only way to achieve happiness is by rejecting sin and freely choosing to do what is right. Through God's law and God's grace, we are called upon to form our consciences and make moral decisions as followers of Christ and members of the Church. The Church itself is the authentic teacher of the ways of Christ and the manner in which we are to live a moral life in the world.

Within this deeper framework of moral decision making, we explore the Ten Commandments in greater detail. Likewise, we concentrate on gospel formation (the Beatitudes) and what it means to live a life of virtue. This course will enable young people to navigate through challenging times with a clear and positive moral attitude that is essential for Catholics in the new millennium.

Liturgy and Worship A Course on Prayer and Sacraments

It is in the Church's liturgy, especially the seven sacraments, that Catholics celebrate all that God has done for us in Christ Jesus through the working of the Holy Spirit. Our salvation was made possible through the paschal mystery of Christ's passion, death, resurrection, and ascension. This mystery is made present to us in the sacred actions of the Church's liturgy.

As members of the Church, we are called upon to enter into this mystery of faith and truly be people of both word and sacrament. This is where our lives of faith are proclaimed, formed, and nourished. If young people are to be strong and faithful followers of Christ, they must make the liturgical life of the Church their own.

New Testament An Introduction

Young Catholics need to rub shoulders with the culture of Jesus and his times. Likewise, they need to know that in Scripture things are not always what they appear to be. Scripture presents so much more, and young people should never be afraid of the truth as presented in Scripture. This text will introduce them to questions people have asked over the ages: Were the Magi historical figures? Did Jesus really raise people

from the dead, or were they just asleep? Did Jesus really die, and did his body really come out of the tomb? By tackling such questions, this course will help young people to appreciate the contemporary Catholic understanding of Scripture and give them tools to avoid fundamentalistic leanings that distort real Catholic doctrine and Scripture itself.

Creed A Course on Catholic Belief in Two Parts

It is through divine revelation that we come to know God through the knowledge God has of himself. The gift of faith enables us to respond to this divine revelation.

Because our first parents rejected God's plan of original holiness and justice, the whole human race is born in the state of original sin. God promised us a savior and that promise was fulfilled through his only Son, who became flesh and took on our human nature. Jesus, the

Son of God and the son of Mary, is true God and true Man. He offered himself as the perfect sacrifice for us and for our salvation.

We are the Church, the people of God. Jesus promised that he would be with the Church until the end of time. He sent the Holy Spirit to guide the Church in all things. The course concludes with Mary and the saints and our belief in the communion of saints and life everlasting.

Church History A Course on the People of God

How important it is for young Catholics to be in touch with their roots, roots that took hold about two thousand years ago!

Beginning with the apostolic age and the age of persecution, young people will be introduced to the accomplishments of men and women of faith throughout the centuries. The successes and difficulties that the Church

has faced, both within and without, will be studied, but always with a view to help young Catholics of today face the challenges of their own time. As Catholics, we stand on the shoulders of giants. In helping others to know the story of this great Church community, we are preparing leaders for the new millennium.

New Testament
Scope and Sequence

Chapter 1

ALIVE IN CHRIST: an invitation to a deeper understanding of Jesus through study of the New Testament; Jesus, a historical figure; ancient "outside" sources and witnesses

Chapter 2

UNLIKE ANY OTHER: oral tradition in the Church; first official writings; the meaning of *testament;* the books of the Bible

Chapter 3

THE DIVINE WORD: authorship of the New Testament; divine inspiration; theories concerning authorship

Chapter 4

THE CHURCH'S BOOK: from tradition to Scripture; understanding inspiration; truths of faith; the canon of Scripture

Chapter 5

MORE THAN HISTORY: divine revelation; modern history—ancient history; process of formation of the New Testament

Chapter 6

GETTING AT THE TRUTH: awareness of literary forms in the Bible; gospel: a literary form; other literary forms in the New Testament

Chapter 7

JESUS AND HIS PEOPLE: Jewish religion and culture; political and biblical covenants; the new and everlasting covenant

Chapter 8

MORE ABOUT JESUS AND HIS PEOPLE: Temple sacrifice and priesthood; the presence of God in his people, in the Temple, and in God's law; prayer, Sabbath observance, feasts, and observance of God's law

Chapter 9

JESUS AND HIS WORLD: geography and customs of Israel; Roman occupation; Galilee and Nazareth; variety of languages

Chapter 10

JESUS AND HIS TIMES: life in Nazareth; home life and education; readiness to hear the good news

Chapter 11

THE GOOD NEWS ABOUT JESUS: the gospels: four different points of view; the evangelists; the synoptic gospels: a comparison

Chapter 12

FOUR POINTS OF VIEW: characteristics of each gospel: a synopsis of the messages and literary styles of Matthew, Mark, Luke, and John

Chapter 13

HUMAN AND DIVINE: Jesus, the Word made flesh; Jesus, the second Person of the Blessed Trinity; Jesus, the only Son of God; meeting Jesus in the gospels; Jesus speaks about himself

Chapter 14

CHRIST THE LORD: Jesus' divinity shown in forgiveness of sins and in miracles; Jesus Christ, Messiah and Lord; the Lord's Prayer

COURSE OVERVIEW

Why a Course on the New Testament?

The cover of this New Testament guide provides a graphic answer to this question. As we read in the new *General Directory for Catechesis:*

The parable of the sower going out to sow is the source of inspiration for evangelization. The seed is the word of God (Luke 8:11). The sower is Jesus Christ. Two thousand years ago he proclaimed the Gospel in Palestine and sent the disciples to sow the Gospel in the world. Today, Jesus Christ, present in the Church through his Spirit, continues to scatter the word of the Father ever more widely in the field of the world. *(Introduction)*

If our young people are to be evangelizers, if they are to share in the ministry of Christ, they must grow in an understanding and love of the New Testament. This course gives young people the tools they must have in order to enter into the world of the New Testament with a truly Catholic understanding. They learn to read it; they are led to believe it; they are challenged to live it. They are beginning an exciting adventure that can give them the impetus and encouragement to become evangelizers who "scatter the word of the Father ever more widely" in their world today.

Objectives

◆ To introduce junior high youth to the New Testament as the announcement of the good news of our salvation in Jesus Christ; to develop persons of commitment to and faith in him.

◆ To challenge the young people to enter into this study of God's revealed word with intensity and enthusiasm; to help them develop a solid Catholic understanding of Scripture so as to avoid fundamentalist distortions.

◆ To help them become truly people of the word who find in Scripture the encouragement, challenge, and hope they need to bring the good news of Christ to the world.

Faith in Action

Active, attentive, responsible service of others should be the hallmark of the Christian life of faith. Involve your group in individual or communal service projects to be carried out throughout this course. The young people should reflect on their commitment in their journals and give a report at the end of the course. (*Note:* All projects will need your support and coordinating efforts.) Some suggestions follow.

◆ The young people might form a "lectors' group" whose purpose is to prepare themselves to do the readings at Mass each week. They should offer their services to the parish liturgical committee.

◆ In performing this service the young people will discover in a new and deeper way the power and beauty of Scripture. They will also find what it means to be active participants in the spreading of the good news of Jesus Christ.

◆ Some young people may feel that belonging to the community of the Church is unimportant. Some may have had unpleasant experiences with organized religion. Among their acquaintances, the young people may know someone who is turning a deaf ear to the message of Christ.

The young people might invite such a friend to accompany them to one of their parish functions for teens or to a retreat weekend. They could simply speak with their friends about their feelings and sincerely attempt to express why they find meaning and value in their faith. In one of these ways they could possibly serve as catalysts in leading someone else to Christ.

Cross Curriculum Projects

◆ Young people who have an interest in language arts might do a study of the literary forms of the Bible and literary forms in modern literature. Besides prose and poetry can they find instances of modern parables, letters, genealogies, apocalyptic writing?

◆ Those who are interested in history might prepare a presentation on the development of the early Church based on eye-witness accounts, letters, and documents. A source could be Sadlier's *Church History: A Course on the People of God*, Chapters 1 and 2.

◆ Young people with an interest in music might put together a tape of hymns and songs based on the words of the New Testament. They might include "Be Not Afraid," "I Am the Bread of Life," "Blest Are They," "Lord, To Whom Shall We Go?". A possible source: *Glory & Praise* hymnal.

How To Use This Guide

Preparation

Well in advance:

◆ Read the entire text before meeting for the first time.

◆ Carefully prepare each session, using both text and guide.

Planning

◆ Go over *Teaching Resources.*

◆ Gather materials.

◆ Plan each *Forum* assignment.

◆ Estimate time you will allot for *Introduction, Presentation,* and *Conclusion* of the session. A place is provided to write your estimate beside each head on the guide.

◆ Prayer is an integral part of the catechetical process. It should be a priority in each session.

◆ At this age young people like to feel ownership and some control of the work of the session. If at all possible, encourage them to bring the text home so that they can become familiar with the theme, identify main ideas, and prepare for the *Forum.* (See page G20.)

◆ In order to become active partners and participants in the learning process, it is essential that the young people have time to prepare and that they be encouraged to assume responsibility for their learning. The *Forum* and the opening prayer especially require their preparation and interaction. All of this presumes that the young people can take their books home.

◆ Preview any videos or films to be used; listen to suggested music.

◆ Learn as much as possible about the young people with whom you will be meeting.

◆ Interaction and dialogue are key to the development of a deep and personal understanding of the ideas presented. We urge you to use the *Forum* activity to this end.

Other Options

If your situation does not allow for the books to be taken home, be creative. Find ways to help the group be ready to participate actively and fully in the work of the chapter. Here are some ideas:

◆ Have a small group prepare the chapter presentation and do the *Forum.* Select a different group each week.

◆ Provide reading and *Forum* preparation time at the beginning of each session. *This would work best with sessions of 90 minutes or longer.*

◆ Prepare and begin each session with a summary presentation of the key ideas of the chapter. *Invite and encourage discussion before moving on.*

Features

Adult Focus

helps you to focus on and be comfortable with the theme of the chapter.

Enrichment Activities

provide additional activities to enhance the sessions.

Teaching Resources

give an overview of the session including opening prayer suggestions and optional supplemental resources.

Journaling

Suggestions are provided for each session. A separate *Faith and Witness* Journal is available for each course. There is one journal for *Creed Part I* and *Creed Part II*.

Assessment

An optional assessment in standardized test format is provided as a blackline master. There is one at the end of each chapter in the guide. A blackline-master test book will be provided for use with the program.

Highlights for Home

This blackline master is provided as a communication to encourage family involvement.

The **Faith and Witness Program** provides a genuine opportunity for young people—with your guidance—to come to a powerful understanding of the faith through study, dialogue, and prayer. You, the catechist, have the challenging role of preparing them and calling them to be people of faith and witness.

The semester courses that together comprise Sadlier's **Faith and Witness Program** may be used for young people at the junior-high and high-school levels. You have the opportunity to develop the curriculum to suit your own needs.

Some considerations in choosing your semester course combination are:

- diocesan guidelines for specific grade levels
- maturity of students
- pre-Confirmation catechesis guidelines.

ALIVE IN CHRIST

Adult Focus

Put out into deep water.
                    Luke 5:4

This invitation of Jesus is an invitation to all of us, especially to our young people. They are about to launch out into the deeper water of the New Testament. Be aware that, as you help them to take the plunge, you are helping them to deepen their understanding of and relationship with Jesus, the Word of God.

In Chapter 1, the young people take a brief look at the "outside" sources of testimony about Jesus. They learn that these nonbiblical sources and non-Christian written sources verify the fact that Jesus of Nazareth did exist and that he made an impact on history.

Most young people need and want a secure and personal relationship with Jesus. As one girl expressed prayerfully, "Lord, be there for me. And I'll try to be there for you." Help the young people understand that they deepen their relationship with Jesus and strengthen their faith in him by seeking his message of God's love in the pages of the New Testament.

Catechism Focus

The theme of Chapter 1 corresponds to paragraphs 80–82, 121, and 450 of the *Catechism of the Catholic Church*.

Enrichment Activities

Center on Jesus

Involve the young people in putting together a collection of books, music, videos, art, and stories about Jesus. Find a permanent home for the collection (a set of shelves or milk crates covered in decorated posterboard). Get the collection started with a few videos: *Jesus of Nazareth* and *The Revolutionary* (available from Videos With Values). Encourage the young people to build up and use this collection throughout the course.

A. "T.I.N.T." Question Box

Make a question box with a slot in the top and clearly marked with the acronym "T.I.N.T." (Teen Issues in the New Testament). Encourage the young people to write any questions they have about the teachings of Jesus or his disciples, especially as they relate to issues of particular interest to them. Share questions and responses a few times a month. If possible, invite Scripture scholars, priests, or Scripture study leaders to field the questions once or twice during the course. Keep the question box displayed in the Jesus Center.

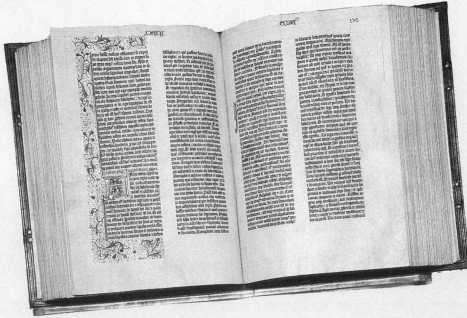

Teaching Resources

Overview

To discover the value of deepening our relationship with Jesus; to explore "outside" sources of evidence about Jesus.

Opening Prayer Ideas

Reflect on Luke 11:9. Pray the intercession taken from the Blessing for a Catechetical Meeting.

or

Read 2 Timothy 3:16–17. Pray: Lord, equip us for every good work through our study of Scripture.

Materials

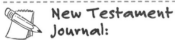 **New Testament Journal:**
For Chapter 1, use pages 1–5.

- Bibles, journals, and highlighters
- sponge ball or beanbag
- assignments written on index cards (See page 11.)

REPRODUCIBLE MASTERS
- handout *Jump In*, page 6C
- *Chapter 1 Assessment*, page 13A
- *Highlights for Home*, page 13B

Supplemental Resources

VIDEOS
- *Discovering the Bible Series:* "Getting Acquainted"
- *One Who Was There*

Gateway Films/Vision Video
2030 Wentz Church Road
P.O. Box 540
Worcester, PA 19490–0540

Jump In

For the first mind web, write words or short phrases to describe what you know about the New Testament.

For the second mind web, write words or short phrases to identify what topics you want to explore in the New Testament semester course.

What you know

to explore

Lord Jesus, it is you who call us out into deep water. Give us the courage, the desire, and the ability to plunge into the sea of faith. Be the force that upholds, protects, and guides us.

Alive in Christ

Ask and you will receive; seek and you will find; knock and the door will be opened to you.
Luke 11:9

Objectives: To discover the value of deepening our relationship with Jesus; to explore "outside" sources of evidence about Jesus.

Introduction ___ min.

Note: Encourage the young people to assume leadership roles in preparing and leading the opening prayer in each session. The time allotted for this prayer should be about ten minutes. Also, if your opening-prayer time is brief, use one of the ideas listed on the *Teaching Resources* chart at the beginning of each chapter. Let the volunteer prayer-leader teams read these ideas and add or adapt them for your group's needs and circumstances.

Opening Prayer: Have the young people look at the photo on pages 6 and 7. Proclaim together Luke 11:9. Ask the group to stand and form a prayer circle. Have them extend their arms and hands. Pray the following intercession that is part of the Blessing for a Catechetical Meeting:

Christ, Son of God, the Father's favor rested on you, and he commanded us to listen to you; give us the gift of understanding, so that we may contemplate your word and experience its gentle power.

Forum: Distribute the handout *Jump In*. Allow a few minutes for the young people to complete the first mind web. Then invite the group to look through their texts to become familiar with the territory that you will be covering together during this course. Explain that this course will give them an opportunity to achieve a deeper understanding of:

• who Jesus is;
• what the New Testament is, where it comes from, and what its purpose is.

Allow a few minutes for the young people to complete the second mind web. Invite volunteers to share what they have written. Then pray together the prayer at the bottom of the handout sheet.

Presentation ___ min.

◆ Take a few minutes to explain the *Forum*—its purpose and the young people's participation in and responsibility for it. Here are some points to cover.

Forum is a Latin word for the place where the ideas and work of the community were explored and discussed. It was the center of public life in a Roman city. So important was this concept that the word *forum* refers to an intense exchange of ideas, thoughts, and opinions.

Each session's work will begin with this kind of exchange and dialogue. The *Forum Assignment* is given in the *Conclusion* section of each chapter. It includes two steps to be prepared before the next meeting.

1. The next lesson is read thoroughly. Key ideas are underlined in pencil.

2. The *forum* activity or question is prepared for discussion. Stress the importance of both preparation for and participation in the *forum*.

◆ Have a volunteer read the opening questions at the top of page 8. Call for a few responses. Then have volunteers read pages 8 and 9. Ask all to underline in color or highlight the key concepts highlighted on the reduced pupil pages. Emphasize that Jesus shares his good news with us through Sacred Scripture and the Church's living witness and tradition. We need both if we hope to live as his disciples.

Do you remember what it was like when you were very young and were learning to swim? What do you remember most, and why?

Deeper Water

When parents bring their young children to the beach to go swimming, they do not send them out to the deep water right away. That would be frightening to the children and perhaps dangerous. Instead children need to get used to the water gradually. Only after they have become comfortable in the water and enjoy it will they learn to swim. Only then can they venture out and experience the excitement of deeper water.

Many things in our lives can be compared to the experience of going out into deep water. For example, we cannot get a real education until we know how to read. We cannot explore cyberspace until we know something about computers. We cannot excel in a game or a sport until we have mastered the rules.

8

In many ways the same can be said about our life of faith. When we were little children, we were introduced to the beauty of our Catholic faith. We began to learn the basics of our religion at the appropriate age level. Once that was done, we could begin to practice our faith and come to know God in our lives. But now it is time for a change. It is time to go out into deeper water.

Jesus himself once invited some people to "put out into deep water" (Luke 5:4). These people were fishermen. They had been working hard fishing all night long but had been unsuccessful in catching anything. When they answered Jesus' invitation, something wonderful happened. They caught more fish than their nets could hold. Once the fishermen saw this, they left everything and followed him.

In a wonderful way Jesus is inviting you now to put out into deep water, too. He is the center of our faith, and he wants you to know him in a deeper and more mature way. Jesus wants you to come closer to him than you have ever been before. He wants you to explore the questions you have about him, about his life and teachings, and about following him in your life.

The invitation might seem almost overwhelming. How can a person even begin to respond to it? To do this, people for the last twenty centuries and in all parts of the world have turned to the Church. After all, it was Jesus who founded the Church and who sent the Holy Spirit upon it. Today it is through the Church that we experience Jesus and learn about him.

For the Church "the key, the center, and the purpose of the whole of man's history is to be found in its Lord and Master" (*Catechism of the Catholic Church*, 450). By being faithful members of the Church, we are able to respond to Jesus' invitation and come closer to him.

We hear the story of Jesus and begin to live the good news that he came to share with us. This good news comes to us in Sacred Scripture and in the Church's living witness and tradition.

Knowing all about the good news of Jesus is more than the work of one lifetime! The purpose of this book is to help us enter more deeply into one part of Sacred Scripture, the New Testament. Catholics who participate in Mass and have attended religion classes have already been introduced to the New Testament. But now it is time to plunge into it more deeply.

Will we learn everything about the New Testament? That would be impossible! Some scholars spend a lifetime studying one part of the New Testament and never exhaust what can be found there. They learn the original language spoken by Jesus and travel to the places where he lived and walked. They do this so that we might have a clearer understanding of Jesus and what he means for us and for the world. In this course some of their discoveries will become ours.

We are about to launch out into the deeper water of the New Testament. Are you ready to plunge in?

What is the one question you have always wanted to ask Jesus about his life? Write it in your journal.

◆ Write the following questions on the board:

• What fears, doubts, or questions do you have about heading out into the deep waters of a more mature discipleship?

• What results and rewards might you expect if you accept Jesus' challenge to delve deeper?

Allow a minute's silent reflection before leading a general discussion.

Note: Throughout the young people's text you will see the sunburst icon. The directives or questions featured here are meant to be thought provoking. They will help the young people to internalize the key concepts presented. Throughout the guide these directives and questions will be referred to as **thought provokers**.

Invite the young people to respond to the **thought provoker** on page 9 in their journals. Take a few minutes to present the concept of journaling to the group. (Go over the ideas on page G19.) Sadlier publishes a journal that reflects the journaling activities suggested in this text and guide. Each person should keep a journal during this course.

Presentation ___ min.

Note: For an active, orderly way to conduct general group sharing you may want to keep on hand a sponge ball or beanbag to toss to the young people as an invitation to contribute responses. Explain to the group three simple rules: They may speak only after catching the ball; they may not repeat another's response; they may not speak a second time until all have contributed once.

◆ Have the young people imagine the following:

> One of your descendants five hundred years from now wants to prove that you existed and to verify what kind of person you were.

Then have the young people share ways they want to be remembered and ways that their descendants will be able to verify their generosity, talent, friendliness, faithfulness, and other qualities.

Encourage the young people to conclude that their descendants may present videos, audio tapes, photos, letters, newspaper clippings, and other works.

◆ Have volunteers read pages 10 and 11. Discuss the statements that the young people consider to be important. Have the group highlight the main ideas highlighted here.

Note: *FYI* (*For Your Information*) is a feature that will appear frequently throughout this guide. Its purpose is to provide you with some additional information about one of the topics mentioned on the pages. If you wish, share this information with your group.

The Truth from Outside

We are going to spend the rest of this chapter and the next few chapters on background material for our study of the New Testament. Several important questions need to be asked. Chief among these questions is: Did Jesus really exist at all? How do we answer this question? What proof do we have outside of the New Testament and the testimony of the Church?

Actually a number of nonbiblical and non-Christian written sources are available to anyone who wishes to read them. They verify the fact that Jesus of Nazareth was a historical figure. He lived in a small country on the eastern shores of the Mediterranean Sea. This was the land of the Jews, and Jesus himself was a Jew. At the time of his birth, his country was a part of the Roman Empire. In fact both the Romans and the Jews give witness to his existence.

One ancient Roman writer was named Pliny the Younger (A.D. 61–113). He was a Roman governor in a province of Asia Minor and was a great letter writer. In one of his letters, he asked the advice of the Roman emperor Trajan on dealing with a religious group called Christians. In the course of the letter, Pliny mentioned that Christianity was causing the revenue from pagan temples and shrines to decline. Because these temples and shrines were being used less and less, the animals used for sacrifice were not being sold. He told the emperor that he was trying to get the Christians to reject Jesus Christ and to accept the pagan gods of the empire. If the Christians continued to profess their faith in Jesus, Pliny said that he would have to put them to death.

In his letter of response, Trajan praised Pliny for the way he was handling the Christian problem. Like Pliny, Trajan did not say much about Jesus himself, but he presumed that Jesus existed because he had so many followers.

Another ancient Roman writer was Tacitus (about A.D. 56–120). He was a historian and wrote about many things, including the great fire that happened in Rome during the reign of the emperor Nero.

Detail from painting of Christ by Giotto di Bondone

Ruins of the Roman Forum

10

Although Nero himself probably started the fire, he successfully blamed the Christians for burning the city and put many of them to death. Writing about Nero and the fire, Tacitus said of the Christians, "Their name comes from Christ, who, during the reign of Tiberius, had been executed by the procurator Pontius Pilate" (*Annals*, 15, 44).

Another Ancient Witness

A Jewish historian named Josephus is another important nonbiblical witness. He was born around A.D. 37 and wrote a twenty-volume history of the Jewish people. In that history he mentioned Jesus and the early Christians. Josephus himself was not a Christian and had no reason to lie about the facts. This is what he wrote about Jesus:

> He was a doer of startling deeds, a teacher of people who received the truth with pleasure. And he gained a following both among many Jews and among many of Greek origin. . . . And when Pilate, because of an accusation made by the leading men among us, condemned him to the cross, those who had loved him previously did not cease to do so. . . . And up until this very day the tribe of Christians, named after him, has not died out.
> *Antiquities of the Jews*, 18

11

◆ Have the young people form "Two-Minute Troupes." Give the following assignments on index cards to group directors.

- Group A: Present an improvised skit in which Pliny the Younger, who is hoping for a promotion, consults the Emperor Trajan about ways to deal with the "fanatic followers" of Jesus.
- Group B: Present an improvised skit in which Tacitus interviews people on the street about who they believe started the great fire that nearly destroyed Rome.
- Group C: Present an improvised skit in which Josephus and his assistant researchers present their findings about Jesus.

Allow preparation time before the troupes present their two-minute skits.

Just in case...
some pronunciation helps

Pliny	**Pleh**-nee
Tacitus	**Ta**-seh-tus
Josephus	Joh-**see**-fus

FYI The ancient Roman philosopher Cicero once wrote that historians should adhere to the following three laws:

- Never dare utter an untruth.
- Never suppress a truth.
- Express no partiality or malice.

As non-Christians, Tacitus and Josephus might have suppressed any mention of Jesus Christ. Yet God used the testimony of a pagan and of a Jew to verify that Jesus was indeed a historical figure. Historians who adhere to Cicero's three laws make the writing of history a sacred pursuit.

Presentation (cont'd)

◆ Have the young people read *Scripture Insight* on page 12. Ask them to look at the map of the Mediterranean world on page 127. Have a volunteer point out Egypt and the Nile River.

◆ Allow a few moments of silence for the young people to respond to the 🖐 **thought provoker** on page 12.

◆ Ask the young people to share their responses to *Things to Think About* and *Things to Share* on page 13. Encourage everyone to participate actively with questions, comments, and suggestions.

Conclusion ___ min.

◆ *On Line with the Parish*, which appears in each chapter, will suggest ways the young people can connect with, participate in, and serve their parish. Take time to talk about these suggestions with the young people and find ways to facilitate their parish endeavors.

◆ Direct attention to *Words to Remember* on page 13. Have the young people identify *Tacitus* and *Josephus*. Refer the group to pages 10 and 11.

Assessment: On page 13A of this guide you will find a blackline master test for this chapter in standardized format. If you plan to administer *Chapter 1 Assessment*, allow about ten minutes for its completion.

It is clear, then, from the witness of Pliny, Tacitus, Josephus, and other ancient writers as well that Jesus did exist. This fact is accepted by believers and nonbelievers alike. When we talk about Jesus in Scripture, we are talking about someone real. It is not like talking about the gods and goddesses of ancient mythology or other imaginary individuals. Our conclusion must be that the New Testament rests on the very solid fact that Jesus existed and that he made an impact on history. Now it is time for us to turn from the truth we know from the outside to the truth we know from the inside.

🖐 *You are invited to look at Jesus Christ in a new way. Are you willing to launch out into the deep water?*

Scripture INSIGHT

The words of Sacred Scripture and other ancient documents were not written originally on paper. They were written on papyrus, an inexpensive material made from a plant that grew in the marshes along the Nile River in Egypt. Parts of the plant were pressed together. After these were dried and rubbed smooth, they could be written upon. The papyrus was formed into long sheets and rolled around a cylinder, making a scroll. Sometimes smaller pieces of papyrus were cut off the scroll to use for short letters or notes. Typically, however, a long scroll would be used for lengthy documents, such as a book of the Bible or other important works.

Later on, parchment was more widely used for writing. Parchment was a writing material made from animal skin. It was washed and the fur removed; then the skin was treated, stretched on a frame, and rolled into scrolls.

Fragments of ancient scrolls that contain parts of the Bible can be found around the world. Many of them are in the Vatican Library.

A fragment of the Dead Sea Scrolls, discovered in the late 1940s; some of the Dead Sea Scrolls contain the oldest texts of the Hebrew Bible.

12

Answers for Chapter 1 Assessment				
1. d	**2.** b	**3.** a	**4.** b	**5.** c
6. a	**7.** c	**8.** d	**9.** c	**10.** Accept reasonable responses.

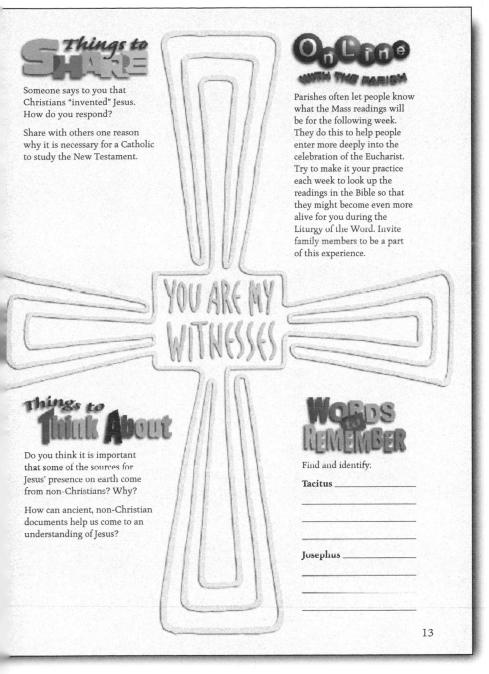

Things to SHARE

Someone says to you that Christians "invented" Jesus. How do you respond?

Share with others one reason why it is necessary for a Catholic to study the New Testament.

OnLine WITH THE PARISH

Parishes often let people know what the Mass readings will be for the following week. They do this to help people enter more deeply into the celebration of the Eucharist. Try to make it your practice each week to look up the readings in the Bible so that they might become even more alive for you during the Liturgy of the Word. Invite family members to be a part of this experience.

Things to Think About

Do you think it is important that some of the sources for Jesus' presence on earth come from non-Christians? Why?

How can ancient, non-Christian documents help us come to an understanding of Jesus?

Words to REMEMBER

Find and identify:

Tacitus _____

_____

_____

_____

Josephus _____

_____

_____

_____

YOU ARE MY WITNESSES

13

Conclusion (cont'd)

◆ Distribute copies of *Highlights for Home*, page 13B. You will do this in each session. Encourage the young people to share these pages each week with their families.

FORUM Assignment

✔ Read pages 14–21. Underline in pencil the statements that express six key ideas.

✔ Choose a person from history whom you admire and would like others to know and to admire in the future. How did you learn this person's story? How will you pass on this person's story to others?

Closing Prayer: Invite the young people to gather near the prayer table on which you have placed an open Bible. Pray, "Jesus, help us to know you through God's word." Then invite all to take turns holding their right hands on the open Bible and proclaiming "Amen."

Evaluation: Do the young people understand that the truth of Jesus' existence is verified by nonbiblical and non-Christian historians? Have they discovered the value of deepening their relationships with Jesus through the study of the New Testament?

FOR CHAPTER 2

- preparations for opening prayer
- texts, Bibles, journals, highlighters
- copies of handout *Flashback*, page 14C
- copies of *Chapter 2 Assessment*, page 21A (optional)
- copies of *Highlights for Home*, page 21B
- drawing paper for scrivener activity

Assessment

1 Through the Church we
- **a.** experience Jesus.
- **b.** grow in knowledge of Jesus.
- **c.** live the good news of Jesus.
- **d.** all of the above

2 At the time of Jesus' birth, Israel was
- **a.** independent.
- **b.** a part of the Roman Empire.
- **c.** a part of Egypt.
- **d.** very large.

3 A Roman governor who wrote for advice about dealing with Christians was
- **a.** Pliny.
- **b.** Tacitus.
- **c.** Josephus.
- **d.** none of the above

4 The Roman historian Tacitus
- **a.** denied Jesus' existence.
- **b.** blamed Christians for burning Rome.
- **c.** verified Jesus and his followers.
- **d.** did not mention Jesus.

5 The Jewish historian Josephus
- **a.** denied Jesus' existence.
- **b.** blamed Christians for burning Rome.
- **c.** verified Jesus and his followers.
- **d.** did not mention Jesus.

6 Circle the one that does *not* belong. Jesus' good news comes to us in
- **a.** non-Christian written sources.
- **b.** Sacred Scripture.
- **c.** the Church's living witness.
- **d.** the Church's tradition.

7 _____ is an inexpensive material made from a plant that grew along the Nile.
- **a.** Parchment
- **b.** Pliny
- **c.** Papyrus
- **d.** none of the above

8 The center of our faith is
- **a.** the Church's tradition.
- **b.** the New Testament.
- **c.** the Church's living witness.
- **d.** Jesus.

9 Like other teachers of his time, Jesus
- **a.** taught only by reading Scripture.
- **b.** never taught in the synagogue.
- **c.** taught by the spoken word.
- **d.** taught weekly in the Temple.

10 In what ways can you respond to Jesus' invitation to "put out into deep water" (Luke 5:4)?

_____

_____

_____

CHAPTER 1

Highlights for Home

Focus on Faith

Rituals are the glue that helps hold families together. As your son or daughter begins this course on the New Testament, you have an opportunity to initiate a ritual that will fortify both faith and family.

Consider gathering one evening each week to talk, listen, inquire, and pray about the current chapter theme in the text. Light a candle. Sing or play some quiet music. Read aloud your favorite passages in the New Testament. Your commitment will be well rewarded. Consider blessing each other at your first gathering with the words of Saint Isaac of Stella:

> Let Jesus grow in you, for Jesus is formed in you and from you, and may become to you a great smile and exultation and perfect joy which no one can take from you.

Conversation Starters

. . . . a few ideas to talk about together . . . .

◆ How might I personally benefit by exploring the New Testament and getting to know Jesus better?

◆ If a person asked, "Why are you wasting your time studying an ancient book like the Bible?" my response would be. . . .

Feature Focus

The *Scripture Insight* feature on page 11 presents the description of the material on which the words of Sacred Scripture were first written. These words and other ancient documents were written on papyrus, a material made from a plant that grew in the marshes along the Nile River. Later on the words of Scripture were written on parchment, a writing material made from animal skin.

If possible, help your son or daughter use a multimedia encyclopedia, such as *The New Grolier Multimedia Encyclopedia,*™ or the reference feature of an online information service, to find information on these writing materials.

Reflection

The following intercession is from *Book of Blessings*. It is part of the Blessing for a Catechetical or Prayer Meeting. Reflect on this request as you plunge into the New Testament more deeply.

> *Christ, Son of God, the Father's favor rested on you and he commanded us to listen to you; give us the gift of understanding, so that we may contemplate your word and experience its gentle power.*

Unlike Any Other

Adult Focus

Like other teachers of his time, Jesus taught by the spoken word. His disciples remembered his words and discussed them. But after Jesus' resurrection and his original followers' deaths, the early Christians felt a great need to hand on the truth about Jesus and his teaching to future generations. Saint Paul began writing letters to various Christian communities, and the gospels began to appear about fifteen years after Paul began his letter writing. Eventually the Church recognized and determined that Paul's letters and four gospel accounts would be part of what we now call the New Testament. This "new" testament about Jesus was understood as a completion and fulfillment of the writings of the Old Testament.

When presenting this chapter, help the young people to understand that the Old and the New Testaments come from God and from the lived experience of God's people. Help them to realize that the Bible is a book "unlike any other" because each book is inspired by God and was written to hand on a message about faith in God.

Catechism Focus

The theme of Chapter 2 corresponds to paragraphs 124–130 of the *Catechism*.

Enrichment Activities

A Prayer Tent

Have the young people design and build a prayer tent as a sacred space for group or private reflection. Explain that the tent symbolizes a place where God comes to dwell with the people of God. Suggested materials include canvas tarps or sheets for the roof (suspended by twine or fishing line from the ceiling) and sheets or wide fabric streamers for the sides. Furnish the tent with a Bible on a low stand; a battery-operated candle; CDs or tapes and appropriate player; a plant; and floor pillows or carpet remnants.

Scripture Treasures

Encourage the young people to become familiar with the treasure of Sacred Scripture. On slips of paper write brief quotes from the Bible. Place them in a basket or a box decorated as a treasure chest. At the beginning of each session, invite each person to draw a slip. The words on the Scripture slip are the individual's to think about and to keep. This practice helps young people become familiar with the words of Scripture, draws them into prayer, and encourages them to make the words their own.

Teaching Resources

Overview

To discover that the New Testament came out of the lived experiences of the Church and was written under the guidance of the Holy Spirit.

Opening Prayer Ideas

Look at the photo of the Grand Canyon on pages 14 and 15. Proclaim together Mark 2:12.

or

Pray together Psalm 119:105–112.

Materials

New Testament Journal:
For Chapter 2, use pages 6–7.

- Bibles, journals, and highlighters
- stone, shell, or other natural object for each person
- icon or picture of Jesus

REPRODUCIBLE MASTERS
- *Flashback,* page 14C
- *Chapter 2 Assessment,* page 21A
- *Highlights for Home,* page 21B

Supplemental Resources

VIDEO

From Christ to Constantine: The Trial and Testimony of the Early Church: Tape 2—"The Spread"

Gateway Films/Vision Video
www.catholicvideo.com

CHAPTER two

Flashback

Far from rejecting the Old Testament, the early Christians saw a deep meaning in it. They understood that both the Old and the New Testaments come from God and both come from the lived experiences of God's people.

Place yourself in one of the scenes referenced below. Read the account in a book of the Old Testament. Imagine you are reacting with one or more of these faith ancestors in the particular time period. Write a dialogue between the person (or persons) and yourself after the scene you have chosen takes place. (Use the reverse side of this page.) Then write a brief explanation of a few ways the scriptural account enriches your life of faith.

Moses and Aaron Before Pharaoh

After God gives Moses his mission to lead the people out of Egypt, he returns to confront the Pharaoh. (*See Exodus 5:18–31.*)

Judith Speaks to the Leaders

The Jews, suffering from drought, were discouraged. Their leader, Uzziah, and the elders of their city were going to surrender to the Assyrians. Judith speaks to the men. (*See Judith 8:9–36.*)

Solomon's Judgment

Solomon was known for his love of God and for exercising God's gift of wisdom. The following is an example of Solomon's judgment. (*See 1 Kings 3:16–28.*)

Saul and David Discuss Fighting Goliath

After David is sent for to play the harp for King Saul, the young shepherd addresses Saul. (*See 1 Samuel 17:32–37.*)

Unlike Any Other

They were all astounded and glorified God, saying, "We have never seen anything like this."
Mark 2:12

Objective: To discover that the New Testament came out of the lived experiences of the Church and was written under the guidance of the Holy Spirit.

Introduction ___ min.

Opening Prayer: Invite the young people to look at the photo of the Grand Canyon on pages 14 and 15. Play a song with the theme of Jesus' invitation to deepen friendship with and knowledge of him. "Jesus on the Mountain Peak" by Bob Moore (*When the Lord in Glory Comes*, GIA) is appropriate.

Then give each young person a stone, a shell, or any other natural object each of which is "unlike any other." If possible, have the young people use permanent markers or paint to inscribe their initials on the object. Display a picture or icon of Jesus that is appealing. Play an instrumental recording while the young people come forward to place their stones and shells around the Jesus icon. The Dameans' "There Is One Lord" (*Reflection*, Vol. 1, GIA) would be appropriate. Pray together:

• Jesus, Son of God, you are unlike any other.

• May we come to know you by reading the Bible, a book unlike any other.

• May we appreciate ourselves as images of God, unlike any other.

Close by praying together the Sign of the Cross.

Forum: Have the young people gather in a "Storytellers" circle. Use a speaker's symbol (a microphone or a small megaphone) to pass from one to the next. Have each person tell the story of the person in history whom he or she admires. Also ask the "Storyteller" to explain the ways he or she will pass on the person's story.

Presentation ___ min.

◆ Invite the young people to form small groups to discuss the introductory questions on page 16. Have a reporter from each group share its response to the second question.

Allow a few minutes for the young people to write their own responses to these questions in their journals.

◆ Write *oral tradition* on the board. Have a volunteer define the term. Ask, "How and why did the earliest members of the Church use oral tradition?"

◆ Ask the young people to share the key concepts they underlined on pages 16 and 17. Then have them highlight or underline in color the statements highlighted on the reduced pages.

◆ On the board draw a tree with five large roots. Label the tree "New Testament." Ask a volunteer to write on each root one of the sources we consider to be roots of the New Testament. The following should be included:

• oral tradition

• hymns and creeds

• collected sayings

• letters of Saint Paul (after Jesus' death and resurrection)

• gospels begin to appear (about 15 years after Paul began his letters).

An apostle giving testimony about Jesus at a public gathering, Raphael, 16th century

What do you think it must have been like to have been a follower and close friend of Jesus? What would you have wanted to tell others about him?

The Truth from Inside

A person does not need faith to establish the fact that Jesus of Nazareth existed and that he had a profound influence on the history of the world. None of this can be denied. For a person of faith, however, there is so much more to Jesus than a few bare facts from history. What do we as people of faith know about him? Where can we connect with this individual who changed the world and who is at the center of the Christian religion?

Our roots go back to the apostles, who were Jesus' closest friends and followers. They were chosen by him, and for about three years they lived with him and walked with him and listened to all he taught them. What they passed on to the other disciples about these experiences has been faithfully preserved by the Church for all time.

16

How did the Church community do this? At first it was done through *oral tradition*. This means that what the apostles experienced about Jesus and what they learned from him were passed on by word of mouth. The earliest members of the Church saw no need to write anything down in the form of an official record of Jesus. After all, the Lord Jesus himself left no written document of his life or teaching.

Moreover, like other teachers of his time, Jesus taught by the spoken word. His disciples, like the disciples of all great teachers of that time, remembered his words and discussed them. This was not unusual; the disciples were people of their time. They were not highly educated, nor were they practiced in the art of writing. Like many ancient people, however, they were accustomed to committing words and ideas to memory.

Even after the resurrection there was still no need to write down anything because the apostles and other eyewitnesses to Jesus were still alive. If people wanted to know something about Jesus, all they had to do was talk to these eyewitnesses and close friends of the Lord. They could also speak to Mary, his mother. Another reason formal written records were not kept from the start was that the community expected that Jesus would return to them very soon.

More Than Word of Mouth

Oral tradition was not the only way people expressed their faith in Jesus. Whenever the Christian community gathered for liturgy, they sang psalms from the Old Testament as well as other hymns that had been composed about Jesus and what he meant for the world. Many of these hymns were written down, as were creeds and other statements of belief. Early on, people also collected the sayings of Jesus that they had heard from Jesus himself or from the preaching and teaching of the apostles. Nevertheless, these were private collections and had no official standing or authority in the Church.

It was not long, however, before things changed for the early Church community. People began to realize that the second coming of Jesus was not going to happen immediately, that it would take place at some future time. Then the first apostles began to die. Many feared that soon none of the original followers of Jesus would be left. Where could people turn to make sure that the truth about Jesus and his teaching was being handed on? About twenty years after the death and resurrection of Jesus, what we now describe as the first official writings of the Church began to appear. These were the letters written by Saint Paul to various Christian communities.

Such good news about the life and teachings of Jesus could not be contained in letters alone. Something more was needed, and the gospel accounts emerged in answer to that need. These gospels began to appear about fifteen years after Paul began to write his letters. Eventually the Church recognized and determined that Paul's letters and four gospel accounts would be part of what we now call the New Testament. These writings came out of the lived experience of the Church and were written under the guidance of the Holy Spirit. They addressed the needs of different Church communities and took shape over a long period of time.

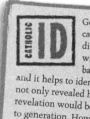

CATHOLIC ID
God making himself known to us is called *divine revelation*. Understanding divine revelation is essential to our whole life of faith. In fact it is the basis of everything Christians believe, and it helps to identify who we are as Catholics. God not only revealed himself but made sure that his revelation would be passed on from generation to generation. How did this happen? It happened through the passing on of tradition and the writing of Sacred Scripture. God's revealing activity took place in the history of the community. It also took place over a long period of time and reached its high point in Jesus Christ.

◆ Have the young people form three "Witness Groups." Give each group leader an assignment card. Provide the "Sayings" group with drawing paper and ribbons for scrolls.

• Oral Tradition: Read Jesus' words about paying taxes to the emperor in Matthew 22:15–22. Learn this gospel story by heart. Be prepared to tell it to others.

• Songs and Creeds: Read about the resurrection of Jesus in Matthew 28: 1–10. Compose a short song or creed, a prayer stating basic beliefs, to help others remember this gospel story.

• Sayings: Read Jesus' teaching about dependence on God in Matthew 6:25–34. Select any three sayings of Jesus about our attitudes towards food, drink, and/or clothing. Write them on a scroll to be shared with others.

◆ Have a volunteer summarize *Catholic ID* on page 17. Ask the young people to highlight or underline in color the last sentence.

FYI Jerome is one of the great saints of the Catholic Church. Born around A.D. 347, he devoted much of his life to the study of Sacred Scripture. He wrote many commentaries about the Bible and is best known for his translation of the Bible into the Latin language. He died in Bethlehem in 420 and is honored as the patron saint of Scripture scholars. Jerome loved God's word so much that he said, "Ignorance of the Scriptures is ignorance of Christ."

Presentation (cont'd)

◆ Have a volunteer read the 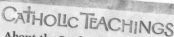 **thought provoker** on page 18. Allow a few minutes for the young people to write their responses in the space provided on page 18.

◆ Direct the young people's attention to the photo of the illuminated Bible pages on page 18. Print *scrivener* on the board. Explain that, in the Middle Ages, a scrivener or scribe carefully and prayerfully copied passages from the Scriptures. He or she may also have illuminated, or decorated, the border of these passages with imaginative lettering or symbols.

Have the young people imagine that they are scriveners. Distribute drawing paper and invite the young people to copy the verse from the Gospel of Mark on page 15. If time permits have them begin illuminating. Explain that completing the illumination is part of the *Forum Assignment*.

While the young people are working, play a thematic recording. "Here Begins the Good News" by Marty Haugen (*The Song of Mark*, GIA) would be appropriate.

◆ Write the word *testament* on the board. Call for a synonym (*covenant*) and have someone explain why the two major divisions in the Bible are called "testaments." (*They are concerned with God's covenant with us. They describe how God keeps the covenant made through Moses and fulfilled in Jesus.*)

CATHOLIC TEACHINGS
About the Books of the Bible

After the time of Jesus, the Jewish rabbis who lived in Palestine accepted thirty-nine books as their Scripture. It was written in Hebrew. The early Christians used the Greek translation of the Hebrew Bible. This translation, called the Septuagint, included seven additional books. These were First and Second Maccabees, Tobit, Judith, Sirach, Wisdom, and Baruch. On the basis of apostolic tradition, the Catholic Church officially recognized these forty-six books of the Septuagint as the Old Testament. Today the Jews and most Protestants accept only the thirty-nine books agreed upon in Palestine. That is why Catholic versions of the Bible are different. All Christians, however, accept the same twenty-seven books of the New Testament.

Illuminated pages, Wycliffe Bible, 1440

Did the coming of this new testimony about Jesus and his disciples mean that the sacred writings of the Jewish people were no longer needed? No! Nothing could be further from the truth. The early Church revered the writings of the Old Testament and accepted them as the word of God. This "new" testament about Jesus was understood as a completion and fulfillment of what had come before. Far from rejecting the Old Testament, Christians saw even deeper meaning in it.

Imagine that you have the opportunity to talk with Mary, the mother of Jesus. If you could ask her one question about Jesus, what would it be?

18

Two Becoming One

To understand Jesus and the Church fully, we must know both the Old and the New Testaments because they belong with each other. That is why we will explore more about both testaments in the next chapter. As we shall see, both the Old and the New Testaments come from God, and both come from the lived experience of God's people. Together the two testaments form one book that we call the Bible, a book unlike any other.

The Bible may look like any other book when it is sitting on the shelf. But nothing could be further from the truth. It is more than a book; it is a library of books. The very word *bible* comes from a word meaning "the books." This describes exactly what the Bible is. It is a collection of seventy-three books that were written over a period of many centuries. Each book was written to hand on a message about faith in God.

The seventy-three books are divided into the Old Testament and the New Testament. The Old Testament is made up of forty-six books. The New Testament is made up of twenty-seven books. All the books together make up the complete Bible.

Take time to look at the chart on page 20 that gives the names of all seventy-three books of the Bible and how they are divided.

When we use the word *testament*, we are not talking about testifying, or giving witness, as when we speak of a "last will and testament." Rather, *testament* is another word for "covenant." So the Bible is that collection of books that is concerned with God's covenant with us. This was the agreement God made with the people of Israel through Moses (the old covenant). It was brought to fulfillment in Jesus (the new covenant).

Because the Bible is so important in the life of God's people, we generally refer to it as Scripture or Sacred Scripture. The word *scripture* gives us a clue right away that the Bible is the word of God put in writing. As Catholics we know that Scripture cannot stand alone. Scripture and tradition together make present the mystery of Christ in our lives. Scripture and tradition make up "a single sacred deposit" of the word of God (*Catechism*, 97).

Contemporary Christians often meet to discuss and pray over what they read in the Bible.

19

◆ Have the young people share the key concepts they underlined on pages 18 and 19. Have them highlight or underline in color the statements highlighted on the reduced pupil pages.

◆ Have volunteers summarize *Catholic Teachings*. Ask the young people to look at the chart on page 20. Have volunteers identify what type each of the additional books are.

• First and Second Maccabees (*historical*)

• Tobit (*historical*)

• Judith (*historical*)

• Sirach (*wisdom*)

• Baruch (*prophetic*)

Have the young people look through the Old Testament to find the beginning of each of the books listed on the chart.

◆ Ask, "What makes present the mystery of Christ in our lives?" (*Scripture and tradition*) Emphasize that Scripture and tradition make up "a single sacred deposit" of the word of God (*Catechism*, 97).

Presentation (cont'd)

◆ Distribute the handout *Flashback*. Have a volunteer read the scene references described. Have the young people check the chart on page 20 to identify the type of book for each reference given. (*Exodus: Pentateuch; 1 Samuel, 1 Kings, and Judith: historical*)

◆ Discuss with the general group the two questions posed in *Things to Share* on page 21. Have the young people form small groups to discuss the questions for *Things to Think About*.

◆ Direct attention to *Words to Remember* on page 21. The definition of *oral tradition* is on page 17. The definition for *testament* is on page 19.

Conclusion ___ min.

◆ Have a volunteer read *On Line with the Parish*. Ask, "Why is Sacred Scripture so important for the life of the Church?" (*Scripture is concerned with God's covenant with us brought to fulfillment in Jesus. It is the word of God in writing.*)

Assessment: If you wish to administer *Chapter 2 Assessment* on page 21A, allow about ten minutes for its completion.

Books of the Bible

The Old Testament

Pentateuch

Genesis	Numbers
Exodus	Deuteronomy
Leviticus	

Wisdom Books

Job	Song of Songs
Psalms	Wisdom
Proverbs	Sirach
Ecclesiastes	

Historical Books

Joshua	2 Chronicles
Judges	Ezra
Ruth	Nehemiah
1 Samuel	Tobit
2 Samuel	Judith
1 Kings	Esther
2 Kings	1 Maccabees
1 Chronicles	2 Maccabees

Prophetic Books

Isaiah	Obadiah
Jeremiah	Jonah
Lamentations	Micah
Baruch	Nahum
Ezekiel	Habakkuk
Daniel	Zephaniah
Hosea	Haggai
Joel	Zechariah
Amos	Malachi

The New Testament

Gospels

Matthew	Luke
Mark	John

Other Writings

Acts of the Apostles   Revelation

Letters

Romans	1 Thessalonians	James
1 Corinthians	2 Thessalonians	1 Peter
2 Corinthians	1 Timothy	2 Peter
Galatians	2 Timothy	1 John
Ephesians	Titus	2 John
Philippians	Philemon	3 John
Colossians	Hebrews	Jude

20

Answers for Chapter 2 Assessment

1. d	2. c	3. a	4. a	5. b
6. d	7. c	8. c	9. a	10. See page 19.

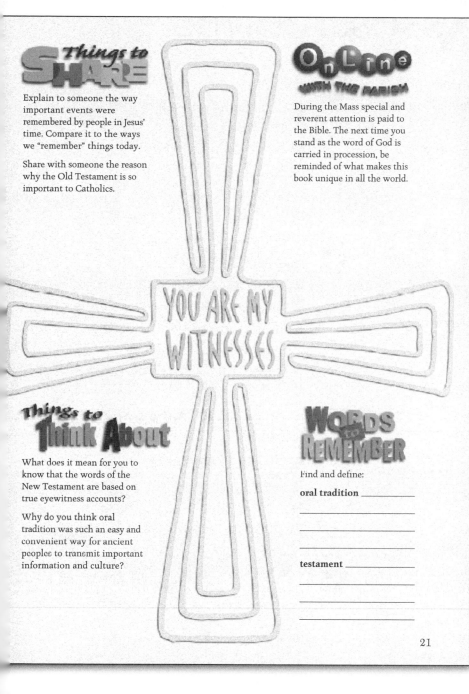

Things to SHARE

Explain to someone the way important events were remembered by people in Jesus' time. Compare it to the ways we "remember" things today.

Share with someone the reason why the Old Testament is so important to Catholics.

OnLine WITH THE PARISH

During the Mass special and reverent attention is paid to the Bible. The next time you stand as the word of God is carried in procession, be reminded of what makes this book unique in all the world.

Things to Think About

What does it mean for you to know that the words of the New Testament are based on true eyewitness accounts?

Why do you think oral tradition was such an easy and convenient way for ancient peoples to transmit important information and culture?

WORDS to REMEMBER

Find and define:

oral tradition _____
_____
_____
_____

testament _____
_____
_____
_____

YOU ARE MY WITNESSES

21

Conclusion (cont'd)

◆ Have a volunteer read the directions for the handout activity *Flashback*. Make sure everyone understands them.

FORUM Assignment

✔ Read pages 22–29. Underline in pencil the statements that express six key ideas.

✔ Complete the handout *Flashback*. Be prepared to share your dialogues and explanations. Complete the scrivener's assignment.

Closing Prayer: Invite the young people to look at the photograph of the Grand Canyon on pages 14 and 15. Then have the young people form two choral-reading groups. Have the groups alternate reading verses two through seven of Psalm 47.

Evaluation: Do the young people understand that the truth of Jesus' existence is verified by the New Testament and Church tradition? Do they appreciate the ways in which the Old and New Testaments together are revered by the Church as the word of God?

FOR CHAPTER 3

• preparations for opening prayer
• copies of handout *Making Plans*, page 22C
• copies of *Chapter 3 Assessment*, page 29A
• copies of *Highlights for Home*, page 29B

Assessment

1 Circle the answer that does *not* belong. The apostles relied on oral tradition because
   a. Jesus taught by the spoken word.
   b. they expected Jesus to return soon.
   c. at first they saw no need for a written record.
   d. no one knew how to write.

2 The first official Church writings
   a. were songs.
   b. were creeds.
   c. were Saint Paul's letters.
   d. were stories.

3 The gospels began to appear
   a. about fifteen years after Paul's letters.
   b. on Good Friday.
   c. about eighty years after Jesus died.
   d. immediately after Pentecost.

4 The four gospel accounts
   a. are part of the New Testament.
   b. are all alike.
   c. pre-date Paul's letters.
   d. were written in the same year.

5 The Bible is
   a. only a history book.
   b. a collection of books.
   c. just like other books.
   d. not inspired.

6 The Old Testament
   a. is made up of seventy-three books.
   b. is the complete Bible.
   c. is divided into ten major categories.
   d. is made up of forty-six books.

7 The New Testament is
   a. made up of thirty-three books.
   b. another word for the gospels.
   c. made up of twenty-seven books.
   d. called the Septuagint.

8 The _____ is the Greek translation of the Hebrew Bible.
   a. Book of Nehemiah
   b. Covenant
   c. Septuagint
   d. none of the above

9 The early Church _____ the writings of the Old Testament.
   a. revered
   b. ignored
   c. criticized
   d. disagreed with

10 Why do we as Catholics need both Scripture and Church tradition?

_____
_____
_____
_____
_____
_____

Chapter 2: Unlike Any Other
Highlights for Home

Focus on Faith

In Chapter 2, the young people trace the roots of the New Testament in the early Church community. These roots go back to the apostles, who for three years lived with Jesus and listened to all he taught them. They passed on these experiences to other disciples through oral tradition. The earliest Church members committed to memory what the apostles told them about Jesus. The early community did not keep written records because they expected Jesus to return to them soon. When the early Christians realized that the second coming of Jesus was not immediate and with the deaths of the apostles, they became concerned. They wanted to make sure that the truth about Jesus and his teaching was being handed on. About twenty years after Jesus' death and resurrection, Saint Paul's letters written to various Christian communities, are now considered to be the first official writings of the Church. The gospel accounts emerged about fifteen years after Paul began writing his letters. Eventually, the Church recognized and determined that Paul's letters and four gospel accounts would be part of the New Testament.

Conversation Starters

. . . . a few ideas to talk about together . . . .

◆ What can I do today to show my gratitude for the Bible?

◆ At this particular time of my life, what book or books do I find most enriching?

Feature Focus

The *Catholic Teachings* feature on page 18 clarifies differences between Catholic versions of the Bible and those of most Protestants. On the basis of apostolic tradition the Church recognizes seven more Old Testament books than do Protestants and Jews. These seven books were included in the Septuagint, the Greek translation of the Hebrew Bible. This translation was used by the early Christians. All Christians, however, accept the same twenty-seven books of the New Testament.

Reflection

When the early Christians gathered for liturgy, they sang psalms from the Old Testament. The words of the psalms have been sung for centuries. Choose your favorite psalm. Pray it slowly. Imagine that you hear many ancestors of faith praying these words with you.

If possible, prayerfully view one or more psalm segments on the videos *Holy Darkness* (the music of Dan Schutte) or *Visions of Gregorian Chants*. Both are available from Oblate Media and Communications Corporation. The address is:

Video with Values
1944 Innerbelt Business Center Drive
St. Louis, MO 63114–5718

THE DIVINE WORD

Adult Focus

In Chapter 3 the young people learn that the Bible is in a class of one. No other book has been authored by God acting in and by means of inspired human authors. The authors of the Bible were human authors; they chose the words, the stories, the characters themselves. At the same time, *God* is the author of Scripture since everything in the Bible was written under the inspiration of the Holy Spirit. Therefore, when presenting this chapter, it is important to emphasize the Church's teaching about divine inspiration:

> God is the author of Sacred Scripture because he inspired its human authors; he acts in them and by means of them. He thus gives us assurance that their writings teach without error his saving truth. (*Catechism*, 136).

Go over the mistaken notions about divine inspiration: dictation theory, God-as-assistant theory, and the later-approval theory. You will want to be able to explain these clearly to the young people and to discuss with them why the theories are erroneous. It is quite possible that our young people will encounter theories like these from those who take a fundamentalist or literalist approach to the Bible. Such an approach distorts the truth of God's message.

Catechism Focus

The theme of Chapter 3 corresponds to paragraphs 80-82, 121-123, and 136-137 of the *Catechism*.

Enrichment Activities

The Video Crew

Invite a rotating crew of volunteers to work with you in selecting, previewing, and showing video segments to illustrate and amplify chapter themes. For Chapter 3, crew members might choose one or more segments of the musical video *The Word* for opening-prayer experiences. Have presenters introduce video segments by providing an explanation of the context. Then have them follow through with dialogue questions and prayer.

Computer Connection

Invite the young people to share their reflections on 2 Peter 1:19. (See page 23 of the text.) Have the group think of messages they would like to give to others about being attentive to God's word. Then invite the young people to use a paint program such as *Flying Colors*™ to design the illustrated messages. If your group is using *Flying Colors*™, have the young people choose an appropriate background canvas, and then access Text Tool, "T" on the side menu, to write their messages on the canvas. Point out the alphabet that appears at the bottom of the screen and explain that letters can be clicked on and dragged to any position. Direct the young people to string together words and sentences to enter their messages. Encourage them to use the paint tools and stamps to fill in their canvases.

Teaching Resources

Overview

To discover the meaning of divine inspiration; to explore mistaken notions about inspiration.

Opening Prayer Ideas

Look at the photo on pages 22 and 23. Reflect on 2 Peter 1:19.

or

Light a battery-operated candle or a lamp. Reflect on ways God's word is a lamp in our lives.

Materials

- Bibles, journals, and highlighters

New Testament Journal:
For Chapter 3, use pages 8–9.

REPRODUCIBLE MASTERS
- *Making Plans*, page 22C
- *Chapter 3 Assessment*, page 29A
- *Highlights for Home*, page 29B

Supplemental Resources

VIDEOS
The Word
Gateway Films/Vision Video
P.O. Box 540
Worcester, PA 19490-0540

Understanding the Bible
Part 1: "God's Word: An Invitation"
St. Anthony Messenger Press
1615 Republic Street
Cincinnati, OH 45210-1298

CHAPTER three

Making Plans

There are many ways of reading and praying with Scripture in our everyday lives. In the Mass each day, the Liturgy of the Word offers us two readings and a responsorial psalm for our instruction and reflection. Or, we can choose one book of the Bible (perhaps a gospel or an epistle) to read straight through, as few as five verses a day. Or, we may want to look ahead to the Sunday readings for the coming week. We can read the three readings and psalm during the week in preparation for the celebration of the coming Sunday.

A plan for the prayerful daily or weekly reading of the Scriptures is outlined here. Make your plans now!

Plans

Step 1: Choose a weekly or daily time and place to get to know God's word.

Time:_____

Place:_____

Step 2: Make a plan for becoming familiar with the gospels.

Gospel I will begin with:_____

Reasons for my choice:_____

How I will proceed:_____

Step 3: Decide in what ways and with whom you will share your Bible experiences.

Way of sharing:_____

With: _____

Step 4: Pray that Jesus will keep you faithful to your plan.

My prayer:_____

> Be attentive to God's word
> "as to a lamp shining in a dark place,
> until day dawns and the morning
> star rises in your hearts."
> *2 Peter 1:19*

The Divine Word

Objectives: To discover the meaning of divine inspiration; to explore mistaken notions about inspiration.

Introduction ___ min.

Opening Prayer: Before the session begins, on the board draw a sketch of the photo on pages 22 and 23. Begin the prayer by directing the young people's attention to the photo. Then use the following directions to conduct a shared reflection with the general group.

• Imagine you are in a dark cavern. No natural light is coming in to guide your way. You have no artificial means of light. What are your feelings? How do you react? (*Pause.*)

Your feelings in this situation can be compared to the ones you may experience when you are puzzled or not receiving counsel or guidance. Name words or phrases that describe your feelings in these situations. (*Have a recorder write the words on the cavern in your drawing.*)

• Imagine that you suddenly see light streaming in to guide your way. What are your feelings? How do you react? (*Pause.*)

Your feelings in this situation can be compared to the ones you may experience when you have made a decision, solved your problem, or taken the advice of a counselor. Name words or phrases that describe your feelings. (*Have a second recorder write the words on the beam of light in your drawing.*)

• What resources are available to you for enlightenment or guidance when you face these situations? (*Have a third recorder write the resources in the pool in the drawing. If the young people do not name prayer or Scripture, ask the recorder to write these spiritual resources.*)

Then invite the young people to proclaim 2 Peter 1:19 on page 23.

Forum: Have the young people form small groups in which to share their dialogues written for the handout *Flashback*. Then have each group choose one dialogue, make necessary changes, and present it to the general group.

Then invite the young people to show each other their illuminations of Luke 11:9.

Presentation ___ min.

◆ Ask the young people to discuss the key concepts they underlined on page 24 and 25. Write *divine inspiration* on the board. Ask the young people to define the term. (*the special influence of the Holy Spirit on the human authors of the Bible*) Ask, "Why is inspiration an extremely important concept in the study of and appreciation of Sacred Scripture?" (See right column on page 25.)

Have the group highlight the statements highlighted on page 25. Emphasize that the Bible is unique in its divine origin and authority. God acts through human authors while respecting their identities and gifts.

Two pages from the *Codex Sinaiticus*, the oldest complete New Testament known to exist

*W*ho wrote the books of the New Testament? of the Old Testament? Who are the authors— or the author—of the Bible? What do you think?

A Question of Authorship

Whenever we write something down, we cannot help but leave clues about ourselves simply by the way we write. Such clues might include a favorite word or phrase, the point of view that we use, a peculiar style of expression, or even the choice of subject. There are also regional expressions that can hint at the identity of a writer. Depending on where one lives in the United States, for example, soft drinks are called either "soda" or "pop." In some areas of the country, a person is described as standing "in line"; in other places, the expression is standing "on line."

It is easy to see that what we say and what we write tell us many things. We can guess at people's educational background, their place of birth and the neighborhood where they grew up, their experiences and the type of work they do, and even the kind of people with whom they have associated. Obviously our guesswork will not tell us everything, but it can provide many pieces to help fit together the puzzle of human identity.

24

24

The Bible, too, gives us clues about its authorship. When we move from book to book among the seventy-three books of Sacred Scripture, we detect the hands of different authors at work. We become aware of different expressions and styles of writing, different points of view and reasons for writing. Some books are more exciting and more colorful than others. Some writers, such as the author of Luke's Gospel and the Acts of the Apostles, were better storytellers than others. Some came from a background of power and influence, and others came from more humble surroundings. A few of the writers may have been teachers or lawyers. Some of the writers of the Old Testament may have been priests of the Jewish religion. In any event it does not take much time and effort to determine that the Bible is the work of many different authors.

Is the Bible only a collection of various authors' works? Yes and no. As Catholics we believe that the Bible had many authors and, at the same time, that the Bible had only one author. This means two things:

- The many authors of the Bible were its human authors. They were the literary sources of the books. Like the authors of any writings, they themselves chose the words, the expressions, the stories, the names of characters, and all things that go into the making of a written document. No one else did it for them.

- At the same time God is the author of Scripture. This is because all the books of the Bible and all the words in them were written under the influence of the Holy Spirit. This is what we call divine inspiration.

Divine inspiration is the special influence of the Holy Spirit on the human authors of the Bible. Because of this influence, God himself becomes the authority behind Scripture and therefore becomes in the deepest sense its author, too. For this reason we call the Bible the word of God. That is why the sublime message of Scripture surpasses mere human invention.

Inspiration is an extremely important concept in the study and appreciation of Sacred Scripture. If we do not have a clear and well-grounded understanding of inspiration, the true meaning of Scripture—both the Old Testament and the New Testament—will be lost. If we do not have this understanding, the Bible becomes just like any other book sitting on a library shelf.

The Bible, however, is not like any other book. It has a divine origin and authority. This is what the Catholic Church teaches us: "God is the author of Sacred Scripture because he inspired its human authors; he acts in them and by means of them. He thus gives assurance that their writings teach without error his saving truth" (*Catechism*, 136).

Let's explore this wonderful mystery of the Bible's authorship more fully.

What was your first clue that the Bible is more than the product of human hands alone?

25

◆ Direct attention to the thought provoker on page 25. As you are writing the following "clue" references on the board (2 Timothy 3:15, Luke 24:32, Romans 15:4), explain to the young people that you don't want them to be "clueless." Have them investigate each clue. After a volunteer reads each one, ask, "What is the human author saying about Scripture being more than the product of human authorship?"

◆ To encourage reverence and appreciation for Scripture, choose a few books of the Old Testament and a few books of the New Testament. Use the following prayer script as the young people open to each book.

- Let us open our Bibles to the Gospel of _____.
- Let us thank God for the human author of this book.
- We thank you, God. We know this is your word.

Play and/or sing "Take the Word of God with You" by Christopher Walker (*Christ Is Here,* Oregon Catholic Press).

FYI The American poet Emily Dickinson (1830-1886) wrote the following verse. Do you agree with the poet? Think about the power of the words written by divinely inspired human authors of the Bible.

> A word is dead
> When it is said,
> Some say.
> I say it just
> Begins to live
> That day.

Presentation (cont'd)

◆ Discuss with the young people the ways the photo montage on page 26 illustrates the concept of divine inspiration of the Bible's human authors.

Have the young people imagine they are photographers. Invite them to describe in their journals the photos they would take or the photos they would combine to illustrate the concept of divine inspiration.

Choose a volunteer photo-exhibit director. The director is to call on the young people to share their descriptions of the photos.

◆ On the board, write the names of the theories of inspiration described on pages 26 and 27. Have volunteers explain these mistaken notions.

Then have the young people form panels of four. Ask each panel to have someone represent a person who thinks each of the following mistaken notions about divine inspiration is correct: dictation theory, God-as-assistant theory, and later-approval theory. Have the fourth panelist represent a person who adheres to the Church's teaching. Allow about ten minutes for the panel discussion. During the discussions visit each panel to make sure the panelists are on the right track.

A Divine Author

What do most people think of when they hear the word *author*? They probably think of someone using a keyboard or paper and pen to put down his or her thoughts. There are some authors, however, who dictate their words and ideas into a machine or to another person who copies them down.

Is this what we mean when we say that God is the author of the Bible? Did God himself actually write down the words or dictate them to the human authors of the Bible? Not at all. God did not do either one of these things. Many people, however, used to think that God worked in that way. We call this the *dictation theory of inspiration*.

According to the dictation theory, God alone is the author of the Bible. He dictated every single word—and the punctuation, too! The human being who copied down God's words was nothing more than a robot and made no contribution to God's dictation.

This is a simple theory, but it is really too simple. The problem with such a theory is that God would never act in that way. After all, God created human beings in his own image and would never treat them in such a manner. He would want each human author of the Bible to make his own particular contribution to the writing and reflect his own personality. God would never use human beings as if they were unthinking machines.

26

For all these reasons the Catholic Church rejects the dictation theory of inspiration. The Second Vatican Council taught that God, the divine author, speaks in Sacred Scripture "through men in human fashion" (*Divine Revelation*, 12).

Other Mistaken Notions

The dictation theory, which makes God alone the author of the Bible, is not the only mistake people have made about divine inspiration. Some people have gone to the other extreme. They hold that human beings alone were the authors of the Bible. According to this theory God did not really have much to do with the writing of Scripture except to prevent the human author from falling into error. God provided no new information. We call this idea the *God-as-assistant theory*.

Such a theory reduces Scripture to a mere human enterprise and makes it more like a textbook on faithful living. Then Scripture is no longer God's word; it is not the divine word. Naturally the Church rejects this theory, too.

Another approach to inspiration suggested by some people might be called the *later-approval theory*. According to this idea the Bible was written in the same way as every other book. Then, when the Church accepted the writings as sacred, it was understood that the Holy Spirit was approving them. But the problem with this theory is the idea that the Holy Spirit had nothing to do with the biblical writings before the Church approved them. Like the God-as-assistant theory, this type of thinking makes Scripture a nice book but not the word of God. That is why the Church rejects this theory, too.

These mistaken notions about divine inspiration were thought up in the past. Unfortunately they still have an effect on people's thinking today. People who accept some form of the dictation theory can be described as strict fundamentalists. They take every word of the Bible literally. They accept every word at its face value and never look at the deeper meaning behind it.

CATHOLIC ID In the liturgy of the Catholic Church, we often read Sacred Scripture from both the Old Testament and the New Testament. After the first two readings, the lector says, "The word of the Lord." After the gospel is proclaimed, the priest or deacon says, "The gospel of the Lord." In each case we respond, "Thanks be to God" or "Praise to you, Lord Jesus Christ." We acknowledge that God is the author of Sacred Scripture. In practice, then, Catholics profess their belief in divine inspiration at every liturgy.

27

Note: The following story sharing is optional.

◆ Share the following story with the young people. Discuss LT's attitude.

LT, a person who took every word of the Bible literally, was reading Psalm 37:5:

Commit your way to the LORD;
trust that God will act. . . .

Suddenly a dam burst and the street was flooded. LT climbed to the roof and prayed for God to act.

Three times a helicopter rescue team flew by, but LT would not grab on to the rope to be rescued. Eventually the water swallowed his house and him with it.

In heaven LT complained to God, "I trusted you, but you did not act." And God said, "What about the helicopter rescue team I sent to you three times?"

◆ Have a volunteer summarize *Catholic ID* on page 27. Then play for reflection a song with the theme of God's word. A suggestion is "Here Begins the Good News" by Marty Haugen (*The Song of Mark*, GIA).

Invite the young people to write their reflections in their journals.

◆ Have the young people highlight the statements highlighted on pages 26 and 27.

Presentation (cont'd)

◆ Invite the young people to write in the space provided their responses to the ☼ **thought provoker** on page 28. Then have them form small groups to discuss their responses.

In these same groups, have them take turns role-playing the two situations described in *Things to Share.*

◆ Have a volunteer read *On Line with the Parish.* If your parish does not conduct summer Bible classes, suggest that those who wish may want to prepare a puppet reenactment of a Bible story.

Invite a preschool, kindergarten, or first-grade group to your meeting room for the presentation.

Conclusion ___ min.

◆ With the entire group, discuss the questions in *Things to Think About.* Then direct attention to *Words to Remember.*

The definition for *divine inspiration* is on page 25. The explanation of *dictation theory* is on page 26.

Assessment: If you wish to administer *Chapter 3 Assessment,* page 29A, allow about ten minutes for its completion.

Why do you think people are tempted to accept mistaken notions about inspiration?

Consider, for example, the following saying of Jesus: "It is easier for a camel to pass through the eye of a needle than for one who is rich to enter the kingdom of God" (Matthew 19:24). If we take these words literally, no rich person would have a chance to get to heaven. But that is not what is meant here. These words are obviously an exaggeration for effect. They teach a message in a clear and colorful way that people can understand, but they should never be taken literally. To take them literally distorts the truth of God's message.

On the other hand, some people hold an opposite view and do not take God's word seriously at all. For these people the words of Scripture carry about as much importance as a book of recipes. This is because for them God really is not the author, if he had anything at all to do with Scripture. Sadly, these people often want to interpret Scripture to serve themselves.

The real truth about divine inspiration is more complex but also much more exciting and satisfying. This is because it respects both divine authorship and human authorship.

28

Answers for Chapter 3 Assessment
1. d   2. b   3. c   4. d   5. c
6. d   7. c   8. a   9. c   10. See page 25.

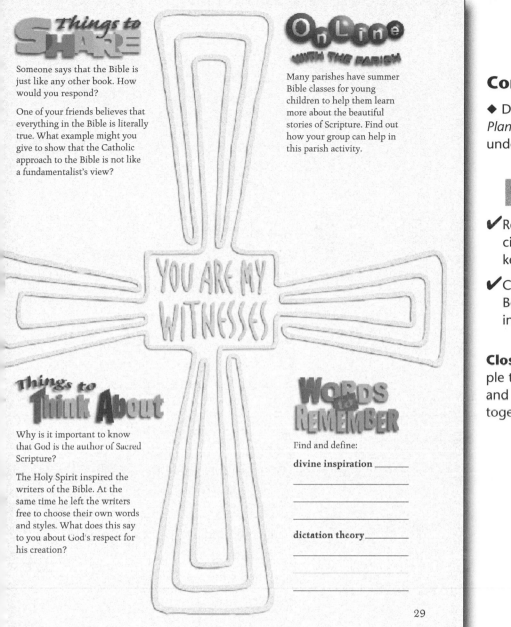

Things to SHARE

Someone says that the Bible is just like any other book. How would you respond?

One of your friends believes that everything in the Bible is literally true. What example might you give to show that the Catholic approach to the Bible is not like a fundamentalist's view?

OnLine WITH THE PARISH

Many parishes have summer Bible classes for young children to help them learn more about the beautiful stories of Scripture. Find out how your group can help in this parish activity.

YOU ARE MY WITNESSES

Things to Think About

Why is it important to know that God is the author of Sacred Scripture?

The Holy Spirit inspired the writers of the Bible. At the same time he left the writers free to choose their own words and styles. What does this say to you about God's respect for his creation?

WORDS to REMEMBER

Find and define:

divine inspiration _____

_____

_____

_____

dictation theory _____

_____

_____

_____

29

Conclusion (cont'd)

◆ Distribute copies of handout *Making Plans*. Make sure the young people understand the directions.

FORUM Assignment

✔ Read pages 30–37. Underline in pencil the statement that expresses six key ideas.

✔ Complete the handout *Making Plans*. Be prepared to share your plans during the next *forum*.

Closing Prayer: Invite the young people to look at the photo on pages 22 and 23. Then have the group pray together Psalm 1:1-3.

Evaluation: Do the young people understand that human authors wrote Scripture under the inspiration of the Holy Spirit? Have they examined mistaken notions about inspiration?

FOR CHAPTER 4

• preparations for opening prayer
• copies of handout *True Colors*, page 30C
• copies of *Chapter 4 Assessment*, page 37A
• copies of *Highlights for Home*, page 37B
• box or bag decorated like a treasure chest

Assessment

1 The Bible has
a. one author.
b. four authors.
c. many authors.
d. both a and c

2 *Divine Inspiration* means
a. angelic assistance.
b. the Holy Spirit's influence on the biblical authors.
c. a feeling of holiness.
d. none of the above

3 The dictation theory of inspiration
a. is Church-approved.
b. is for secretaries.
c. holds that God dictated each word of the Bible to human authors.
d. honors human authors.

4 To take every word of the Bible literally is to
a. distort God's message.
b. misunderstand intended exaggerations.
c. confuse truths of faith with truths of science and history.
d. all of the above

5 The God-as-assistant theory of inspiration is that _____ alone were the authors of the Bible.
a. the Father, Son, and Holy Spirit
b. the apostles
c. human beings
d. the Holy Family

6 Catholics profess their belief in divine inspiration
a. at every liturgy.
b. only after the gospel.
c. in their responses after all the readings.
d. both a and c

7 The theory that says that the Bible was written like any other book and eventually approved by the Church is called the
a. God-as-assistant theory.
b. divine inspiration theory.
c. later-approval theory.
d. dictation theory of inspiration.

8 Circle the one that does *not* belong.
The many authors of the Bible
a. all came from the same background.
b. came from different backgrounds.
c. used different styles of writing.
d. expressed different points of view.

9 Those who take every word of the Bible at face value without looking at the deeper meaning are
a. authors.
b. Church Scripture scholars.
c. fundamentalists.
d. lectors.

10 Describe clues that the Bible gives us about its authorship.

Highlights for Home

Focus on Faith

When Dante wrote "The Divine Comedy," people exclaimed, "Ah! What an inspired work!" But when we say that the Bible is "inspired," we mean so much more than this.

As Catholics we believe that the Bible had many authors and, at the same time, only one author. The many authors are its human authors who were the literary sources of the books. At the same time, God is the author of Scripture. This is because all the books of the Bible and all the words in them were written under the influence of the Holy Spirit.

Inspiration in its precise religious meaning refers to the influence of the Holy Spirit. The Scriptures are sacred and inspired as no other work can be because they are literally "in-Spirited." When we venture into the Bible with the young people, we can assure them that they are walking on sacred ground. They are opening themselves to the power of God's word.

Conversation Starters

. . . . a few ideas to talk about together . . . .

◆ Why shouldn't I take every word of the Bible literally?

◆ How might I encourage one other person to become more familiar with the word of God?

Feature Focus

In *Catholic ID* the young people are reminded that, in the liturgy, we often listen to readings from the Old Testament and the New Testament. As we say the responses after the readings, Catholics profess their belief that God is the author of Sacred Scripture. Give good example to your son or daughter by saying these responses in an enthusiastic, faith-filled manner.

Reflection

Spend a moment looking at the photograph on pages 22 and 23. Among the earth's natural phenomena, caves may be among the most inviting yet the most challenging. The darkness of a cave can overwhelm even the most eager explorer. In order to experience the natural wonders within, one must be prepared, above all, to carry one's own light. Life can be like a cave—dark, full of twists and turns. But we can explore freely, because we carry the light of the word of God with us, our "lamp shining in a dark place" as Saint Peter wrote (2 Peter 1:19).

Peter may have been recalling a familiar psalm. Carry this verse with you as you explore the darkness and transform it with light, the inspired word of God:

Your word is a lamp for my feet,
a light for my path. . . .
My life is always at risk,
but I do not forget your teaching.
Psalm 119:105, 109

THE CHURCH'S BOOK

Adult Focus

This chapter clarifies three important concepts in the historical process of the formation of the biblical writings we call the Scriptures: *revelation* passed on through *tradition*, recorded in writing under the *inspiration* of the Holy Spirit, thus becoming Scripture, the written word of God.

The inspiration of the Holy Spirit guided the human authors in discerning "what God wanted put into the sacred writings." The Holy Spirit guided the human authors in both the content of their writing and in choosing the truth God wanted taught. The Holy Spirit used their human gifts of language and expression to transmit the truth God intended for all people.

Does this mean that the Bible teaches every kind of truth in the world? No. In earlier ages, the truths of faith were not distinguished from the truths of history or science. Gradually we came to realize that Scripture was written to teach the truths of faith, not of science or of history.

Continue to encourage the young people to consider Scripture a source of guidance, strength, comfort, and correction so that they may be "equipped for every good work" (2 Timothy 3:1–7). For it is in Scripture that "the Father who is in heaven comes lovingly to meet his children, and talk with them" (*Catechism*, 104).

Catechism Focus

The theme of Chapter 4 corresponds to paragraphs 83, 104–107, 113, 120, and 134–135 of the *Catechism*.

Enrichment Activities

🖥 Computer Connection

Invite the young people to use a crossword software program, such as *WordCross®*, to make crossword puzzles that feature terms and names presented in Chapters 1 through 4.

Have the young people work in small groups. Direct each group to confer among themselves to make up a list of words and corresponding clues. If necessary, allow the groups to refer to the text. When all are ready, direct the groups to enter their words and clues into the computer to be processed into crossword puzzles. Then have the groups print and exchange puzzles. Allow ample time for the young people to solve one another's puzzles.

Easier Access

If the young people have their own Bibles or New Testaments, suggest that they make tabs to indicate the different books.

They may want to use tabs available for purchase from a stationery or office-supply store or make their own. This can be done by cutting small strips of paper, writing the names of the books on the strips, and then placing clear tape over both sides of the tabs. Then tape each tab to the first page of the particular book.

Suggest that the young people use a color code for the different types of books. The following is an example:

• historical books—tan
• prophets—green
• gospels—red

Teaching Resources

Overview

To discover that the Bible does not contain any errors about the truths of faith; to learn why the Bible is the Church's book.

Opening Prayer Ideas

Read and reflect on Matthew 6:19-21.

or

Pray together Psalm 1:1-3. Make a commitment to study and to pray God's word.

Materials

- Bibles, journals, and highlighters
- box or bag decorated like a treasure chest

New Testament Journal:
For Chapter 4, use pages 10–11.

REPRODUCIBLE MASTERS
- *True Colors*, page 30C
- *Chapter 4 Assessment*, page 37A
- *Highlights for Home*, page 37B

Supplemental Resources

VIDEOS
Journeys to the Edge of Creation
Ignatius Press
P.O. Box 1339
Ft. Collins, CO 80522

Understanding the Bible
Part 1: "God's Word: An Invitation"
St. Anthony Messenger Press
1615 Republic Street
Cincinnati, OH 45210-1298

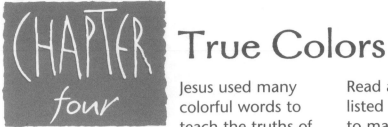

True Colors

Jesus used many colorful words to teach the truths of our faith. Reading and meditating on his teaching may help you to distinguish between the times you disguise yourself under false, colorful layers of selfishness and times when you reflect the true colors of God's love.

Read and reflect on each of the passages listed in the left column below. Draw a line to match it with the theme-related petition in the right column. Then try writing your own colorful prayer of petition. Don't forget to list the gospel chapter and verse.

Luke 19:1–10

Help me to scrape off the green layer of jealousy or envy for what others have. Help me to remember that green is a symbol of growth and hope in your promises.

Luke 11:29–37

Help me to remove the yellow layer of cowardice. Help me to follow the yellow and orange light of your guidance.

Matthew 20:20–28

Help me to scrape off the blue layer of coldness to others. Help me to remain a true-blue friend to you by showing my concern and serving others.

John 6:60–71

Help me to remove the purple layer of false pride. Help me to remember that purple symbolizes reconciliation and peace.

The Church's Book

All scripture is inspired by God.
2 Timothy 3:16

31

Objectives: To discover that the Bible does not contain any errors about the truths of faith; to learn why the Bible is the Church's book.

Introduction ___ min.

Note: Before the session begins, decorate a large box or gift bag to serve as a treasure chest. Place a Bible inside the chest. Then keep the treasure chest from the young people's view until the point suggested.

Opening Prayer: Invite a prepared volunteer to read Matthew 6:19–21. Allow about five minutes for reflection. Then ask the young people to list in their journals their treasures—people, places, things, qualities, talents, gifts.

Then present to the group the treasure chest you have prepared. Have a volunteer open the chest and show the group the treasure he or she has found. Ask the young people—if they have not done so—to add the Bible to their list of treasures. Ask, "Why does the Church consider the Bible a treasure?"

Then invite the young people to look at the photos on pages 30 and 31. Ask, "How do the various readings from Scripture give us uplifting thoughts and add color to our lives?" Then share the following prayer with the group:

> Write upon our hearts, O Lord God, the lessons of your holy word. Help us to be doers of the same, and not forgetful hearers only.

Forum: Have a "Principal Planner" call on volunteers to share the plans they have written on the handout *Making Plans*. Ask the young people to listen carefully to each presenter. This will give them practice in listening when the word of God is read at Mass.

Presentation ___ min.

◆ Before the session begins, draw a flow chart on the board that is helpful in conveying information about the *Dogmatic Constitution on Divine Revelation*. (See "God's Revealing Activity.") The designed outline should include topics listed below. During the session invite the young people to help you complete the chart by filling in the information (indicated here in parentheses) in the appropriate places.

• the two major areas of information with which it deals (*God's revelation of himself to us and how that revelation is transmitted through time*)

• the two communities to which God revealed himself (*community of Israel and apostolic community of the Church*)

• the ways in which God's revelation was made known (*testimony given by word of mouth—tradition; recorded in writing under the inspiration of the Holy Spirit—Scripture*).

◆ Discuss with the young people the key statements they underlined on pages 32 and 33. Have the group highlight the main ideas highlighted on the reduced pupil pages.

What is the origin of Sacred Scripture?
Why do you think the Bible is a book unlike any other?

God's Revealing Activity

When Jesus and members of the early Church used the word *Scripture*, they were referring to what we now call the Old Testament. They believed that these sacred writings were divinely inspired, and this belief was handed down to them from their Jewish heritage. Before the time of Christ, belief in biblical inspiration was common in Judaism. So it was a part of Jesus' beliefs and those of the early Church, too.

From the earliest days of the Church, the idea of inspiration was accepted and applied to the writings of the New Testament as well. For almost nineteen centuries belief in divine inspiration remained unquestioned. But in modern times people began to question everything, and different theories about inspiration were developed, some of which we have already seen. It was not until the Second Vatican Council opened in 1962 that the Church considered writing a document giving a clear and detailed teaching about divine inspiration and its importance.

Old and New Testament figures, detail from painting by Fra Angelico, 14th century

32

The document produced by the council is called the *Dogmatic Constitution on Divine Revelation*. It deals with God's revelation of himself to us and how that revelation is transmitted through time. God revealed himself and his intentions for us at a particular time in history to a particular group of people. He did this first in the community of Israel and later in the apostolic community of the Church. God's revelation was made known by the testimony of those who received it. Passed on by word of mouth, it became *tradition*. Recorded in writing under the inspiration of the Holy Spirit, it became *Scripture*.

In presenting a clear explanation of inspiration, the Vatican II document indicates the strong New Testament foundation for our belief in divine inspiration. Here are two important passages with which Catholics should be familiar.

- "All scripture is inspired by God" (2 Timothy 3:16).

- "There is no prophecy of scripture that is a matter of personal interpretation, for no prophecy ever came through human will; but rather human beings moved by the holy Spirit spoke under the influence of God" (2 Peter 1:20–21).

Understanding Inspiration

A book that has both divine and human authorship is unique in human history. We cannot compare the Bible and its origins with any other book or type of writing. So when we talk about inspiration, we are dealing with a mystery of faith. By calling it a mystery, we do not mean that it is totally beyond our understanding. It simply means that there is much more to inspiration than we will ever fully understand.

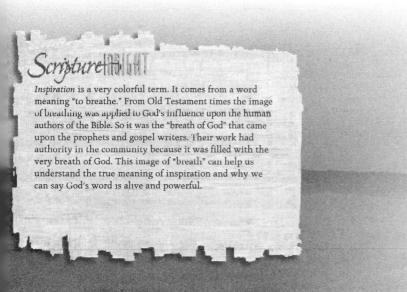

Scripture INSIGHT

Inspiration is a very colorful term. It comes from a word meaning "to breathe." From Old Testament times the image of breathing was applied to God's influence upon the human authors of the Bible. So it was the "breath of God" that came upon the prophets and gospel writers. Their work had authority in the community because it was filled with the very breath of God. This image of "breath" can help us understand the true meaning of inspiration and why we can say God's word is alive and powerful.

33

◆ Have the young people read the 👑 **thought provoker** on page 34. Encourage the young people to pray in this manner during the coming week.

◆ Ask a volunteer to summarize *Scripture Insight* on page 33. Then invite the young people to do a breath meditation in which they close their eyes and breathe deeply. Guide them with the following directions, speaking slowly and softly:

- As you breathe in, be conscious of the Holy Spirit entering into you.

- As you breathe out, feel yourself expelling negative thoughts and fears.

- Enjoy the sensation of the Holy Spirit breathing in you, a beloved son or daughter of God.

◆ Direct attention to the reproduction of Fra Angelico's painting on page 32. Share the identifications of the biblical figures shown.

- outer circle, moving clockwise from top: Ezekiel, Jeremiah, Micah, Jonas, Joel, Malachi, Ezra, Daniel, Isaac, King David, Moses, King Solomon

- inner circle: Peter, Mark, Jude, Luke, Jacob, Matthew, Paul, John

Note: Jacob connects the Old and New Testaments because he was the father of Joseph, the husband of Mary.

FYI

Giugo II, a monk and Christian mystic, gave this advice on ways to be fed by the Bible:

- Choose a short passage that appeals to you.
- Savor the words by reading or saying them slowly.
- Give the words time to become part of you, to "go into your heart."
- Ask the Holy Spirit to give you a taste of the passage's true meaning.

Presentation (cont'd)

◆ Have the young people form small time-traveling groups. Each group is visiting the sixteenth century. The group members are with people who have just heard Copernicus's theory about the Earth and the Sun. Have the groups roleplay the reactions in the crowd. Then work together to prepare explanations about the truths in Scripture.

Allow about ten minutes for the groups to "get their acts together;" then have them give their presentations to the entire group.

◆ Have volunteers summarize "The Real Truth." Ask, "What truth of faith does the Genesis account of creation teach us?"

Discuss with the young people the statements they underlined on pages 34 through 36. Have them highlight the key concepts highlighted here.

Use one of the Scripture passages in today's lesson as part of your evening prayer. Write your passage here.

That being the case, what can we say about God's activity in inspiring the human authors? In a marvelous way God somehow moved the minds of the human authors. He did this so that they could produce works they otherwise would not have been able to write. For example, the powerful and yet loving portrait of God given to us by Paul in his letters could never have come from Paul alone. Nevertheless, in moving Paul's mind and heart, God respected his freedom. That is why Paul's letters are different from other books of the Bible. The letters are truly the work of Paul and inspired by God, too. Both God and Paul are the authors.

How exactly did the Holy Spirit inspire the human authors? The Holy Spirit guided them in the content of their writing and in choosing the truth God wanted taught. The human authors looked at the traditions of the faith community and the opinions that were held by different members of that community. Under the influence of the Holy Spirit, they made the right choices that would transmit the truth God intended for all people.

When people of faith come to the Bible and enter more deeply into the mystery of inspiration, they come face-to-face with the divine word. The *Catechism* expresses this beautifully: "In Sacred Scripture, the Church constantly finds her nourishment and her strength, for she welcomes it not as a human word, 'but as what it really is, the word of God.' 'In the sacred books, the Father who is in heaven comes lovingly to meet his children, and talks with them'" (104).

The Real Truth

Does being inspired mean that the Bible cannot contain any errors? The answer is yes if we mean that the Bible does not contain any errors about the truths of faith. But what about the truths of history and science? Before modern times, questions of faith, history, and science were all mixed together without any distinctions. In fact most people felt that the Bible was concerned with more than just questions of faith. They looked to the Bible to answer just about every kind of question, even those dealing with science.

Things began to change in the sixteenth century, during the time of Copernicus. He was a Polish astronomer whose theories about the movement of the Sun challenged the way people looked at their world. Until that time people thought that the whole universe revolved around planet Earth. Earth and humankind formed the center of everything.

34

The evidence for this Earth-centered existence was easy to see. People's everyday experience led them to believe that the Sun revolved around Earth. The Sun "rose" in the east and "set" in the west.

There was more than visual evidence, however. People thought the Bible itself, God's holy word, testified to an Earth-centered world. According to their reading of Scripture, God put the Sun, the Moon, and the stars in the sky for our benefit. Think what happened when Copernicus said that Earth revolved around the Sun. No longer was Earth the center of the universe. Copernicus's theory seemed to mean that we could not trust our experience and that the Bible was in error. If the Bible was wrong about this, could it be wrong in other areas?

Over time it has become clear that the truth of Scripture is the truth of faith, truths for our salvation. The Bible does not teach every kind of truth in the world. It is not our primary source for the truth of history or science, for example. The Church teaches that "the books of Scripture must be acknowledged as teaching firmly, faithfully, and without error that truth which God wanted put into the sacred writings for the sake of our salvation" (*Divine Revelation*, 11).

The Church's Book

Knowing about inspiration helps us to understand how the Church chose the writings that would be part of the Bible. After all, there were many important writings that were held in high esteem and circulated among the various communities of the early Church. Along with the seventy-three books chosen to be in the Bible, there were the beautiful letters of Ignatius of Antioch and those of Clement of Rome, just to name a few. There were even other gospel accounts besides those of Matthew, Mark, Luke, and John. One of the most famous was called the Gospel of Thomas.

35

◆ Ask the young people to explain the Church's use of the word *canon*. (*the measuring rod of faith*) On the board write *canon of Scripture*. Have a volunteer define the term. (*the official list of biblical books*)

◆ Have volunteers explain why we say that the Bible is the Church's book. They should include the points explained in the last paragraph of "The Church's Book" on page 36.

◆ Have a volunteer summarize *Catholic Teachings* on page 36.

FYI Share the following excerpt from the Letter to the Trallians (9) written by Ignatius of Antioch.

Close your ears, then, to any talk that ignores Jesus Christ, of David's lineage, of Mary. He was really born, ate and drank; was really persecuted in the days of Pontius Pilate, was really crucified and died, in the sight of all heaven and earth and the underworld. He was really raised from the dead.

Presentation (cont'd)

◆ Discuss the  thought provoker on page 36.

◆ Direct the young people's attention to the photo on page 36. Explain that the person is holding up the lectionary used during liturgical celebrations. Explain that listening intently to the Scripture read during these celebrations will help us to realize that "the Church carries in her Tradition the living memorial of God's Word" (*Catechism*, 113).

◆ Distribute the handout *True Colors*. Have the young people work with a partner. Invite volunteers to share their colorful petitions.

Conclusion ___ min.

Have the young people respond in their journals to the first question of *Things to Share* and the second question of *Things to Think About*.

Then discuss together the first question of *Things to Think About*.

◆ Direct attention to *Words to Remember*. Both terms are on page 36.

Assessment: If you plan to administer *Chapter 4 Assessment*, page 37A, allow about ten minutes for its completion.

In the Church it came to signify a measuring rod of faith. Catholics use the word when speaking about the official list of biblical books, the *canon of Scripture*.

From all this we can truly see that the Bible is the Church's book. It was the Church that assembled these books. It is the Church that has passed them on through the centuries. It is the Church that interprets them in the light of its own tradition. The Bible comes from the Church and serves the Church. The *Catechism* states this very beautifully: "Sacred Scripture is written principally in the Church's heart rather than in documents and records, for the Church carries in her Tradition the living memorial of God's Word" (113).

The *Catechism* also states that in Scripture "the Father who is in heaven comes lovingly to meet his children and talk with them" (104). How might these words affect you each time you read or listen to Scripture?

From all the writings that were in circulation, the Church, guided by the Holy Spirit, recognized only seventy-three as being truly inspired by God. How did the Church do this? For one thing, it saw in these books a certain sublime quality that other works just did not have. More than this, the books seen as sacred played a special role in the faith life of the Church. They expressed the Church's apostolic tradition and origin. They had a real authority about them. Most important, the Church saw in these books a true and necessary reflection that mirrored its own faith.

Already in apostolic times the books of the Old Testament were accepted as Scripture. By the beginning of the second century, official lists of New Testament books were being developed. In fact, by A.D. 200 a Christian writer named Tertullian was the first to use the term *New Testament*. Christians saw in these books standards of their faith and practice.

The seventy-three books of the Bible are called the canon of Sacred Scripture. The English word *canon* comes from a Greek word meaning "measuring rod."

CATHOLIC TEACHINGS

About Inspiration

This is what the Second Vatican Council has to say about inspiration: "Holy Mother Church, relying on the belief of the apostles, holds that the books of both the Old and New Testament in their entirety, with all their parts, are sacred and canonical because, having been written under the inspiration of the Holy Spirit they have God as their author and have been handed on as such to the Church" (*Divine Revelation*, 11).

36

Answers for Chapter 4 Assessment

1. a	2. c	3. b	4. a	5. b
6. c	7. d	8. a	9. b	10. See page 36.

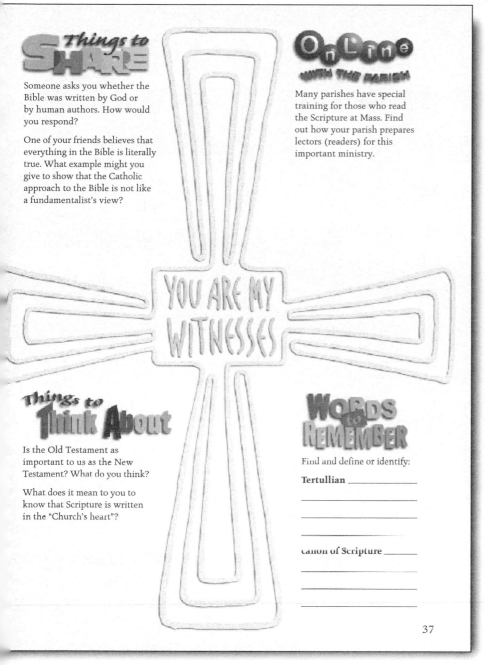

Things to SHARE

Someone asks you whether the Bible was written by God or by human authors. How would you respond?

One of your friends believes that everything in the Bible is literally true. What example might you give to show that the Catholic approach to the Bible is not like a fundamentalist's view?

OnLine WITH THE PARISH

Many parishes have special training for those who read the Scripture at Mass. Find out how your parish prepares lectors (readers) for this important ministry.

Things to Think About

Is the Old Testament as important to us as the New Testament? What do you think?

What does it mean to you to know that Scripture is written in the "Church's heart"?

WORDS to REMEMBER

Find and define or identify:

Tertullian _____

_____

_____

_____

canon of Scripture _____

_____

_____

_____

37

Conclusion (cont'd)

FORUM Assignment

✔ Read pages 38–45. Underline in pencil the statements that express six main ideas.

✔ Prepare your response for the second question of *Things to Share*. Be prepared to share your response at the beginning of the next session.

◆ Encourage the young people to share *Highlights for Home*, page 37B, with their families.

Closing Prayer: Write on the board the following Prayer Before Reading Scripture. Pray the words together.

Give me a word,
O Word of the Father,
touch my heart:
enlighten the understandings
of my heart:
open my lips and fill them
with your praise

Evaluation: Do the young people understand that human authors wrote Scripture under the inspiration of the Holy Spirit? Do they appreciate that the Bible contains no errors about the truths of faith?

FOR CHAPTER 5

- copies of handout *The Truth of History*, page 38C
- copies of *Chapter 5 Assessment*, page 45A
- copies of *Highlights for Home,* page 45B
- lyrics of a song about Jesus, the Light of the World
- drawing paper

Assessment

1 In the Bible
- **a.** there are no errors about the truths of faith.
- **b.** the scientific theory of evolution is explained.
- **c.** God is not heard.
- **d.** all authors write in the same way.

2 The image of inspiration that best helps us to understand its true meaning is
- **a.** a flowing stream.
- **b.** a quill pen.
- **c.** the "breath of God."
- **d.** rainbow of color.

3 The Church chose the books of the canon for their
- **a.** interesting stories.
- **b.** authority.
- **c.** non-expression of tradition.
- **d.** "headline" quality.

4 Both the Old and New Testaments
- **a.** are sacred and canonical.
- **b.** teach accurate science.
- **c.** teach accurate geography.
- **d.** are completely historical.

5 Jesus and members of the early Church used the word *Scripture* to refer to
- **a.** the Gospel of Thomas.
- **b.** the Old Testament.
- **c.** all the gospels.
- **d.** the New Testament.

6 Before the time of Christ, belief in biblical inspiration was ___ in Judaism.
- **a.** not considered
- **b.** not common
- **c.** common
- **d.** condemned

7 ___ was the first person to use the term *New Testament*.
- **a.** Thomas
- **b.** The Second Vatican Council
- **c.** Saint Paul
- **d.** Tertullian

8 God's revelation, passed on by word of mouth, became
- **a.** tradition.
- **b.** unacceptable.
- **c.** unimportant.
- **d.** unnecessary.

9 ___ books of the Bible are called the canon of Sacred Scripture
- **a.** Only the Old Testament
- **b.** The seventy-three
- **c.** Only the New Testament
- **d.** Only the historical

10 Explain briefly why we say that Scripture is written "principally in the Church's heart."

_____

_____

_____

_____

_____

Highlights for Home

Focus on Faith

This chapter helps our young people to clarify two simple facts about the Bible. The first is that "All scripture is inspired by God" (2 Timothy 3:16). The second is that the truth of Scripture is the truth of faith, truths for our salvation. It is important for us to realize that the Bible does not teach every kind of truth in the world. We do not depend on the Bible for accuracy in the truths of history or science. The Bible teaches us "that truth which God wanted to put into the sacred writings," as the Second Vatican Council explained in its document on *Divine Revelation* (11).

The Holy Spirit, inspired the human authors in the content of their writing and in choosing the truth God wanted taught. It was under the inspiration of the Holy Spirit that the human authors of the Bible made the right choices, choices that would transmit the truth God intended for all people.

Conversation Starters

. . . . a few ideas to talk about together. . . .

◆ What do we mean when we say, "The Bible does not teach every kind of truth in the world"?

◆ For me, why is it important to know that the Bible is the Church's book?

Feature Focus

The *Catholic Teachings* feature on page 36 assures us that all the books in the canon of Scripture were inspired by the Holy Spirit and chosen by the Church to express its apostolic tradition and its faith.

Reflection

The photograph on pages 30 and 31 is a photo of the Northern Lights, enhanced by the addition of color. The Northern Lights, usually white in a dark sky, can now be seen in a new dimension. They remain the Northern Lights, but, through color, they engage our senses in a new way.

The authors of the Bible wrote human words under the inspiration of the Holy Spirit. How does the word of God color your life in a new way?

The writers of the Old Testament used the cycles of nature and the heavenly bodies—the rising of the sun and its setting, the order of the stars, the thunder and lightning of a sudden storm—to express their relationship with God. Think of the splendor of the Northern Lights as you pray:

Your word, LORD, stands forever;
it is firm as the heavens.
                              Psalm 119:89

MORE THAN HISTORY

Adult Focus

It is important to understand that when we are talking about the Bible, we are talking about "more than history." Of course there are many historical facts in the Bible, but not everything mentioned in the Bible is history. In this chapter, the young people learn that, although historical information is sometimes part of biblical writing, its real focus is religious truth.

The inspired writers of the Bible had wonderful memories, told exciting stories, and depended primarily on oral tradition for the passing on of information in the community of faith. This becomes clear when we look at the three stage formation process of the gospels in the New Testament: the life and teachings of Jesus, the oral tradition, and the written gospels. Review this information presented in a chart on page 44 of the text. Emphasize with the young people that the gospels are our chief source for the life and teaching of Jesus, our Savior.

Catechism Focus

The theme of Chapter 5 corresponds to paragraphs 107, 109–110, 124–127 and 129 of the *Catechism*.

Enrichment Activities

Computer Connection

The *Visit* is an interactive CD/ROM produced by the American Bible Society. The young people can explore the history and customs of Palestine in the first century.

Requires Multimedia IBM-compatible 486DX/33 (66mhz or better recommended)

◆ Have the young people use a word-processing program, such as *The Writing Center,*™ to compose a newspaper article recapping an imaginary interview with the human author of the Book of Jonah.

Have the young people work in pairs to prepare a list of questions they would like to ask. Tell them also to write responses the person might give. Then have the pairs turn the questions and answers into magazine articles on the computer. If the young people are using *The Writing Center,*™ have them arrange a two- or three-column layout for their articles. Have all the reporter teams print their articles and present them to the group.

Teaching Resources

Overview

To clarify the difference between historical fact and religious truth in the Bible.

Opening Prayer Ideas

Read together John 1:5. Sing or reflect on the lyrics of a song about Jesus, the Light of the World.

or

Pray together Psalm 132:11-18.

Materials

- Bibles, journals, highlighters
- lyrics of a song about Jesus, the Light of the World
- drawing paper

REPRODUCIBLE MASTERS
- *The Truth of History,* page 38C
- *Chapter 5 Assessment,* page 45A
- *Highlights for Home,* page 45B

New Testament Journal:
For Chapter 5, use pages 12–13.

Supplemental Resources

VIDEOS
The Bible:
What's It All About
St. Anthony Messenger Press
1615 Republic Street
Cincinnati, OH 45210-1298

The Story of
Jonah and the Whale
Videos with Values
1509 Washington Ave.
Suite 550
Saint Louis, MO 63103

The Truth of History

Read the following two statements. For each statement, write three examples that would help you explain the statement to another person.

What happened in history was very important to biblical writers, for it was in the events of history that God dealt with his people.

1._____

_____

2._____

_____

3._____

_____

Modern people approach the truth of history differently from ancient people.

1._____

_____

2._____

_____

3._____

_____

CHAPTERS

More Than History

The light shines in the darkness,
and the darkness has not overcome it.
John 1:5

Objective: To clarify the difference between historical fact and religious truth in the Bible.

Introduction ___ min.

Opening Prayer: Invite the young people to look at the photo on pages 38 and 39. Read together John 1:5. Then read the following two verses of a prayer taken from a blessing in *Catholic Household Blessings & Prayers.* Ask the young people to repeat the prayer phrase each time you pause.

> Lord our God,
> we praise you for the light
> of creation: (*Pause.*)
> the sun, the moon, and the
> stars of the night. (*Pause.*)
>
> We praise you for the light
> of Israel: (*Pause.*)
> the Law, the prophets, and the
> wisdom of the Scriptures. (*Pause.*)

> We praise you for Jesus Christ,
> your Son: (*Pause.*)
> he is Emmanuel, God-with-us,
> the Prince of Peace,
> who fills us with the wonder
> of your love. (*Pause.*)

Then sing together or reflect on the lyrics of a song about Jesus, the Light of the World. "Canticle of Isaiah" in the *Glory & Praise* hymnal would be appropriate.

Forum: Have the young people form small groups to discuss their responses to the second question in *Things to Share* for Chapter 4:

> One of your friends believes that everything in the Bible is literally true. What example might you give to show that the Catholic approach to the Bible is not like a fundamentalist's view?

Presentation ___ min.

◆ Write on the board the historical fact: The *Titanic,* the British luxury passenger liner, sank on April 14–15, 1912. Explain that this event has been written about in song, in non-fictional accounts, and most recently in fictional screen and stage plays. Ask:

• How does learning about this event in different formats influence your views about society in the early 1900s?

• What lessons about life can you gain from these different accounts?

◆ Direct the young people's attention to the photograph on page 40. Have a volunteer read the introduction. Discuss responses to the questions.

Note: To review the story of Jonah, you may want to show the children's video *The Story of Jonah and the Whale.* (See *Supplemental Resources.*)

◆ Allow about five minutes of quiet time for the young people to read pages 40 and 41. Then ask the following questions:

• What lesson about responsibility does the story of Jonah teach us?

• What meaning did Jesus give to this story?

For responses see the second paragraph in the left column on page 41. Then ask, "What was the primary concern of the biblical writers?" (*The sacred writers wanted to transmit a written record of the revealing activity of God.*)

*J*esus used the story of Jonah, one of the best-known characters of the Old Testament, to get a point across to his disciples. According to the story, Jonah was swallowed by a whale and lived in its belly for three days. Would you be surprised if someone told you that this story was not based on historical fact but was told to teach a lesson of faith? Why?

Inspiration and History

Actually there are many people who would be surprised to learn that Jonah and his whale were not historical characters. After all, the Bible is the inspired word of God. They think this means that everything in the Bible must be history and therefore based on facts.

Is this true? Does inspiration make everything history? Of course not. Obviously there are many historical facts in the Bible, but not everything mentioned in the Bible is history. The Book of Jonah, to which Jesus referred, is a good example. It is not inspired history. Rather, it is an inspired parable, a story used to teach a lesson.

40

In the parable Jonah is commissioned by God to preach to the people of a far-off city. But Jonah is afraid and takes a ship and sails away from his responsibility. The ship is caught in a storm, and Jonah is thrown overboard and swallowed by a great whale. After three days and nights, the whale spits Jonah out onto the shore, and he sets off to carry out the mission given to him by God.

The story of Jonah teaches many important lessons. One lesson is the truth that God wants people to face their responsibilities and never be afraid of doing God's work. Jesus himself gave another meaning to the story of Jonah. He said, "Just as Jonah was in the belly of the whale three days and three nights, so will the Son of Man be in the heart of the earth three days and three nights" (Matthew 12:40). Jesus used the story of Jonah and the whale to teach about his own death and resurrection. Whether or not Jonah was a historical figure makes no difference to the inspired writing or the truth of these lessons.

There are, however, numerous examples of history in the Bible. In the Old Testament the many stories of King David are based on the truth of a famous king of Israel who lived about three thousand years ago. In the New Testament the missionary journeys of Saint Paul show how the Church undertook the spread of the gospel in the first century. David and Paul were not like Jonah; they were real people. They are part of the history of God's people, not imaginary characters only used to make a point in a parable.

So the Bible has some history in it, but it is more than just a listing of cold, hard facts about people and events. The Bible is an inspired book about religious truth. What does this mean? It means that the human authors of the Bible, under the inspiration of the Holy Spirit, interpreted events and people. The authors looked for deeper meaning behind the things that went on in their lives. They looked for religious truth, the truth that God intended to reveal. In seeking after this truth,

the writers were more than reporters simply giving facts about what they observed. For the writers of Scripture, the truth was more than the eye could see or more than meets the eye!

What, then, was the primary concern of the biblical writers? Can we describe it in one word or phrase? Yes, we can: *divine revelation,* which is God making himself known to us. The sacred writers wanted to transmit a written record of that revealing activity of God. That is why historical events and even scientific facts were of secondary importance to them.

The fullness of God's revelation comes to us in Jesus, the Word made flesh. John's Gospel summarizes it this way: "No one has ever seen God. The only Son, God, who is at the Father's side, has revealed him" (John 1:18). Jesus is this only Son. When we go to Scripture to discover more about him, we are not looking at Scripture as we would look at a modern history book. We are looking for religious truth, the deeper meaning that God intends to reveal to us. We are looking to encounter Jesus Christ, the Son of God, the second person of the Blessed Trinity who took on flesh at the incarnation.

Can you explain the difference between historical fact and religious truth in the Bible? Share your thoughts with the group.

Have the young people write in their journals their personal reflections about the Book of Jonah. While they are writing, you may want to play a recording of instrumental music.

◆ Discuss the **thought provoker** on page 41. Have the young people highlight the statements highlighted on the reduced pupil pages.

◆ Invite the young people to look at the photo on pages 38 and 39. Have a volunteer read the last paragraph on page 41. Have all respond with the words of John 1:5 on page 39.

FYI You may want to share and discuss the following statement of Thomas Merton in his book *Opening the Bible.*

The "word of God" is recognized in actual experience because it does something to anyone who really "hears" it: it transforms his [or her] entire existence.

Presentation (cont'd)

◆ Ask the young people to share the statements they underlined. Have the group highlight or underline in color the key concepts highlighted on pages 42 through 44.

◆ At this time you may want to show *Jesus: The Story Begins.* This first tape in the *Jesus and His Times* series includes daily life in Nazareth. The tape is available from St. Anthony Messenger Press/Franciscan Communications at the following web site.

http://www.americancatholic.org

◆ Distribute the handout *The Truth of History.* Allow about seven minutes of quiet time for individuals to write their responses.

Then have the young people form two groups. Ask the members of the first group to explain the first statement on the handout to members of the second group. In their explanations the Group One members should use the examples they have written on the handout. The members of the second group may ask questions or discuss the statements given.

Then have the second group explain the second statement to the first group. The procedure used for the first presentation should be followed.

Passing on tradition by word of mouth

It was in history that Jesus chose his apostles and founded the Church. The bottom line is this: The inspired word of God was written in human history, not outside it.

As we look back into history, we often have questions about the day-to-day lives of our ancestors in faith. We may even wonder about the unknown details of Jesus' life. Did he have a favorite sport that he liked to play? What was his favorite meal? Did he enjoy music? Did he like to sing? Did he have a dog or other pet?

These are the kinds of questions that biographers and historians like to answer when writing about well-known people of history. Answers to questions such as these help to make the "story" of history come alive. Food, music, sports and pets are part of life. They have a human interest to which people relate very easily.

So, did Jesus have a dog or didn't he? We will never know. That question or detail would never have crossed the minds of the biblical writers. When writing about historical people and real events, their approach was completely different from that of modern biographers and historians.

People with a History

When we say that the primary interest of the biblical writers was religious truth, we are not trying to say they were not at all interested in the facts of history. What happened in history was certainly important to them, for it was in the events of history that God dealt with his people. It was in history that Abraham was called by God. It was in history that the only Son of God was born into the world.

CATHOLIC ID

Saint Thérèse of Lisieux is one of the Church's most popular saints. In her autobiography she spoke about her love of Sacred Scripture: "Above all it's the gospels that occupy my mind when I'm at prayer." Why would she say this? Because the gospels are "the heart of all the Scriptures" (*Catechism*, 125). The gospels are our chief source for the life and teaching of Jesus, our Savior.

42

History and History

Modern people approach the truth of history differently from ancient people. Modern people can read, and books and other written materials are readily available. In the ancient world this was not always the case. Few people could read; there were no corner bookstores or libraries. What did ancient people do? They memorized things and passed them on by word of mouth. That is why ancient writers frequently set facts and events into the form of a story that was easy to remember. This might explain their seeming disinterest in reporting exact facts and specific dates. They were more interested in interpreting an event than in describing it as a reporter would.

An important characteristic of ancient writers was their dependence on oral tradition rather than on written records. Unlike modern writers, they did not depend on research and written documents. Modern writers become very involved in giving specific dates, listing the sequence of events exactly, and being able to document all facts. Ancient writers would not feel at home or comfortable in reporting the news of the day!

Nonetheless, ancient writers transmitted the truth in their own way. Although this way was different from ours, it was still based on the truth of history. The inspired writers of the Bible were no different from other ancient writers. They, too, took the events of their history and wrote about them as other people of their time did. They felt free to interpret their history and discover its meaning. They had wonderful memories, told exciting stories, and depended primarily on oral tradition for the passing on of information in the community of faith.

One of the many modern means of communication

43

◆ Have a volunteer read *Catholic ID* on page 42. You may want to explain to the young people that Thérèse died from tuberculosis at age twenty-four. Near the end of her life she would read nothing but the gospels. She said all other books left her "cold and dry."

◆ Have the young people work in pairs to design time lines for the process of the formation of the gospels in the New Testament. (See the chart on the following page.) They should use key words, dates, and symbols to illustrate each stage of the process.

Before the young people begin, remind them that B.C. means "Before Christ" and A.D. means "Anno Domini" (in the year of our Lord). The abbreviation A.D. is used for the years after Christ's birth. Then call attention to the dates given for the first stage.

Note: You may want to explain that errors were made in the calculations of early Christian calendars. Invite the young people who are interested to find information about the development of these calendars.

FYI The Second Vatican Council initiated and encouraged a profound renewal of Catholic biblical study. The following excerpt is from the *Dogmatic Constitution on Divine Revelation:*

For the correct understanding of what the sacred author wanted to assert, due attention must be paid to the customary and characteristic styles of perceiving speaking and narrating which prevailed at the time of the sacred writer, and to the customs men normally followed at that period in their everyday dealings with one another (12).

Presentation (cont'd)

◆ Have the young people share and discuss the time lines that they have made.

◆ In small groups have the young people discuss the ☼ **thought provoker** on page 44. The groups should also discuss the questions in *Things to Share* and *Things to Think About.*

◆ Direct attention to *Words to Remember.* The definition of *divine revelation* is on page 41.

Conclusion ___ min.

◆ Review the poetic form of haiku. Remind the group that it is a poem that has three lines. The first and third lines have five syllables; the second line has seven syllables. Explain to the young people that their *forum assignment* is to write a poem about Jesus. They may choose to write a haiku or use rhyming or free verse. Suggest that reflecting on the photo opening this chapter or Chapter 6 may help them.

Assessment: If you plan to administer Chapter 5 Assessment, page 45A, allow about ten minutes for the young people to complete the test.

This is clear when we look at the formation of the gospels in the New Testament. This process took place in three stages:

Stage 1: *The life and teachings of Jesus*
Jesus actually lived and moved among us in history. The gospel accounts are based on the ministry of Jesus, what he did and taught from about the years A.D. 28 to 30.

Stage 2: *The oral tradition*
The followers of Jesus spread the good news about him. The apostolic preaching, in which the early Church interpreted the meaning of what Jesus said and did, lasted until about the year A.D. 65. By this date many of the apostles may have died.

Stage 3: *The written gospels*
Finally the gospel writers selected what was important from oral tradition and put it into written form. They did this under the inspiration of the Holy Spirit. This happened in the first century A.D. between the late 60s and the early 90s.

Now we know the difference between ancient and modern writings about history. That is why we can say there is history, and there is history.

☼ *Are you disappointed about not knowing whether or not Jesus had a dog? Why or why not?*

Answers for Chapter 5 Assessment
1. a   2. c   3. d   4. b   5. d
6. c   7. b   8. a   9. b   10. See page 41.

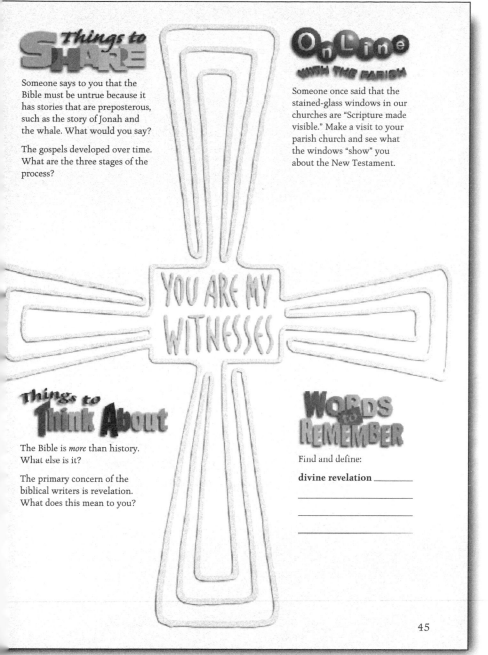

Things to SHARE

Someone says to you that the Bible must be untrue because it has stories that are preposterous, such as the story of Jonah and the whale. What would you say?

The gospels developed over time. What are the three stages of the process?

OnLine WITH THE PARISH

Someone once said that the stained-glass windows in our churches are "Scripture made visible." Make a visit to your parish church and see what the windows "show" you about the New Testament.

Things to Think About

The Bible is *more* than history. What else is it?

The primary concern of the biblical writers is revelation. What does this mean to you?

WORDS TO REMEMBER

Find and define:

divine revelation _____
_____
_____
_____

45

Conclusion (cont'd)

◆ Encourage the young people to share *Highlights for Home,* page 45B, with their families.

FORUM Assignment

✔ Read pages 46–53. Underline in pencil the sentences that express six main ideas.

✔ Use a poetic form of your choice to write a short poem about Jesus.

Closing Prayer: Have the young people form two choral-reading groups. Have the groups alternate reading the verses of Jonah's thanksgiving prayer (Jonah 2:3-10).

Evaluation: Do the young people understand that the Bible is more than history? Do they see the difference between historical fact and religious truth in the Bible?

FOR CHAPTER 6

• copies of handout *Identifying with Parable Characters,* page 46C
• copies of *Chapter 6 Assessment,* page 53A
• copies of *Highlights for Home,* page 53B
• lyrics for "Companions on the Journey" (optional)
• words of one or more religious poems (optional)

Assessment

1 Circle the one that does *not* belong.

The Book of Jonah
  a. is an inspired historical book.
  b. is an inspired parable.
  c. is in the Old Testament.
  d. has meaning for us today.

2 An important characteristic of ancient writers was their dependence on
  a. written records.
  b. specific dates.
  c. oral tradition.
  d. sequence of events.

3 What happened in history was _____ biblical writers.
  a. not important to
  b. completely ignored by
  c. never mentioned by
  d. important to

4 The primary concern of the biblical writers was
  a. reporting facts.
  b. divine revelation.
  c. telling parables.
  d. being popular storytellers.

5 Jesus used the story of Jonah and the whale to teach about
  a. the meaning of parables.
  b. punishment.
  c. lack of fear.
  d. his own death and resurrection.

6-8 Put the stages of the formation of the gospels in the correct sequence:
  a. stage 1; b. stage 2; c. stage 3.
  ___ written gospels
  ___ oral tradition
  ___ life and teachings of Jesus

9 Divine revelation is
  a. God making himself known to us.
  b. the primary concern of biblical authors.
  c. fulfilled in Jesus Christ.
  d. all of the above

10 Explain briefly what we mean by saying that the Bible is an inspired book about religious truth?

_____
_____
_____
_____
_____
_____
_____
_____
_____

Highlights for Home

Focus on Faith

It is important to understand that when we are talking about the Bible, we are talking about "more than history." Of course there are many historical facts in the Bible, but not everything mentioned in the Bible is history. In this chapter, the young people have learned that, although historical information is sometimes part of biblical writing, its real focus is religious truth.

The inspired writers of the Bible had wonderful memories, told exciting stories, and depended primarily on oral tradition for the passing on of information in the community of faith. This becomes clear when we look at the three-stage formation process of the gospels in the New Testament: the life and teachings of Jesus, the oral tradition, and the written gospels. Review this information presented in a chart on page 44 of the text. Emphasize with your son or daughter that the gospels are our chief source for the life and teaching of Jesus, our Savior.

Conversation Starters

. . . . a few ideas to talk about together . . . .

◆ If I could interview Jesus, what questions about the details of his daily life would I most want to ask? Why?

◆ How does it help me to know that the Bible is more than history?

Feature Focus

The *Catholic ID* feature on page 42 focuses on Saint Thérèse of Lisieux, Doctor of the Church, who encourages us to become more familiar with the gospels. Her love for Jesus drew her constantly back to reading, studying, and praying the gospels in his presence. It is important for everyone in every age to remember that the gospels are "the heart of all the Scriptures" (*Catechism*, 125).

Reflection

Look at the photo in the text on pages 38 and 39. Read Matthew 4:12–17. Imagine you see Jesus approaching Capernaum by the sea. Imagine you hear him say, "Repent, for the kingdom of heaven is at hand." How do you respond to Jesus' exhortation?

CHAPTER 6

Adult Focus

Awareness of literary forms is important in understanding literature. This awareness is important when we read the Bible, for the Bible is literature, too. Knowing the difference between prose and poetry will help the young people unlock the meaning of the Bible. In so doing, it will release the power of the divine and human word for modern people.

In this chapter the prominent literary forms of the New Testament are introduced. Foremost among these is the gospel, a literary form used by Matthew, Mark, Luke, and John, to announce the good news of salvation and to proclaim in faith what Jesus, the Son of God, did for the world.

As the young people explore other literary forms (epistles, parables, hymns, genealogies, midrash, and apocalyptic writing), help them to see that religious truth is larger than any single literary form can contain.

Catechism Focus

The theme of Chapter 6 corresponds to paragraphs 110 and 125 of the *Catechism*.

Enrichment Activities

Literary Expression

Write the heading *Prose* on the board. Have volunteers list types of fiction and non-fiction books under the heading. The following are possible listings:

◆ fiction—historical, mystery, adventure, science fiction, fables

◆ non-fiction—biography, true adventure, travel.

Ask the young people to choose their favorite type of book. Have them each write a prayer to thank God for what he or she enjoys and learns when reading this type of book. The following is an example:

> Thank you, God, for science fiction. Thank you for my imagination that helps me to go beyond my gravity-bound self to see ways of sharing your good news in the future. Help me to work with my fellow earthlings.

Designing Parable T-Shirts

Have the young people design and decorate parable T-shirts as an evangelization project. You may want to provide the following examples to help them get started:

• Bring the Lost Home

• Good Samaritans Get Great Rewards

• Invest your Talents Now Before It's Too Late.

Teaching Resources

Overview

To recognize and appreciate the literary forms of the New Testament.

Opening Prayer Ideas

Read John 15:9-17 or John 21:1-14.

or

Thank God for faith ancestors, especially the inspired authors of the Bible.

Materials

- Bibles, journals, highlighters
- lyrics for "Companions on the Journey" (optional)
- words of one or more religious poems (optional)

REPRODUCIBLE MASTERS
- *Identifying with Parable Characters, page 46C*
- *Chapter 6 Assessment, page 53A*
- *Highlights for Home, page 53B*

New Testament Journal:

For Chapter 6, see pages 14–15.

Supplemental Resources

VIDEOS
Jesus and His Times
"Among the People"
Vision Video
www.catholicvideo.com

God's Trombones
Part 2: "The Prodigal Son"
Videos with Values
1509 Washington Ave.
St. Louis, MO 63103

Identifying with Parable Characters

Choose one of the following parables that most appeals to you. Read it carefully in the Gospel of Luke. Then decide the parable character with whom you most want to identify. Read the gospel passage again, placing yourself in the shoes of your chosen character. Complete the statements below.

- The Lost Son (Luke 15:11–32)
- The Good Samaritan (Luke 10:29–37)

I am

because

My actions are motivated by

(in the beginning, later, throughout the parable).

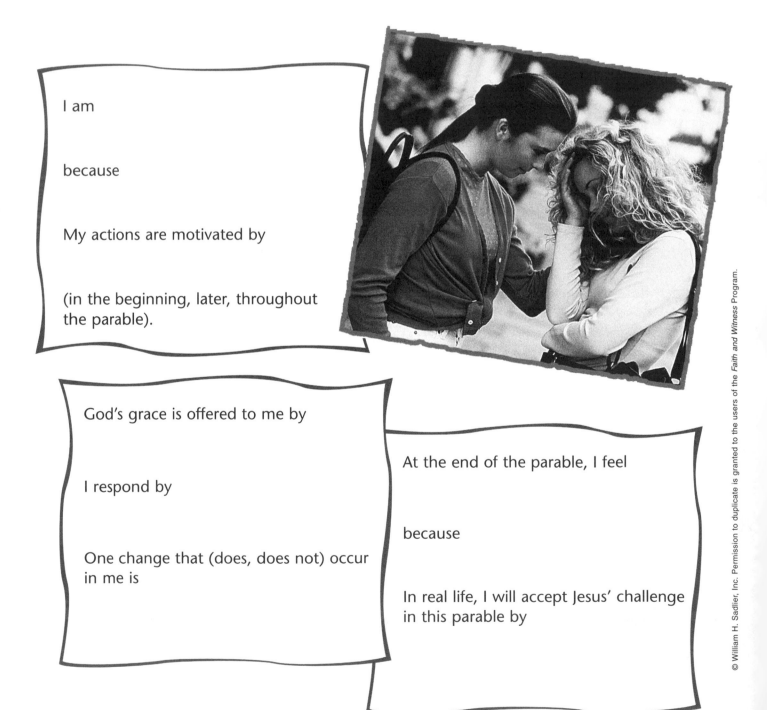

God's grace is offered to me by

I respond by

One change that (does, does not) occur in me is

At the end of the parable, I feel

because

In real life, I will accept Jesus' challenge in this parable by

Getting at the Truth

Oh, the depth of the riches and wisdom
and knowledge of God!
Romans 11:33

Objective: To recognize and appreciate the literary forms of the New Testament.

Introduction ___ min.

Opening Prayer: Invite the young people to look at the photo on pages 46 and 47. Proclaim together Romans 11:33. You may want to use the following script to guide a reflection about friendship:

> The divers in the photograph are about to explore the richness of God's creation of the sea. Right now many of you are interested in adventure and making new friends as well as deepening the friendships you have. Therefore, it is important to remember that a true friend helps a person recognize and experience the "depth of the riches and wisdom and knowledge of God"(Romans 11:33).

> A rich, deep friendship is shared between two people who want to deepen their friendship with Jesus and their understanding of his teaching. A false,

shallow friendship disables both people in seeking God's love. Take a few quiet moments to think about your current friendships. Which are helping you to begin to experience the depth and richness of God's love? What can you change about your attitude to live as a true friend of Jesus Christ?

Ask a volunteer to read John 15:9–17 or John 21:1–14. Then listen to a recording or sing "Companions on the Journey." The lyrics are based on Micah 6:8 in the Old Testament and Matthew 7:7 in the New Testament. The words and music can be found in the *Glory & Praise* hymnal.

Forum: Before the session begins, you may want to ask volunteer artists to make a poster or banner having a seascape at dawn on it.

Hang the poster behind the lectern. During the *forum* have the young people take turns standing at the lectern and reading their poems about Jesus.

Presentation ___ min.

◆ Call the young people's attention to the introductory paragraph on page 48. Discuss the two questions posed.

◆ Have volunteers define the literary forms *prose* and *poetry*. Ask, "Why is it important to realize that the Bible contains these literary forms?" *(This realization will help us to unlock the meaning of the Bible, releasing the power of this divine and human word for modern people.)*

◆ Discuss with the young people the statements they underlined for "Prose and Poetry" on pages 48 and 49. Then have the group highlight the key concepts highlighted here.

◆ Have someone read aloud the poem at the bottom of page 48. Call on volunteers to describe the kind of language the poet uses and what the effect is on the reader. Find out who in the group enjoys writing poetry and what topics the poets favor. Ask, "Why might poetry be a good way to express our religious feelings?"

You may want to share a few religious poems. The following are suggestions: "Pied Beauty" and "As Kingfishers Catch Fire" by Gerard Manley Hopkins; "The Creation" by James Weldon Johnson; "The Pillar of the Cloud" by John Henry Newman.

When he received the Nobel Prize for literature, William Faulkner, a great American writer, said that it is the privilege of a writer to help people face life with courage, hope, compassion, and sacrifice.

Do you think Faulkner was right? Is the written word of human beings that powerful?

Prose and Poetry

The written word can be a powerful thing. It can make people fall down with laughter, or it can bring people to tears. It can transmit such important information that it will move people to change their lives. Nowhere is this more true than in the Bible. This written word of God has been changing people's lives for centuries. The biblical writings, however, are from the past. Do writers from the past share anything in common with modern-day writers?

All writers, whether ancient or modern, have to answer the same question: "What form will my writing take?" Every piece of literature—and this includes the Bible—has its own appropriate literary form. A *literary form* is the type of writing that an author uses to get a message across. The two most basic literary forms are prose and poetry.

This book, for example, is written in prose. Why? Because *prose* is the literary form closest to our spoken language, and this makes it more appropriate for study. We use prose when we want to make direct statements about something or to present facts. We also use it to give a running narration in a story.

Poetry, on the other hand, is a different type of literary form. It expresses the truth in another way. *Poetry* is not like our everyday language; it is a more imaginative type of writing that uses symbols, sounds, and rhythms that express things about our life in a more emotional way.

If I could walk in the meadow of sky
with the sickle moon in my hand,
I'd cut all the blossoming point-petaled flowers
'til knee-deep in stars I'd stand.

48

e use poetry to describe experiences that the
nguage of prose really cannot express. Consider, for
ample, the figurative images in the following lines:

If I could walk in the meadow of sky
with the sickle moon in my hand,
I'd cut all the blossoming point-petaled flowers
'til knee-deep in stars I'd stand.

hat a beautiful picture these words give us.
hen we look up into the starry sky, it is almost as
we could be knee-deep in stars. Could this ever
expressed more powerfully by using prose? It
uld not. Poetry is the better literary form in this
se. Sometimes poetry can get us into the deeper
eaning of things. That is why the words of a song
often in poetic form.

wareness of literary forms is important in
derstanding literature. There is a big difference
the way one reads prose and poetry. This
areness is important when we read the Bible,
the Bible is literature, too. It contains the
literary forms of prose and poetry. Knowing this
will help us to unlock the meaning of this ancient
text. In doing so, it will release the power of this
divine and human word for modern people.

Gospel: A Literary Form

The Old Testament and the New Testament have
many other literary forms. In this text, however,
we will be concentrating on the literary forms that
are characteristic of the New Testament. The first
and most recognizable literary form is the gospel.

A *gospel* is an announcement of good news. In fact,
the word itself means "good tidings." In the New
Testament there are four gospels: the Gospels of
Matthew, Mark, Luke, and John. Each one announces
the good news of salvation in Jesus Christ. It does
this not simply to tell the story of Jesus but also to
proclaim in faith what Jesus, the Son of God, did
for the world. The inspired words of the gospel are
not only meant to share the message of Jesus.

CATHOLIC TEACHINGS

About Bible Translations

The Bible is always being translated from
Latin, Greek, and Hebrew into modern
languages. In this way people around
the world have access to God's word.
The Church is very careful that these
translations be as correct as possible. That
is why all authorized Catholic versions
of the Bible must contain an imprimatur.
Imprimatur is a Latin word meaning
"let it be printed." The imprimatur is an
approval given by a bishop to print a book.
It assures us that a specific translation of
the Bible is faithful to the word of God and
is the result of good scholarship. Look for
the imprimatur statement in the Bible you
are using. It can usually be found in the
first few pages of the book.

49

◆ You may want to point out to the
young people that many prose writers
use imagery and symbolism. As an
example, have a volunteer read
Matthew 6:25–34. Ask, "What is the
symbolic language Jesus uses to teach
this lesson about unnecessary worry
about material goods?"

◆ Have the young people form small
groups. Explain that each group has
been given one minute of air time on
the television networks to explain the
purpose of the four gospels and the
reading of them. The group's task is to
prepare a script in prose or poetic
form.

Then have a director call on the young
people to present their one-minute
scripts about the four gospels. When all
the presentations are given, have the
young people choose their three
favorites. Ask for select volunteers to
polish the scripts and work on formal
presentations for a later session.

◆ Have a volunteer summarize *Catholic
Teachings*. Have the young people
locate the imprimatur in their Bibles
and in their texts.

Presentation (cont'd)

◆ Invite the young people to respond to the  **thought provoker** on page 50. Ask them to name a favorite example of prose and poetry in their responses.

◆ Have the young people form small groups to play "Seven Questions." Try to have an even number of groups (from four to eight). Ask the members of each group to write seven questions about "Gospel: A Literary Form" on pages 49 and 50.

Then have each group write an answer key. When the groups have finished writing, set up the groups in challenge teams: Group A plays Group B, C plays D, and so on. Since most of the questions will be the same, have the challenge teams play simultaneously.

◆ Ask for volunteers to write on the board the literary forms they read about on pages 50 through 52. As the name of each form is written, have another volunteer explain the meaning. Then discuss the statements the young people underlined. Have them highlight the main ideas highlighted on the reduced pages. You may wish the young people to highlight or underline in color the definitions for *hymn* and *apocalyptic writing*. They are not highlighted in the guide.

They are also meant to move those who hear the message to make a commitment to change their lives. That is why Paul could write, "Conduct yourselves in a way worthy of the gospel of Christ, so that, whether I come and see you or am absent, I may hear news of you, that you are standing firm in one spirit, with one mind struggling together for the faith of the gospel" (Philippians 1:27).

More than any other New Testament book, the gospels give the story of Jesus and the most important events of his life. Although there is much biographical detail in the gospels, their primary purpose is not to present a biography of Jesus. Rather they hand on the high point of God's revelation to us in Jesus Christ. That is why they prompt us to change our lives. There is really only one gospel, only one "good news" about Jesus. The four gospel accounts of Matthew, Mark, Luke, and John come to us from different early Christian communities. Their lives as followers of Jesus helped to shape the writing of these gospel proclamations.

Which do you like to read most, prose or poetry? Explain.

Scripture INSIGHT

In some ways the use of different literary forms in the Bible should come as no surprise, especially to modern readers. After all, the Bible is like a library of seventy-three books. When we go to a library, we do not go to the science section to read poetry. We go to the poetry section. When we read the Book of Psalms, we should expect to read a great deal of poetry, not history or biography.

More Literary Forms

Besides prose, poetry, and gospel, there are other literary forms in the New Testament. Here are some that you may easily recognize.

Epistle The word *epistle* means "letter." In the New Testament there are twenty-one epistles of varying lengths and by different authors. The most famous epistle writer was Saint Paul. Most of his letters were written to Church communities. Some letters, however, were written to individuals who had important responsibilities in the community.

50

Parable Parable comes from a word that means "to compare." A *parable* is a fictitious (made-up) short story that uses ordinary experiences of life to teach a deeper spiritual lesson. In a wonderful way parables shake us up and make us see and compare things about life in a whole new way. By twists and turns they challenge us and make us ask questions about our lives. Think of the parables of the sower and the seed (Matthew 13:1–9), the prodigal son (Luke 15:11–32), and the Good Samaritan (Luke 10:29–37). After reading these passages, we can see why Jesus was such a master teller of parables.

Genealogy A *genealogy* is a listing of ancestors. This listing might be done for a person, a family, or a group. It helps us to know where we come from. The most famous New Testament genealogy is in Matthew 1:1–17. In a masterful way it roots Jesus in the history of Israel and in the family of Abraham. When we know who all the people in the genealogy are, we begin to appreciate how God's promises to us are fulfilled in many and varied ways.

Midrash This is a distinctly Jewish literary form. It was popular with rabbis, who reinterpreted the Old Testament texts for the people of their day. *Midrash* is a style of writing that the New Testament authors used to apply Old Testament accounts to people in the New Testament. Like the rabbis, the gospel writers did this to help make the Old Testament texts meaningful for Christians.

An example of midrash is found in Matthew 2:16–23. In this passage the gospel writer reminds his readers of incidents from the Old Testament. In telling the story of the return of Jesus, Mary, and Joseph from Egypt, Matthew quotes Jeremiah 31:15–17. This Old Testament passage refers to the return of the Israelites from their exile in Babylonia. By his reinterpretation of Jeremiah, Matthew shows that Jesus relived the experiences of the Jewish people.

The Good Samaritan (after Delacroix), Vincent Van Gogh, 1890

51

◆ Direct attention to *Scripture Insight* on page 50. Encourage the young people to try to identify the literary forms being used for Scripture passages they will listen to, read, or study in the near future.

◆ Invite a different volunteer to read aloud each of the following passages. The task of the listeners is to identify the literary form as quickly as they recognize it.

• Philippians 1:27–30 (*epistle*)
• Matthew 12:1–9 (*parable*)
• Philippians 2:5–11 (*hymn*)
• Matthew 1:1–17 (*genealogy*)
• Matthew 2:16–23 (*midrash*)
• Matthew 24:29–31 (*apocalyptic*)

At this time, you may want to show a segment of the video *The Bible: What's It All About?* This video explores the origins of the Bible and its literary forms. It includes discussions with young people. (See *Supplemental Resources.*)

◆ Distribute the handout *Identifying with Parable Characters.* Have a volunteer read the directions. Make sure the young people understand them. Explain that working on the activity is the *forum assignment.*

Presentation (cont'd)

Note: The following activity is optional.

◆ Read the names of the following teams and the teams' assignments. Explain that each person should decide which team to join. The decision should be based on an individual's interests or gifts.

- Letter Launcher: Write a short letter to the teenage members of a new Christian community. Use a quote or story from the New Testament to encourage the group to follow Jesus.

- Parable Printers: Write a contemporary edition of one of the parables listed on page 51.

- Hymn Hummers: Write a short verse to an existing melody or one of your own for a hymn that expresses the group's faith in and feelings about Jesus.

- Apocalyptic Artists: Read Matthew 24:29–31. Design a photographic collage or painting to illustrate this passage.

Have the young people form small groups in which to share their responses to the questions in *Things to Think About* and *Things to Share*.

◆ Direct attention to *On Line with the Parish*. Brainstorm and discuss choices of literary forms for parish histories.

Conclusion ___ min.

Assessment: If you plan to administer *Chapter 6 Assessment*, page 53A, allow about ten minutes for the young people to complete the test.

Hymn The members of the early Church, like those of today's Church, sang hymns and songs when they gathered for the liturgy and other celebrations. This music expressed some of their deepest beliefs. Some of the words from these hymns were incorporated into the New Testament text. One of the most beautiful hymns summarized belief in the humanity and divinity of Jesus. It must have been very popular because Paul made it part of his letter to the Philippians (2:5–11).

Apocalyptic Writing This literary form is highly symbolic and often uses images describing future times and the end of the world. In attempting to describe the last moments of world history, it speaks of catastrophes and a struggle in which God finally destroys the forces of evil. One clear example of this type of writing is found in Matthew 24:29–31. In this passage we read about the sun being darkened, the moon not giving light, the stars falling from the sky, and even the sound of trumpets announcing the end of everything. Obviously this type of writing is very symbolic and is not meant to be taken literally.

Is it easy to find all these literary forms in the books of the New Testament? Yes and no. It is easy to spot some of them, especially when we read the text carefully. But we have to be aware that they can be mixed together even in the same chapter of a book. As we shall see, the gospel writers can move very quickly from prose to poetry, from genealogy to midrash to parable. That is why Catholics depend on the guidance of the Church and the insight of Scripture scholars to identify these literary forms.

Why did the biblical writers use so many forms? Because they were dealing with the truth of divine mysteries. One form is not sufficient to express this kind of truth. Poetry gets to the truth in a way different from that of prose. Parables give us the truth in ways different from apocalyptic writings. Yet, the goal of each literary form is the same: to get at the truth. And the truth is larger than any single literary form can contain. Certainly now we can see that the New Testament is much more than history.

Find the hymn in Philippians 2:5–11. Now pray it together.

52

Answers for Chapter 6 Assessment
1. b   2. b   3. c   4. d   5. c
6. a   7. a   8. d   9. d   10. Accept reasonable responses.

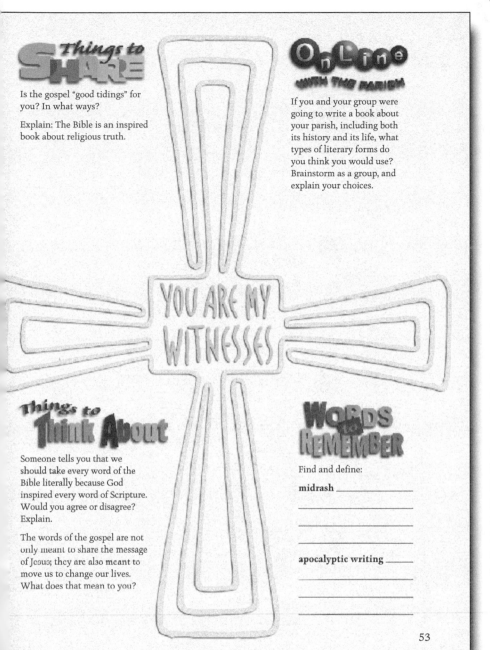

Things to SHARE

Is the gospel "good tidings" for you? In what ways?

Explain: The Bible is an inspired book about religious truth.

OnLine WITH THE PARISH

If you and your group were going to write a book about your parish, including both its history and its life, what types of literary forms do you think you would use? Brainstorm as a group, and explain your choices.

Things to Think About

Someone tells you that we should take every word of the Bible literally because God inspired every word of Scripture. Would you agree or disagree? Explain.

The words of the gospel are not only meant to share the message of Jesus; they are also meant to move us to change our lives. What does that mean to you?

WORDS to REMEMBER

Find and define:

midrash _____

_____

_____

apocalyptic writing _____

_____

_____

_____

53

Conclusion (cont'd)

◆ Direct attention to *Words to Remember* on page 53. The definition for *midrash* is on page 51; the explanation of *apocalyptic writing* is on page 52.

 **FORUM** *Assignment*

✔ Read pages 54–61. Underline in pencil the statements that express six main ideas.

✔ Complete the handout *Identifying with Parable Characters*.

◆ Encourage the young people to share *Highlights for Home*, page 53B, with their families.

Closing Prayer: Ask the young people to form two choral-reading groups. Have the groups bring their Bibles and stand in parallel lines, facing each other, to proclaim Philippians 2:5–11. Have each group alternate reading the verses. All bow slightly when the tenth verse is proclaimed.

Evaluation: Do the young people recognize and appreciate the literary forms of the New Testament?

FOR CHAPTER 7

- preparation of volunteers for prayer
- copies of handout *Living the Covenant*, page 54C
- copies of *Midsemester Assessment*, page 124 (optional)
- copies of *Chapter 7 Assessment*, page 61A (optional)
- copies of *Highlights for Home*, page 61B

Assessment

1 Biblical authors
 a. were all historians.
 b. depended on oral tradition.
 c. never used poetry.
 d. used only prose.

2 The word *epistle* means
 a. "short story."
 b. "letter."
 c. "hymn."
 d. "gospel."

3 The basic literary forms are
 a. symbols and sounds.
 b. metaphors and similes.
 c. prose and poetry.
 d. books and libraries.

4 A gospel is
 a. not a literary form.
 b. a fictional short story.
 c. a listing of Jesus' ancestors.
 d. an announcement of good news.

5 Parables
 a. list ancestors.
 b. are songs of praise.
 c. make surprising comparisons.
 d. are inspiring letters.

6 Midrash
 a. is a Jewish literary form.
 b. is a list of ancestors.
 c. describes the end of the world.
 d. is a fictitious short story.

7 Apocalyptic writing
 a. describes the end of the world.
 b. is highly factual.
 c. is to be taken literally.
 d. is not in the Bible.

8 *Imprimatur* is a Latin word meaning
 a. "good tidings."
 b. "the end of the world."
 c. "prose writing."
 d. "let it be printed."

9 Circle the one that does *not* belong.
 The gospels give
 a. the story of Jesus.
 b. a prompting to change our lives.
 c. the most important events of Jesus' life.
 d. only a biography of Jesus.

10 Explain why it is important to recognize the literary forms of the Bible.

_____

_____

_____

_____

_____

Highlights for Home

Focus on Faith

To communicate their message, the inspired authors of the Bible used different literary forms. Each form reveals the truth in its own way, moving the reader ever closer to the Son of God who is the greatest revelation of the Father.

This chapter concentrates on the literary forms of the New Testament: gospel, epistle, parable, genealogy, midrash, hymn, and apocalyptic writing. It is important to remember that the gospel writers sometimes move very quickly from prose to poetry, from genealogy to midrash to parable. That is why Catholics depend on the guidance of the Church and the insight of Scripture scholars to identify these literary forms.

With your son or daughter, explore several of the literary forms explained in this chapter. Look up the examples given on pages 51 and 52 and share your responses to them. Let yourself be drawn into prayer using the word of God.

Conversation Starters

. . . . a few ideas to talk about together. . . .

◆ Which literary form of the New Testament do you enjoy reading the most? Why?

◆ What can our parish do to encourage more young people and adults to become familiar with the literary forms of the Bible?

Feature Focus

Catholic Teachings on page 49 explains that the Church is very careful that translations of the Bible be as correct as possible. For this reason, all authorized Catholic versions of the Bible must contain an imprimatur. The imprimatur is an approval given by a bishop to print a book. It assures us that a specific translation of the Bible is faithful to the word of God and is the result of good scholarship.

Reflection

To his disciples and those who respected him, Jesus was known as "rabbi" or teacher. He startled and challenged his listeners to change their lives and to turn once again to God. How did he do this? Jesus used examples from everyday life, which he expressed in colorful and picturesque language.

Consider the comparisons Jesus used in Matthew 7:24–29. Consider ways you might build your house on rock at this time in your life. Listen closely to and act on the words of Jesus.

Adult Focus

In this chapter the young people are reminded that Jesus was a Jew; he belonged to a people with a rich history and religious heritage. By becoming more familiar with the religious history and practices of the Jews, we enhance our ability to know Jesus and understand the New Testament. We can appreciate the new and everlasting covenant in which we share as followers of Christ.

In Chapter 7, the young people learn about the biblical covenants of the Old Testament. They learn that the greatest of these was the one God made with his people on Mount Sinai. After the people agreed to this covenant's terms, it was sealed with a sacrifice, and then they participated in the sacrificial meal.

As Moses sprinkled the blood of the sacrifice on the people, he said, "This is the blood of the covenant which the LORD has made with you" (Exodus 24:8)

Jesus used covenant terminology at the Last Supper when he said, "This cup is the new covenant in my blood which will be shed for you" (Luke 22:20). He did this because, like the covenant at Sinai, the new covenant was sealed in blood—the blood of Jesus—and a sacrificial meal.

Help the young people to realize that we belong to a people of the new covenant. This truth should affect every aspect of our lives.

Catechism Focus

The theme of Chapter 7 corresponds to paragraphs 348, 534, 610–611, and 1539–1545 of the *Catechism*.

Enrichment Activities

The Holy Land

Invite a parishioner who has made a pilgrimage to the Holy Land to speak with the young people. If the parishioner is willing to show videotapes about the trip, have the VCR and television set up.

You may want to show selected segments of *Where Jesus Walked* or *Song of the Holy Land*, video pilgrimages to Bethlehem, Nazareth, Jerusalem, Capernaum and other places marked on the map on page 57. They are both available from:
Ignatius Press
P.O. Box 1339
Ft. Collins, CO 80522

Adventures of Faith Ancestors

Have the young people work together in small groups to write and illustrate the lives and adventures of one of the Old Testament heroes or heroines listed on pages 56 and 58. These books may include simple sketches or line drawings that are accompanied by dialogue. The dialogue should be based on the accounts in the Old Testament.

Teaching Resources

Overview

To explore the meaning of the covenant God made with his people on Mount Sinai and the new covenant that was sealed in the Blood of Jesus.

Opening Prayer Ideas

Have a procession and sing "All Glory Laud and Honor" or "The King of Glory."

or

Pray together Luke 1:68–75.

Materials

- Bibles, journals, and highlighters
- something to represent a shepherd's staff (optional)
- set stations with name plaques (See Guide page 54–55.)
- large sheet of paper or posterboard

New Testament Journal:
For Chapter 7, use pages 28–29.

REPRODUCIBLE MASTERS
- *Living the Covenant,* page 54C
- *Chapter 7 Assessment,* page 61A
- *Midsemester Assessment,* page 124
- *Highlights for Home,* page 61B

Supplemental Resources

VIDEOS
Where Jesus Walked
Videos with Values
P.O. Box 3470
Saint Louis, MO 63143

The Singer of Israel: David
Vision Video
P.O. Box 540
Worcester, PA 19490

CHAPTER
seven

Living the Covenant

You belong to the people of the new covenant. This fact should affect every aspect of your life. Today some young people are finding that they can maintain high moral standards if they are involved in a "youth charter." The charter is a community document that out- lines standards of behavior agreed upon by teenagers and adults. The charters that now exist cover sportsmanship, youth activities, and substance abuse (drugs, alcohol, and tobacco).

For each of these categories list at least three issues that you think need to be addressed in your local community.

youth activities

sportsmanship

substance abuse

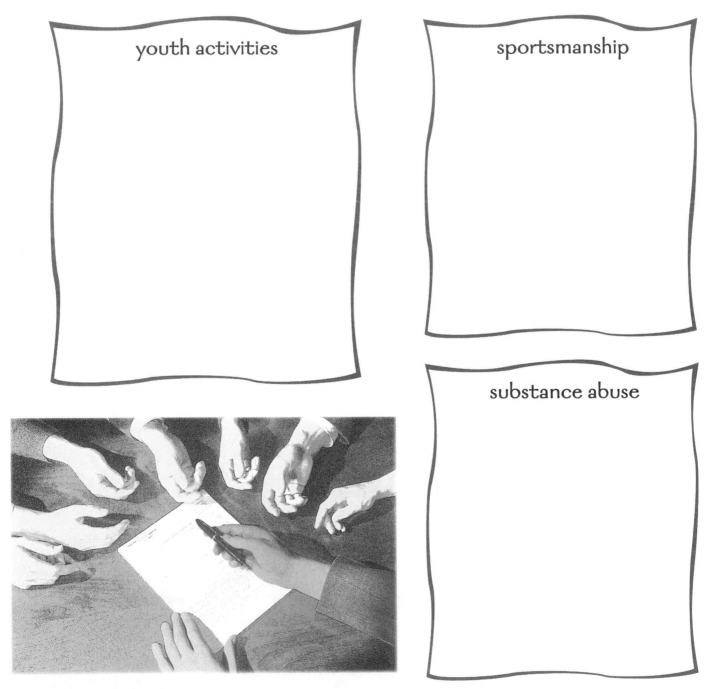

Jesus and His People

Blessed be the Lord,
the God of Israel,
for he has visited and
brought redemption to his people.
Luke 1:68

Objective: To explore the meaning of the covenant God made with his people on Mount Sinai and the new covenant that was sealed in the Blood of Jesus.

Introduction ___ min.

Opening Prayer: Before the session begins, have a large branch or cane available to represent a shepherd's staff. Set up stations around the room, one station for each of the following Old Testament leaders:

- Abraham—a name plaque with stars surrounding his name
- Jacob—a name plaque with the numeral 12 printed on it
- Moses—a name plaque and, if possible, a box of sand placed under the plaque
- Deborah and Samson—one name plaque with *promised land* printed on it

- King David—a name plaque with a crown and harp drawn on it
- Solomon—a name plaque with the outline of the Temple in Jerusalem on it
- Jesus—a name plaque with a picture or statue of Jesus placed under the plaque.

To begin the prayer, invite the young people to form a procession, carrying their texts. Ask someone to lead the procession with the shepherd's staff. Explain that the leader will extend the staff over the group when the young people pray Luke 1:68 (on page 55) at the start of the procession and at each station.

When the procession stops at the Jesus station, invite the young people to sing "All Glory Laud and Honor" or "The King of Glory." The lyrics and music of both songs are in the *Worship* and *Glory & Praise* hymnals.

Place the shepherd's staff in the prayer corner. When the young people return to their seats, ask them to open their Bibles and read Psalm 139:23–24.

Forum: Have the young people form small groups to share their responses on the handout *Identifying with Parable Characters*. Group leaders may have the members exchange papers and present the chosen characters' point of view. Then have one person in each group share with the young people the groups' suggestions about living the two parables.

Presentation ___ min.

◆ If possible, display or pass around a passport as a volunteer reads the introductory paragraph on page 56. Sketch a passport on the board. Fill it in with the young people's responses to the introductory questions.

◆ Have volunteers read "The Son of David" on page 56. Stop at the questions "Who were his ancestors? When did their history begin?" Ask all to underline in color or highlight the key concepts highlighted on this page.

◆ Ask the young people to turn to page 127 in the back of their books and look at the map of the Mediterranean world at the time of Jesus.

Point out Egypt and remind the young people that Abraham, Joseph and his brothers, and Moses spent some time there before the Israelites settled in the promised land.

Then have the young people locate Babylon. Explain that the Jews spent many years in captivity there before returning to their own land.

A passport gives us basic information, including place of birth and nationality. A passport also contains a recent photo to help identify the person. If Jesus were to have a passport, what information about him would we find on it? What would he look like?

The Son of David

Most people are already aware of the basic information about Jesus. He was born in the town of Bethlehem in the province of Judaea, which was located in the country of Israel. Jesus was a Jew. That was his nationality.

As for his looks, no one can say for sure. But this has not stopped artists through the centuries from painting his image. As men and women of faith, these artists wanted people to recognize in Jesus something of themselves and their own culture. So they painted Jesus to look like the people of their own countries. That is why we have many different images of Jesus today. At times he looks Italian; sometimes he is pictured as Dutch or African or Asian.

Jesus, however, was not Dutch or African or Italian or Asian. Jesus was a Jew who lived about two thousand years ago in a world very different from our own. As a Middle Eastern person of that time, he probably had dark brown eyes, dark hair, and olive-colored skin. These are characteristics of the Semitic peoples who inhabited this region.

We also know that Jesus grew up in the small town of Nazareth in Galilee and more than likely lived the life of a country person. Like his foster father, Joseph, he was known as a carpenter and was accustomed to working with his hands. Jesus

56

knew what it meant to work hard and the effort that it took to build something. Contrary to many pictures that present him as someone who never got his hands dirty, Jesus was probably a rugged individual with calloused hands and muscles toughened from work.

Because Jesus was a Jew, he belonged to a people with a rich history and religious heritage. If we want to know Jesus and make sense of the New Testament, we must know and understand the people whose heritage Jesus shared. Who were his ancestors? When did their history begin?

God formed a people of his own beginning with Abraham. He promised that Abraham's descendants would be "as countless as the stars of the sky and the sands of the seashore" (Genesis 22:17). The God who called Abraham would be their God, and they would be his people. God kept this promise with Abraham and with Isaac, Abraham's son. God continued to keep his promise with Jacob, the son of Isaac, and with Jacob's twelve sons. Their names would later be identified with the twelve tribes of Israel. These twelve tribes, as listed in Genesis 49:1–27, are Reuben, Simeon, Levi, Judah, Zebulun, Issachar, Dan, Gad, Asher, Naphtali, Joseph, and Benjamin. It is important to know their names because they are mentioned in the New Testament, too.

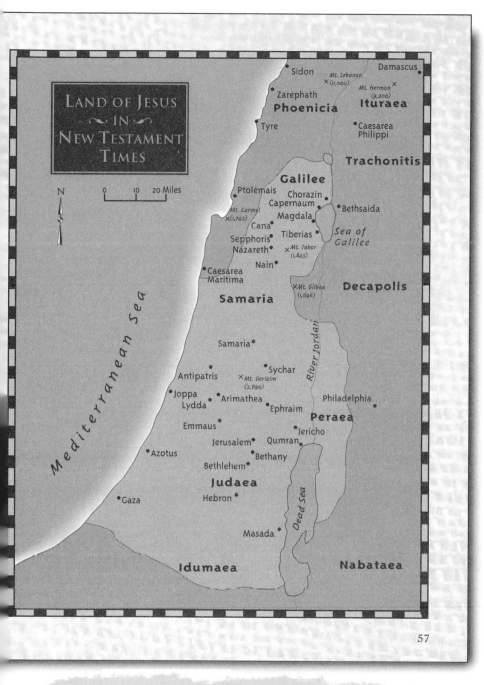

LAND OF JESUS IN NEW TESTAMENT TIMES

N   0   10   20 Miles

◆ Direct the young people's attention to the map on page 57. Have the young people play "Location, Location, Location." Ask the following questions, have volunteers respond, and have the group locate the places on the map.

• What cities are named in Matthew 2:1–2? Name the region in which they are located. (*Bethlehem and Jerusalem in Judaea*)

• What cities are named in Matthew 11:20–24? (*Chorazin, Bethsaida, Tyre, Sidon, Capernaum, Sodom—not on map*)

• What towns in what region are named in Matthew 4:12–16? Describe their directional relationship to Jerusalem in Judaea. (*Nazareth and Capernaum in Galilee are north of Jerusalem.*)

Note: Zebulun and Naphtali are the tribes that lived in this area in the time of Isaiah.

• What town is named in John 2:1? What is its directional relationship to Nazareth? to the Sea of Galilee? (*Cana is north of Nazareth and west of the Sea of Galilee.*)

57

FYI During Advent the custom of making a Jesse tree is practiced in many parishes. On it are hung symbols of Old Testament people and events. In the Church's prayer on December 19, we pray to Jesus:

> O Flower of Jesse's stem,
> you have been raised up
> as a sign for all peoples;
> kings stand silent in your
>   presence;
> the nations bow down
>   in worship before you.
> Come, let nothing keep you
>   from coming to our aid.

Presentation (cont'd)

◆ On a large sheet of paper, draw a large tree branch with many small branches. Have volunteers print on the small branches the names of the ancestral leaders in faith mentioned on pages 56 and 58. Display the branch poster in your prayer space. Place the shepherd's staff used for the opening prayer near the branch.

◆ Have a volunteer define the term *political covenant.* (*a treaty made between nations or individuals*) Refer the young people to the parts listed in the right column on page 58. Then discuss the sealing or completion ceremony.

◆ Write on the board *biblical covenant.* Have the young people highlight the definition found in the left column on page 59. Discuss the parts of the covenant on Mount Sinai. Then have the young people highlight the sealing of this covenant in the first paragraph in the right column on page 59.

◆ Ask, "Why did Jesus use covenant terminology at the Last Supper?" (*Like the covenant at Sinai, this covenant would be sealed in the Blood of Jesus and a sacrificial meal.*)

Have the young people highlight all the key concepts highlighted on pages 58 through 60.

The history of the Jewish people was filled with struggle and hardship as they tried to be faithful to God. We remember that Jesus' ancestors were enslaved in Egypt. Under the leadership of Moses, God led his people to freedom and to the promised land. Guided by judges such as Deborah and Samson, the people conquered and settled this land. God finally gave them kings to rule them, the greatest of whom was King David, a member of the tribe of Judah. Now the Jews would be like other nations, with a king of their own. They would have a great capital, the city of Jerusalem. There David's son Solomon built a magnificent Temple where God could be worshiped.

Later, however, the people forgot God's promise and became careless. They rejected the warnings of the prophets. They turned away from God and were led far away from their homeland into captivity in Babylonia. After many years God, who is always faithful, brought them back to their own land. There the people rebuilt the Temple, which had been destroyed, and they rededicated themselves to the Lord. God, however, was now calling them to be more than a great nation. He was preparing them for the greatest moment in history: the coming of the promised Messiah, the Son of David.

58

People of the Covenant

Jesus and his disciples were people of their time and used the language of the Jewish religion and culture. Many of the words they used took their meanings from ancient times and came from the Old Testament. If we want to get closer to Jesus and appreciate the New Testament, we have to make these words our own.

One of the most important of these words is *covenant*. People who think they know what a covenant is may be surprised to discover how rich in meaning this word really is.

Political Covenants Originally *covenant* was a political word. A *political covenant* was a treaty made between nations or individuals. Often it was made between a victorious king and the conquered people of another nation. So important was the covenant that it was usually sealed with a religious ceremony or solemn ritual action.

Political covenants were common among the pagan peoples of ancient times. Normally these covenants took a standard form and contained several parts:

• a preface naming the parties of the agreement: the powerful king and the conquered people

• a historical introduction listing the good things the king had done for the people

• the terms of the agreement: the duties and obligations that the conquered people would undertake at the king's direction

• proclamation of the terms to all the people

• witness of pagan gods

• the curses and blessings that would be given by the gods to those who either broke or kept the covenant.

Every treaty was completed with a ceremony. It might be the offering of a sacrifice to the gods, but often it was a ritual action. First an animal was cut in two. Then a representative from each side of the treaty would walk through the middle of the divided animal. This showed that the people who made the treaty understood that the gods might destroy in the same way those who failed to live up to the agreement.

Biblical Covenants When the ancient Israelites wanted to describe their relationship with the one true God, they adopted this covenant format and gave it a religious meaning. A *biblical covenant* was a solemn agreement between God and his people, legally binding on both sides and confirmed by offering a sacrifice to God or by a solemn ritual. The form of this biblical covenant looked very much like that of the ancient political covenant.

In the Old Testament the greatest covenant God made with his people was the covenant on Mount Sinai (Exodus 20—24). This covenant, like an ancient political covenant, also had several parts:

- a preface: "I, the LORD, am your God, who brought you out of the land of Egypt." (Exodus 20:2)
- a historical introduction: a reminder of everything God had done for his people
- terms of agreement: the commandments and laws given to Moses by God
- proclamation by Moses of the terms to all the people
- witness of the one and only God
- curses and blessings: God's promised rewards for the good and punishment for the evil.

After the people agreed to the terms of the Sinai covenant, it was sealed with a sacrifice. Then they participated in the sacrificial meal. As Moses sprinkled the blood of the sacrifice on the people, he said, "This is the blood of the covenant which the LORD has made with you" (Exodus 24:8). Now God and the people were united. They became one "blood," one family.

Why should we be so concerned with these ancient covenants? Because they are at the heart of both the Old and the New Testaments. Beginning with Noah and continuing with Abraham, Moses, and David, God established a relationship with his people through covenants. God was always faithful to his promises; yet the people needed to be called again and again to renew their promises to God. Eventually the prophets began to speak of a new covenant. This prophecy was fulfilled in Jesus.

◆ You may want to share with the group the following prayer that the Church prays on Good Friday:

Let us pray
for the Jewish people,
the first to hear the word of God,
that they may continue to grow
    in the love of his name
and in faithfulness to his covenant.

Almighty and eternal God,
long ago you gave your promise
    to Abraham and his posterity.

Listen to your Church as we pray
that the people you first made
    your own
may arrive at the fullness of
    redemption.

We ask this through Christ
    our Lord. Amen.

Presentation (cont'd)

◆ Have a volunteer summarize *Scripture Insight* on page 60. Explain that the next chapter presents more about sacrificial offerings.

◆ Allow about five minutes of quiet time for the young people to write their responses to the ☀ **thought provoker** on page 60.

◆ Have the young people form small groups to discuss the questions in *Things to Share, Things to Think About,* and *On Line with the Parish.*

Conclusion ___ min.

◆ Direct attention to *Words to Remember.* The definition for *biblical covenant* is on page 59.

Assessment: If you wish to use the *Midsemester Assessment,* pages 124 and 125, allow about twenty minutes for its completion.

If you are going to administer *Chapter 7 Assessment,* page 61A, allow about ten minutes for its completion.

Look again at the words of Moses when he sprinkled the people with the blood of the covenant. Do his words remind you of any words in the New Testament? Remember what Jesus said at the Last Supper: "This cup is the new covenant in my blood, which will be shed for you" (Luke 22:20). Jesus was using covenant terminology. He did this for a good reason. Like the covenant at Sinai, this covenant would be sealed in blood—the Blood of Jesus—and a sacrificial meal. Now there was a new covenant between God and his people. It was not sealed with the blood of animals but was ratified once and for all in the Blood of Jesus, the Son of God. This is the new and everlasting covenant in which we share as followers of Christ.

Scripture **INSIGHT**

The people of the Old Testament and of Jesus' time as well were agricultural people, people of the land. When they offered sacrifices to God, they often used animals. They did this, not because they hated animals or wanted to abuse them, but because they wanted to give God the most important things they owned.

☀ *Think about this: You belong to a people of the new covenant. How should this affect your life?*

60

Answers for Chapter 7 Assessment
1. d   2. a   3. a   4. c   5. c
6. c   7. b   8. a   9. a   10. See page 60.

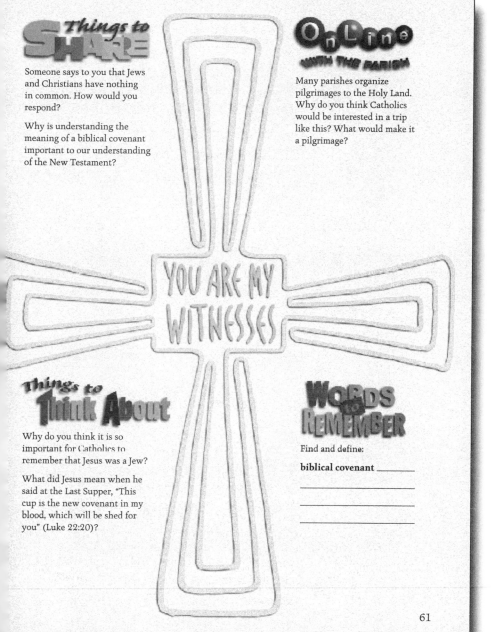

Things to SHARE

Someone says to you that Jews and Christians have nothing in common. How would you respond?

Why is understanding the meaning of a biblical covenant important to our understanding of the New Testament?

OnLine WITH THE PARISH

Many parishes organize pilgrimages to the Holy Land. Why do you think Catholics would be interested in a trip like this? What would make it a pilgrimage?

Things to Think About

Why do you think it is so important for Catholics to remember that Jesus was a Jew?

What did Jesus mean when he said at the Last Supper, "This cup is the new covenant in my blood, which will be shed for you" (Luke 22:20)?

Words to REMEMBER

Find and define:

biblical covenant _____

_____

_____

_____

61

Conclusion (cont'd)

◆ Distribute the handout *Living the Covenant*. Make sure the young people understand the directions.

FORUM Assignment

✔ Read pages 62–69. Underline in pencil the sentences that express six key concepts.

✔ Complete the handout *Living the Covenant*.

Closing Prayer: Have the young people look at the photo on pages 54 and 55. Proclaim together Luke 1:68.

Evaluation: Do the young people appreciate that, if we want to know Jesus and make sense of the New Testament, we must know and understand the Jews whose heritage Jesus shared? Do they understand that the new covenant was ratified in the Blood of Jesus, the Son of God?

FOR CHAPTER 8

• preparations for opening prayer
• copies of handout *For the Record*, page 62C
• copies of *Chapter 8 Assessment*, page 69A
• copies of *Highlights for Home*, page 69B
• *Glory & Praise* hymnals (optional)

Assessment

1 Jesus was
- **a.** a Middle Easterner.
- **b.** a carpenter.
- **c.** a Jew.
- **d.** all of the above

2 The ancestors of Jesus
- **a.** were enslaved in Egypt.
- **b.** were never in captivity.
- **c.** always obeyed God.
- **d.** built no Temples.

3 A political covenant
- **a.** was a treaty between nations or individuals.
- **b.** was sealed by a handshake.
- **c.** ignored pagan gods.
- **d.** was not important.

4 A biblical covenant
- **a.** was never written.
- **b.** was not like a political covenant.
- **c.** was confirmed by offering a sacrifice.
- **d.** had only one part.

5 The new covenant was established by
- **a.** Moses.
- **b.** Abraham.
- **c.** Jesus.
- **d.** David.

6 The names of Jacob's twelve sons were later identified with names of
- **a.** political covenants.
- **b.** certain stars of the sky.
- **c.** the tribes of Israel.
- **d.** biblical covenants.

7 ___ was the capital city of the Jewish people.
- **a.** Babylonia
- **b.** Jerusalem
- **c.** Nazareth
- **d.** Bethlehem

8 The greatest Old Testament covenant God made with his people was
- **a.** on Mount Sinai.
- **b.** after the great flood.
- **c.** after the Babylonian captivity.
- **d.** politically advantageous.

9 The Mount Sinai covenant's terms of agreement were___ given by God to Moses.
- **a.** commandments and laws
- **b.** duties of a conquered people
- **c.** rainbows set in the sky
- **d.** sacrificial offerings

10 What did Jesus mean when he said at the Last Supper, "This cup is the new covenant in my blood, which will be shed for you" (Luke 22:20)?

_____
_____
_____

Highlights for Home

Focus on Faith

In this chapter the young people are reminded that Jesus was a Jew; he belonged to a people with a rich history and religious heritage. By becoming more familiar with the religious history and practices of the Jews, we enhance our ability to know Jesus and understand the New Testament. We can appreciate the new and everlasting covenant in which we share as followers of Christ.

In Chapter 7, the young people learn about the biblical covenants of the Old Testament. They learn that the greatest of these was the one God made with his people on Mount Sinai. After the people agreed to this covenant's terms, it was sealed with a sacrifice, and then they participated in the sacrificial meal. Like this covenant at Sinai, the new covenant was sealed in blood—the Blood of Jesus—and a sacrificial meal.

Emphasize with your son or daughter that we belong to a people of the new covenant. Help them to realize that this should affect every aspect of our lives.

Conversation Starters

. . . . a few ideas to talk about together. . . .

◆ How can we, as a parish and as a family, contribute to a deeper understanding between Catholics and Jews?

◆ In what ways do I show I believe that I belong to a people of the new covenant? What do I have to change?

Feature Focus

Scripture Insight on page 60 points out that the people of the Old Testament and Jesus' time were agricultural people. They often used animals as their sacrificial offerings to God. They did this because they wanted to give God the most important things they owned.

Reflection

Together with your family draw up a family friendship treaty or covenant. List the rules or guidelines that will enable you to live as people of the new covenant. Then have a signing ceremony. After all members have signed the document, share a family favorite meal or snack.

MORE ABOUT JESUS AND HIS PEOPLE

Adult Focus

In this chapter the young people will explore the belief of Jesus and the Jews that God was present in his people, in the Temple, and in God's law. They will learn about three important elements of Jewish life and worship: the Temple, the priesthood, and sacrifice. When presenting this chapter, help the young people to understand that the offering of sacrifices was an important part of the covenant and of Jewish worship.

In the Temple sacrifices were offered to praise and thank God and to atone for sin. Only priests were allowed to offer sacrifices. Only the high priest was permitted to enter the holy of holies, the most sacred part of the Temple, once a year on the Day of Atonement. When the Temple of Jerusalem was destroyed by the Romans in A.D. 70, the Jewish priesthood came to an end. In the new covenant, there would be a new priesthood, one centered in Jesus and the paschal mystery. Jesus is the high priest who offered himself as a sacrifice. He gave up his life on the altar of the cross, and through his Blood we were saved from sin.

It is important to be able to distinguish between the old covenant and the new covenant. As you present this chapter, help the young people to realize that knowing and living God's law as people of the new covenant is our privilege and joy. As they come to understand and appreciate the religious heritage of Jesus, may they, as people of the new covenant, come to understand, to appreciate, and to claim their inheritance of faith.

Catechism Focus

The theme of Chapter 8 corresponds to paragraphs 348, 534, 610–611, and 1539–1545 of the *Catechism*.

Enrichment Activities

The Temple in Jerusalem

Invite the young people to do a research project on the Temple that Solomon built or that the Israelites built after they were freed from the Babylonian captivity. The young people may write a paper, build a model, or prepare a dramatization. All forms should include a description of the Temple's interior.

In the Temple

Have the young people form five groups. Assign one of the following Scripture passages to each group:

- Luke 1:5–25 (Announcement of the Birth of John)
- Luke 2:22–38 (Presentation of Jesus)
- Luke 2:41–52 (The Boy Jesus in the Temple)
- John 10:22–39 (Feast of the Dedication)
- Mark 11:15–19 (Cleansing of the Temple).

Have the group members discuss what is happening in the Temple and its connection to Jewish life and worship at the time of Jesus. Invite the groups to prepare a dramatization of the reading to present to the group in a later session.

Teaching Resources

Overview

To explore the belief of Jesus and the Jews that God was present in his people, in the Temple, and in God's law; to discover the importance of the Temple, the priesthood, and sacrifice to Jewish life and worship.

Opening Prayer Ideas

Read and reflect on John 15:11–17.

or

Read and reflect on Matthew 22:36–39.

Materials

- Bibles, journals, and highlighters
- *Glory & Praise* hymnals (optional)

REPRODUCIBLE MASTERS
- *For the Record*, page 62C
- *Chapter 8 Assessment*, page 69A
- *Highlights for Home*, page 69B

New Testament Journal:
For Chapter 8, use pages 30–31.

Supplemental Resources

VIDEOS
- *The Last Supper*
- *The Passover*
- *The Singer of Israel: David*

Vision Video
P.O. Box 540
Worcester, PA 19490

CHAPTER eight

For the Record

A music producer wants to record a contemporary youth version of Psalm 119. She has chosen to use the verses listed below. For each verse, write the lyrics you would like to use in a rock, country, pop, or rap song. Feel free to write a melody to use for all the verses.

Psalm 119

How can the young walk without fault?
    Only by keeping your words. (9)

Lead me from the way of deceit;
    favor me with your teaching. (29)

I am a friend of all who fear you,
    of all who keep your precepts. (63)

Teaching from your lips is more
        precious to me
    than heaps of silver and gold. (72)

My eyes shed streams of tears
    because your teaching is not
        followed. (136)

Your Lyrics

How can teens stay clean?
Only by tuning in to God's station.

_____

_____

_____

_____

_____

_____

_____

_____

_____

_____

_____

_____

_____

_____

More About
Jesus and His People

From age to age you gather
a people to yourself.
Eucharistic Prayer III

Objectives: To explore the belief of Jesus and the Jews that God was present in his people, in the Temple, and in God's law; to discover the importance of the Temple, the priesthood, and sacrifice to Jewish life and worship.

Introduction ___ min.

Opening Prayer and Forum: Invite the young people to open their texts to pages 62 and 63. Proclaim together the prayer on page 63. Then have two energetic volunteers who have prepared actions or gestures present the following rap:

Don't just sit there in isolation!
Please say yes to Jesus' invitation
To join with past and future
generations
In being people of the new covenant.

Have the young people form small groups to share the issues they have written for the handout *Living the Covenant*. Ask each group to discuss points that will help young people keep God's covenant. Have them also talk about ways they can support and help each other live according to God's law.

Then gather together in a circle. Have a prepared volunteer read John 15:11–17. Then sing together a hymn that is based on the theme of the people of God. "Faithful Family," "Gather Us In," and "We Gather Together" are appropriate. All are in the *Glory & Praise* hymnal.

Presentation ___ min.

Note: If possible, show a diagram of the Temple in Jerusalem. One may be found on page 325 in the introduction to *The Catholic Student Bible* of the *New American Bible*, William H. Sadlier, Inc. for Oxford University Press.

◆ Write the following Latin words and formula on the board:

sacrificium—sacer (sacred) + *facere* (to make)

Explain to the young people that the word *sacrificium* is a noun and means "something that has been made sacred."

Then write the word *sacrifice.* Ask a volunteer to give the definition provided on page 64. *(a gift offered to God by a priest and destroyed in some way to show that it belongs to God alone)*

Have volunteers list on the board possible gifts that people brought to the Temple for the priest to sacrifice. Ask, "Why were these gifts offered?" *(to give praise and thanksgiving to God and as a way of atoning for sin)*

Then have volunteers explain what type of sacrifice a holocaust was.

*E*xcept for one remaining wall, the Temple of Jerusalem was destroyed in A.D. 70. That wall is a place of pilgrimage for Jews today.

Why do you think the wall of the Temple is a place of pilgrimage for so many?

Model of the Temple rebuilt by Herod around 20 B.C.

People of the Temple

The Temple in Jerusalem was a very important place for Jesus and the Jews. The gospels record that Jesus was brought there as an infant and again as a twelve-year-old boy on pilgrimage with his family. During his public life Jesus went to the Temple on important occasions. You might remember the time when he got angry with the money changers and drove them away from the Temple area. Why was the Temple so important? What did it have to do with the Jewish people and their faith in God?

The Temple was the center of Jewish life and worship. It was only at the Temple that sacrifices could be offered to God. The offering of sacrifices was an important part of the covenant and of Jewish worship. Every day there were special morning and evening sacrifices offered to the praise of God. A *sacrifice* was a gift offered to God by a priest and destroyed in some way to show that it belonged to God alone.

64

The different kinds of sacrifices offered in the Temple are listed in the first seven chapters of the Book of Leviticus. The gifts to be sacrificed were brought to the priests. Possible gifts included cattle, sheep, and goats. The poor, such as Mary and Joseph, could offer pigeons or turtledoves. Other sacrificial gifts included grain, flour, frankincense, oil, and bread.

Why were these gifts offered? They were offered to give praise and thanksgiving to God and as a way of atoning for sin. Perhaps the most important sacrifice was the holocaust offering. A *holocaust* was the offering of a whole animal. The person offering the gift would present it to the priest. After the animal was slaughtered, its blood was sprinkled over the altar. Then the offering was totally consumed by fire. Why? To return to God the gift of life that only God could have given in the first place. In the making of this sacrifice, the smoke from the victim went directly up to God. The victim's blood was poured on the altar because blood was considered the force of life itself. Now the gift belonged to God in a special way.

Priesthood and Sacrifice

A *priest* is one authorized to offer a sacrifice. Sacrifice is the highest form of worship one can offer to God, and every sacrifice in the Temple was offered by a priest. In Israel priests were not ordained for sacred service in the way that priests of the new covenant, Catholic priests, are ordained today. The Old Testament priesthood was hereditary, passed on from father to son. God had chosen the tribe of Levi as the priestly class, and a man was a priest simply because he was a member of this tribe.

Moses and Aaron, his brother, were members of the tribe of Levi. Over the long history of the Jewish people, the family of Aaron was singled out by God as the family from which the Temple priests would come. The other members of the tribe of Levi became secondary ministers of the Temple who assisted the priests. These secondary ministers

became known as *Levites*. Do you remember the priest and the Levite who are mentioned in Jesus' parable of the Good Samaritan? Now you know who they are.

With so many members of the tribe of Levi—both priests and Levites—involved in Temple worship, some sort of organization was necessary. The head priest, who exercised overall authority in the Temple, was called the *high priest*. One of his special duties each year was to enter the holy of holies, the most sacred part of the Temple. The high priest alone could do this once a year on the Day of Atonement.

During his trial Jesus was brought before the high priest. Try to find the priest's name in the New Testament. Clue: Read John 18.

◆ Have the young people form small groups. Ask each group to write five statements to summarize "Priesthood and Sacrifice." Then have a reporter from each group read the summary statements to the other groups.

◆ Direct the young people's attention to the **thought provoker** on page 65. Have the young people read John 18 to find the answer. (*Caiaphas*)

◆ Have a volunteer summarize *Catholic ID* on page 66. Read together Leviticus 8:12.

◆ Ask the young people to share the statements they underlined for "People of the Temple" and "Priesthood and Sacrifice" on pages 64 through 66. Have them highlight the key concepts highlighted on the reduced pages.

FYI Share the second stanza of a hymn the Church sings at Easter, "At the Lamb's High Feast We Sing."

Praise we him, whose love divine
Gives his sacred blood for wine,
Gives his body for the feast,
Christ the Victim, Christ the Priest. Alleluia!

Presentation (cont'd)

◆ Write the word *Shema* on the board. Ask volunteers to explain the meaning. You may want to explain that after the time of Jesus, the Shema was written on a small scroll, called a *mezuzah*. The scroll was placed in a container and hung on the doorpost of every Jewish home. All who went in and out touched the mezuzah reverently and prayed the Shema. This practice is still observed today.

Read together the words of the Shema on page 66.

◆ Write the word *synagogue* on the board and have a volunteer provide a definition. (*Every village and town had a synagogue. It was a place of prayer and study; the scrolls containing Sacred Scripture were kept there.*)

Then have volunteers explain the Sabbath service that took place at the main gathering of the week. List each part on the board. The following parts should be included in the correct sequence:

• singing of a psalm

• reciting the Shema and other prayers

• reading of Scripture and a sermon

• closing with a blessing prayer.

Have a volunteer read the prayer of blessing in Numbers 6:24–26.

Priesthood and sacrifice were important for Israel. In fact the entire Book of Leviticus is filled with procedures and regulations about Temple worship and the priesthood. However, when the Temple of Jerusalem was destroyed by the Romans in A.D. 70, the priesthood of the old covenant came to an end. In the new covenant there would be a new priesthood, one centered in Jesus.

In the New Testament we learn that Jesus was both the sacrificial victim and the priest. He gave up his life on the altar of the cross, and through his Blood we were saved from sin. In the Letter to the Hebrews, Jesus Christ is also called our high priest. There we read:

> Every high priest is taken from among men and made their representative before God, to offer gifts and sacrifices for sins. . . . No one takes this honor upon himself but only when called by God, just as Aaron was. In the same way, it was not Christ who glorified himself in becoming high priest, but rather the one who said to him:
>   "You are my son;
>   this day I have begotten you."
> Hebrews 5:1–5

You may wish to find out more about Aaron, the brother of Moses, who was an important person in the Old Testament.

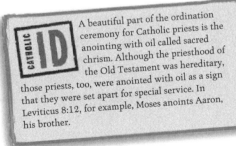

A beautiful part of the ordination ceremony for Catholic priests is the anointing with oil called sacred chrism. Although the priesthood of the Old Testament was hereditary, those priests, too, were anointed with oil as a sign that they were set apart for special service. In Leviticus 8:12, for example, Moses anoints Aaron, his brother.

66

People of Prayer

An important belief of Jesus and the Jews was that God was present in his people, in the Temple, and in God's law. That was the point of the covenant and its fulfillment: The Jews were God's people, and the Lord of heaven and earth was their God.

God, Present in His People   As a covenant people the Jews were to imitate God. Moses had been instructed by God to tell the people, "Be holy, for I, the LORD, your God, am holy" (Leviticus 19:2). That is why Jesus and his people were to be people of prayer. Every morning and every evening, they recited the great Shema. *Shema* is a word meaning "hear," and it was the first word of the prayer:

> HEAR, O ISRAEL! THE LORD IS OUR GOD, THE LORD ALONE! THEREFORE, YOU SHALL LOVE THE LORD, YOUR GOD, WITH ALL YOUR HEART, AND WITH ALL YOUR SOUL, AND WITH ALL YOUR STRENGTH.
> DEUTERONOMY 6:4–5

The words of the Shema tell us that because there is only one God, we must love him with our whole being. Jesus recited the words of the Shema every day. He also made them "the greatest and the first commandment" (Matthew 22: 38).

Besides praying the Shema each day, Jesus went to the synagogue in Nazareth. There was only one Temple, and that was in Jerusalem. But every village and town had a *synagogue*. It was a place of prayer and study; the scrolls containing Sacred Scripture were kept there.

Orthodox Jew playing the shofar (ram's horn) to announce the beginning of a Jewish festival

Daily services were held in the synagogue, but the main gathering of the week was on the Sabbath. The Sabbath service opened with the singing of a psalm and the recitation of the Shema and other prayers. These were followed by the reading of Scripture and a sermon. The service closed with the blessing prayer found in Numbers 6:24–26.

The *Sabbath observance* was an important part of the covenant between God and his people. It was based on the creation story of Genesis, in which God rested on the seventh day after creating the world. Observing the Sabbath was a serious obligation as part of God's law and was a sign of recognizing God's presence with his people. The Sabbath began at sunset on Friday and lasted until sunset on Saturday. Today, we believe that a new day begins at midnight; but at the time of Jesus, a new day was considered to begin at sunset. No work of any kind could be done on the Sabbath, including housework and cooking a meal.

God, Present in the Temple The Temple was the center of the Jewish religion. It was a sacred place and contained the holy of holies. This was God's special dwelling place with his people, for it was there that the ark of the covenant had been kept. Jews living outside Jerusalem made pilgrimages to the Temple. On the great feasts as many as 200,000 made a pilgrimage to Jerusalem, more than doubling the resident population of 150,000. Three feasts were special times of pilgrimage:

• *Passover*, or Pesah, was a feast for remembering that God brought his people out of slavery in Egypt. It was celebrated in the spring. The passover, or paschal, lambs were sacrificed at the Temple, and the families who were there participated in the sacrificial meal.

• *Pentecost*, or the feast of Weeks, was fifty days after Passover. It celebrated the covenant on Mount Sinai and was a time for renewing the covenant. It was like the anniversary of the giving of God's law to Moses.

• *Tabernacles*, or Sukkoth, was the harvest feast celebrated in autumn. It was a special time to thank God for bringing his people out of Egypt and returning them to the promised land.

◆ Ask the young people, "What was the holy of holies?" (*It was God's special dwelling place with his people, for it was there that the ark of the covenant had been kept.*)

Have volunteers explain the three feasts described on page 67. Then ask another volunteer to explain the Day of Atonement, or Yom Kippur. This feast's explanation is on page 68.

◆ Have the young people highlight the main ideas highlighted on pages 66 through 68.

Note: At this time you may want to show the videos *The Last Supper* and/or *The Passover*. Both are available from Gateway Films/Vision Video. The e-mail address is visionvide @aol.com

Just in case...
some pronunciation helps

Shema. . . . . Sheh-**mah**
mezusah . . . . . . meh-**zoo**-zah
Yom Kippur . . . . Yom Ki-**poor**

67

FYI The shofar is a ritual musical instrument made from the horn of ram. In biblical times the shofar was used to announce the Sabbath.

In modern practice it is now sounded in the synagogue to call the Jewish people to a spiritual renewal on Rosh Hashanah, New Year's Day. The shofar is also sounded on Yom Kippur to call the Jews to repentance and love of the Torah (the first five books of the Old Testament, also called the Law).

Presentation (cont'd)

◆ Have the young people reread *Catholic Teachings* on page 68. Observe a moment of silence in which the young people thank Jesus for his great sacrifice.

◆ Have volunteers summarize "God, Present in His Law" on page 68. Ask everyone to read the message of Psalm 119 as stated in the last sentence of this section.

◆ Discuss questions in *Things to Think About* and *Things to Share*. Emphasize that if we want to know Jesus and make sense of the New Testament, we must know and understand the Jewish people whose heritage Jesus shared.

Conclusion ___ min.

◆ Direct attention to *Words to Remember*. The definition of *priest* is on page 65; the definition of *sacrifice* is on page 64.

◆ Have the young people form small groups to share their responses to the questions in *On Line with the Parish*. In the back of this book, artists' depictions of "Jesus Christ in Every Age" are presented.

Assessment: If you wish to give a standardized test, administer *Chapter 8 Assessment* on page 69A.

The western wall of the Temple, an important place of Jewish piety today

CATHOLIC TEACHINGS

About Sacrifice
When speaking about Jesus' sacrifice on the cross, the Church teaches us that "this sacrifice of Christ is unique; it completes and surpasses all other sacrifices" (*Catechism*, 614).

In the autumn calendar the *Day of Atonement*, or *Yom Kippur*, was also an important feast. It was a day of fasting and repentance for sin. On this feast the high priest took two goats as sin offerings. He offered the sacrificial blood of one goat as an offering for sin in the holy of holies, which he alone could enter on this one day each year. He laid his hands upon the head of the other goat and then drove the animal out into the desert. This signified that the sins of Israel would be taken away. The goat that symbolically carried away the sins of the people was known as a *scapegoat*.

God, Present in His Law For the Jews the law of God flowed from the covenant, and the obligation to keep it was a covenant duty. God's will for the people took the form of law. Unlike other peoples, for whom all laws were human inventions, Jesus and the other Jews understood God's law as his revealed will. So knowing and living God's law was a privilege and part of a sacred covenant. This meant that God's law was liberating; obeying it was to be a joy!

One of the psalms Jesus prayed was Psalm 119, a prayer to God, the lawgiver. With 176 verses, it is the longest psalm. But all the verses give the same message: May God be praised and thanked for giving us his law; may we have the wisdom to understand it and the strength to keep it.

Is obeying God's law a joy for you? Try to include part of Psalm 119 in your prayer this week.

68

Answers for Chapter 8 Assessment

1. b	**2.** d	**3.** d	**4.** c	**5.** b
6. a	**7.** b	**8.** b	**9.** d	**10.** See page 66.

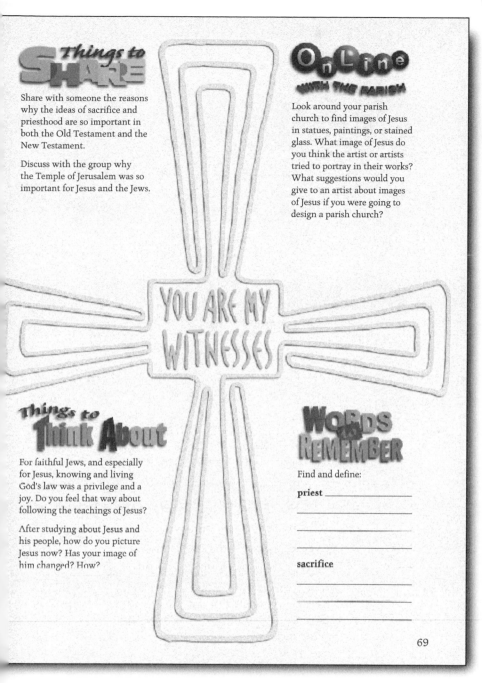

Things to SHARE

Share with someone the reasons why the ideas of sacrifice and priesthood are so important in both the Old Testament and the New Testament.

Discuss with the group why the Temple of Jerusalem was so important for Jesus and the Jews.

OnLine WITH THE PARISH

Look around your parish church to find images of Jesus in statues, paintings, or stained glass. What image of Jesus do you think the artist or artists tried to portray in their works? What suggestions would you give to an artist about images of Jesus if you were going to design a parish church?

Things to Think About

For faithful Jews, and especially for Jesus, knowing and living God's law was a privilege and a joy. Do you feel that way about following the teachings of Jesus?

After studying about Jesus and his people, how do you picture Jesus now? Has your image of him changed? How?

WORDS to REMEMBER

Find and define:

priest _____

_____

_____

_____

sacrifice _____

_____

_____

_____

69

Conclusion (cont'd)

◆ Distribute copies of the handout *For the Record*. Have a volunteer read the directions and make sure the young people understand the assignment.

FORUM *Assignment*

✔ Read pages 70–77. Underline in pencil the statements that express six main ideas.

✔ Complete the handout *For the Record*.

◆ Encourage the young people to share *Highlights for Home*, page 69B, with their families.

Closing Prayer: Have the young people write their responses to the 👑 **thought provoker** question on page 68.

Then ask the young people to form two choral-reading groups. Have the groups bring their Bibles and stand in parallel lines, facing each other, to pray Psalm 119:9–16. Have each group alternate reading the verses.

Evaluation: Have the young people discovered the importance of the Temple, the priesthood, and sacrifice to Jewish life and worship? Have they explored the Jewish belief that God was present in his people, in the Temple, and in God's law?

FOR CHAPTER 9

• copies of handout *Walking on Water*, page 70C
• copies of *Chapter 9 Assessment*, page 77A
• copies of *Highlights for Home*, page 77B

Assessment

1 Sacrifices in the Temple
a. only included animals.
b. were offered only by priests.
c. had no religious meaning.
d. were rarely offered.

2 Jesus and the Jews believed that God was present in
a. the Temple.
b. political covenants.
c. his law.
d. both a and c

3 Jews observed the Sabbath by
a. worshipping in the synagogue.
b. praying the Shema.
c. not working.
d. all of the above

4 Circle the feast that the Jewish people did not celebrate.
a. Passover
b. Pentecost
c. Easter
d. Tabernacles

5 A holocaust was the offering of
a. flour.
b. a whole animal.
c. frankincense.
d. oil and bread.

6 Circle the one that does *not* belong.
In Jesus' time sacrificial gifts were offered to
a. show the greatness of humans.
b. give praise to God.
c. to thank God.
d. to atone for sins.

7 _____ could enter the holy of holies on the Day of Atonement.
a. The Levites
b. The high priest alone
c. The givers of sacrificial offerings
d. All worshippers

8 Scrolls containing Sacred Scripture were kept in the _____ of every Jewish village and town.
a. Temple
b. synagogue
c. private homes
d. holy of holies

9 Circle the one that does *not* belong.
The Day of Atonement was
a. in autumn.
b. an important feast.
c. a day of repentance.
d. also known as Pentecost.

10 Explain why Jesus and his people prayed the Shema every morning and every evening.

_____
_____
_____

CHAPTER 8: More About Jesus and His People

Highlights for Home

Focus on Faith

In this chapter, the young people explored the belief of Jesus and the Jews that God was present in his people, in the Temple, and in God's law. They also examined three important elements of Jewish life and worship: the Temple, the priesthood, and sacrifice.

In the Temple sacrifices were offered to praise and thank God and to atone for sin. Only priests were allowed to offer sacrifices. Only the high priest was to enter the holy of holies, the most sacred part of the Temple, once a year on the Day of Atonement. When the Temple of Jerusalem was destroyed by the Romans in A.D. 70, the Jewish priesthood came to an end. In the new covenant, there would be a new priesthood, one centered in Jesus and the paschal mystery. Jesus is the high priest who offered himself as a sacrifice. He gave up his life on the altar of the cross, and through his Blood we were saved from sin. It is important to be able to distinguish between the old covenant and the new covenant.

Conversation Starters

. . . . a few ideas to talk about together . . . .

◆ How will I show my gratitude to Jesus for offering himself as a sacrifice on the altar of the cross?

◆ Do I consider knowing and living God's law a privilege? a part of the sacred covenant? a great joy?

Feature Focus

The *Catholic ID* feature on page 66 reminds us that our priests are anointed with sacred chrism during the ordination ceremony, just as Jewish priests of the Old Testament were anointed.

Reflection

Hear, O Israel! The LORD is our God, the LORD alone! Therefore, you shall love the LORD, your God, with all your heart, and with all your soul, and with all your strength.

Deuteronomy 6:4–5

Every morning and every evening, Jesus recited the great Shema. In Hebrew, *shema* means "hear" and is the first word of this prayer. Contemporary Jews still pray this prayer morning and evening as a basic affirmation of faith. Because Jesus used these verses in his teaching and called them "the greatest and the first commandment" (Matthew 22:36–38), we also find them very familiar to us.

As people of the new covenant, we are called to be a people of prayer. Reflect on the words of Jesus.

You shall love the Lord, your God, with all your heart, with all your soul, and with all your mind. This is the greatest and the first commandment. The second is like it: You shall love your neighbor as yourself.

Matthew 22:36–39

JESUS AND HIS WORLD

Adult Focus

Essayist Wendell Berry writes of our need to belong to the landscape in which we dwell. His spiritual ambition is to know his environment fully, as fully as the birds and beasts who are native to it. In one of his essays he writes, "The wild creatures belong to the place by nature, but as a man I can belong to it only by understanding and by virtue" (*Recollected Essays 1965–1980*).

From the evidence of his parables and his familiarity with the desert, the mountains, and the Sea of Galilee, we can be sure that Jesus knew fully the place in which he dwelled. To picture him as unconnected with his particular native place, time, or culture is to forego the possibility of knowing Jesus well.

Chapter 9 guides the young people into the first-century world of Jesus so that they can come to know him in his historical context. Awareness of Israel as a small nation located at an important crossroads in the Roman Empire is essential to a real appreciation of Jesus' life and teaching. To know Nazareth as a lower Galilean town near the bustling Roman city of Sepphoris is to better understand the stories and travels of "Jesus the Galilean."

Anyone who makes it his or her spiritual ambition to know fully Jesus' native place and culture will be rewarded. This is our hope for our young people as we prepare them to hear the good news of Jesus of Nazareth.

Catechism Focus

The theme of Chapter 9 corresponds to paragraphs 125, 127, and 514–515 of the *Catechism*.

Enrichment Activities

Describing Where We Dwell

Encourage the young people to keep a daily journal for one week. For each day they are to record details about their home, neighborhood, or community. Encourage awareness of the natural and man-made environment (sights, sounds, smells, structures, other inhabitants). Ask the group to include their observations in their daily prayer.

Computer Connection

Have the young people use a multimedia encyclopedia, such as *The New Grolier Multimedia Encyclopedia*™, or the reference feature of an online information service, such as *America Online*®, to find information about the Sea of Galilee, the Arabian Desert, and the Roman occupation of Israel in the time of Jesus.

In Another Language

If you would like your group to hear the Aramaic language, you may want to order the audiocassette *The Lord's Prayer in Aramaic* at the following address:

The Noohra Foundation
18022 Cowan Street
Suite 100-B
Irvine, CA 92714

Teaching Resources

Overview

To discover the reasons Israel was considered the crossroads of the world at the time of Jesus; to explore the culture of and languages spoken in Galilee.

Opening Prayer Ideas

Share a "desert" experience.

or

Pray Psalm 68:33–36. Consider the meaning these words would have had for the Jews in Jesus' time.

Materials

- Bibles, highlighters, and journals

New Testament Journal:
For Chapter 9, use pages 20–21.

REPRODUCIBLE MASTERS
- *Walking on Water*, page 70C
- *Chapter 9 Assessment*, page 77A
- *Highlights for Home*, page 77B

Supplemental Resources

VIDEOS
Seeking Jesus in His Own Land
- "The Birth of Jesus"
- "Jesus the Prophet"
- "Jesus the Redeemer"

St. Anthony Messenger Press/
Franciscan Communications
1615 Republic Street
Cincinnati, OH 45210

Walking on Water

Read Matthew 14:22–33. Step into Peter's sandals and respond to the questions of a friend who was not in the boat that night.

Peter, what did you think when you saw Jesus coming toward you?

How did you feel? What did Jesus do?

How has this awesome experience changed you?

Jesus and His World

Many prophets and kings desired to see what you see, but did not see it, and to hear what you hear, but did not hear it.

Luke 10:24

71

Objectives: To discover the reasons Israel was considered the crossroads of the world at the time of Jesus; to explore the culture of and languages spoken in Galilee.

Introduction ___ min.

Opening Prayer: Invite the young people to look at the photograph on pages 70 and 71. Have them focus on the swirling motion. Ask, "Do you sometimes feel that so many things are swirling in your mind that you are in overdrive? What do you do?"

Explain that sometimes we need to "escape" from our immediate surroundings (including friends and other people) in order to think things through, to pray, to calm down, to relax, or to reestablish our priorities. Jesus did this often throughout his life. Before he began his public ministry, he went into the desert to find solitude and to pray. Invite the young people to step back from their immediate surroundings "to go into the desert." Use the following script directions:

- Close your eyes. Gradually let the tension flow from your head, your eyes, your face, your neck. Visualize the tension and stress flowing down through your body and out through your toes, leaving you relaxed.

- Picture yourself in a quiet spot. Perhaps you are in a desert-like environment, with sand and rocks as far as the eye can see. Whatever spot you choose, this is your desert place.

- Quietly and peacefully, sort through the issues in your mind today. Choose one to focus on, telling Jesus how you feel about it: excited, happy, indifferent, confused, sad, angry. Find comfort in talking with Jesus, who taught us how to pray—who showed us the way to take time out of very busy days.

Then conclude the prayer by reading together Psalm 121 or singing together "Peace is Flowing Like a River." If you choose to sing the song by Carey Landry, explain that the young people can consider themselves the captives "freed" from being caught in a whirlwind of activity.

Presentation ___ min.

◆ Have a volunteer read the introductory paragraph on page 72. Discuss the conditions of living in a desert.

◆ Write the term *crossroads* on the board and have a volunteer explain its meaning. Ask the young people to identify an area of your local community that would be considered a crossroads.

Have the group highlight the main concepts highlighted in this chapter.

◆ To help the young people see the scope of the Roman Empire, have them look at the map in the back of their books on page 127.

On the board write the names of Israel's three main regions: Galilee, Samaria, and Judaea. Have the young people locate each region on the map.

◆ Discuss the special privileges granted to the Jews by the Romans. Ask, "Do you think that there was a great deal of dissatisfaction about the ruling presence of the Romans?" Discuss the reason that Samaritans were looked down upon by the other Jews of Jesus' time.

A large part of our planet is covered by deserts. Have you ever visited a desert region or seen one on television or in movies? What do you think it would be like to live in a desert?

Crossroads of the World

Jesus grew up and lived in one of the great desert regions of the world. His country, on the edge of a great desert, was called Israel. Later it was called Palestine. Centuries before Jesus the country had been called Canaan and was the land promised by God to Abraham and his descendants.

Israel was a small country, but it had a rich and varied landscape. To the west, it bordered on the Mediterranean Sea. East of the coastal plain was the hill country. This was an area with hills and valleys, excellent for herding sheep and goats and for growing fruits and vegetables. Farther east was a mountain range with high bluffs that descended to the Jordan River valley and finally led to the Arabian Desert.

Because Israel was close to the desert, it is important for readers of the New Testament to understand just what a desert is. The word *desert* covers a variety of landscapes, from shifting sand dunes to rocky cliffs to a hardened mixture of sand and pebbles. Travel in the desert is difficult, even for some animals. Besides the overwhelming heat, the desert is dry and barren, and water wells are found only occasionally on oases.

In an arid country surrounded by so much desert, the Jordan valley was an important place, for it was there that the Jordan River flowed. There, too, was the Sea of Galilee, a beautiful freshwater lake. But the valley also contained the Dead Sea, a salty and lifeless body of water about thirteen hundred feet below sea level (the lowest point on the surface of the earth).

72

The Romans are mentioned often in the New Testament. They ruled a mighty empire that stretched from Britain to Egypt. The empire was divided into provinces, each one overseen by a governor or administrator appointed by the emperor in Rome. Supported by a vast army, the governors were to keep order throughout the empire. The day-to-day running of governments was left to the local rulers and kings. But the Roman governors retained overall control. They saw to it that taxes were levied for Rome, and they had the last word in all disputes.

Among all the provinces of the mighty empire, the tiny province of Israel had special privileges. The Jews hated the presence of the pagan Romans in their country and fiercely opposed them. To keep peace, the Romans allowed the Jews to worship their God publicly and did not force them to worship the gods of Rome. In addition the Jews were not subject to military service, could keep the Sabbath, and were allowed to pay a special tax for the upkeep of the Temple.

At the time of Jesus, Israel was made up of three main regions: Galilee, Samaria, and Judaea. Galilee in the north gave its name to the Sea of Galilee. Nazareth was in Galilee, and Jesus was known both as a Nazorean and as a Galilean. Samaria was the middle region in Israel and was populated by a mixed race of people. The Samaritans were descendants of Jews who centuries before had intermarried with pagans. For that reason they were looked down upon by the other Jews of Jesus' time.

Even though Israel could be a harsh land in which to live, it was still known as a crossroads for peoples of the ancient world. A narrow strip of territory along the seacoast, it formed a natural highway for merchants going between the great centers of Mesopotamia and Egypt. But this also made it a highway for the invading armies of ancient empires. Israel, being so small, was often conquered and ruled by one of these foreign powers. At the time of Christ, Israel was part of the Roman Empire.

◆ During this session, you may want to show the following videos that make up the series *Seeking Jesus in His Own Land:*

- *The Birth of Jesus*—The young people will see places that commemorate Jesus' birth.

- *Jesus the Prophet*—The young people will visit the settings of the wedding feast of Cana, Jesus' baptism, and the Sermon on the Mount.

- *Jesus the Redeemer*—The young people will visit the sites of Jesus' passion, death, and resurrection.

◆ Have the young people locate Capernaum on the map on page 73. Ask them to identify the town's region. *(Galilee)*

Then ask the young people to look up the following passages in the Bible. For each reading, have them identify a reason the town would be listed as a place to visit on a pilgrimage to the Holy Land.

- Matthew 4:13—After Jesus left Nazareth, he went to live in Capernaum.

- Mark 1:21—After calling the first disciples, Jesus taught in the Capernaum synagogue on the Sabbath.

- Luke 7:1–10—After reentering the town, Jesus healed the centurion's slave.

Have the young people look at the map on page 57 as a prepared volunteer reads Mark 1:2–8. Ask the young people to write in their journals any obstacles that may block their way along their journey of faith. Ask them to write one thing that they can do to clear the path.

73

Presentation (cont'd)

◆ Discuss the ⚜ **thought provoker** on page 74. Encourage the young people to recognize that the history of the Jewish people at times included bearing the hardships of the desert and being conquered by rulers of other lands. Jesus was proclaiming the good news to his listeners who were living under Roman rule with special privileges to practice their faith.

◆ Have the young people look at the map on page 73. Have them locate the town of Nazareth and the city of Sepphoris. Ask, "In what direction would you be traveling if you were fishing on the Sea of Galilee near Capernaum and then bringing the fish to market in Sepphoris?" (*southeast*)

◆ Have a volunteer summarize *Scripture Insight.* Explain that there were two kinds of fish caught in the Sea of Galilee and the Jordan River: The "clean" fish, which included tilapia, bleak, and lake sardines, could be eaten by the Jews. The "unclean," which included catfish, eel, and lamprey, were separated from the others and sold to those who were not Jewish.

Judaea was south of Samaria and was the center for Jewish worship. No matter where they lived, Jews looked to Judaea, for Jerusalem and its Temple were there. It was the political capital and the seat of religious authority. Jesus was born in Judaea in the town of Bethlehem. In the desert region of Judaea, John the Baptist lived and preached. It was in the district of Judaea that Jesus carried on much of his ministry and was crucified. So Israel was more than at a crossroads of the world; it was at the crossroads of faith.

⚜ *How do you think a knowledge of Israel will help you to understand Jesus and his message in a deeper way?*

Open-air market

A View from Nazareth

Knowing more about Galilee helps us to know more about Jesus. The upper part of this region was very mountainous and sparsely populated. It was a place where someone could get away from the busyness of life and enjoy the solitude of the countryside. The lower part of Galilee, however, was a heavily populated area that included both Gentiles and Jews. It was the place where Jesus grew up. One reason for the larger population in this area was its closeness to the Sea of Galilee and the big fishing industry there. In fact, fish that swam in these waters were caught and then sold throughout the Roman Empire.

Nazareth, the town where Jesus spent most of his life, was in lower Galilee. The Jews who lived there were exposed to many outside influences. Perched on a hillside, Nazareth looked down on a major trading route called the *Via Maris* ("Seaway").

74

Caravans of merchants passed close to Nazareth every day, bringing their wares from countries all around the Mediterranean. It is not hard to imagine the boy Jesus and his friends encountering these caravans, learning about the customs of other peoples and hearing other languages spoken.

The people of Nazareth were also influenced by *Sepphoris*, the main city of the region during New Testament times. Excavations during the 1980s confirmed the fact that Sepphoris was a large and thriving city filled with different people from around the world. Because it was a little more than three miles away, Sepphoris could be seen easily from Nazareth. Even though it is never mentioned in the New Testament, Sepphoris undoubtedly affected the lives of everyone in Nazareth and the surrounding region.

It is interesting to know that Jesus lived so close to Sepphoris, only an hour's walk from his home. Did Jesus spend a great deal of time there? Probably not, because it was not a traditionally Jewish town. It was controlled

by Roman forces, and perhaps it did not even have a synagogue. Whatever the case, Jesus must have walked its streets at one time or another and maybe did business there. But as far as we know, Jesus' preaching ministry was restricted to traditional Jewish towns and villages.

Scripture

Many of the apostles are described as fishing in the Sea of Galilee. They would never have been able to fish in the Dead Sea, however, because its water is twenty-five percent salt. Nothing can live in it, and that is why it is called the Dead Sea.

Large catch of fish, Sea of Galilee

75

◆ Play a quick round of fill-in-the-blanks by asking the following questions and having the general group respond.

• When Jesus spoke with foreigners, he probably was glad he knew ___. (*Greek*)

• When Jesus prayed in the synagogue, he spoke in ___. (*Hebrew*)

• When Jesus told his parables out in the countryside, he spoke to the crowd in ___. (*Aramaic*)

• When Jesus heard Roman soldiers talking, he may not have understood them because they were speaking ___. (*Latin*)

◆ Explain to the young people that speaking more than one language can be a necessity as it was for Jesus. For example, in Europe, many people must speak more than one language because their countries are very close together. Compare this to your geographical situation. Ask, "What if people in a neighboring state or town spoke another language? How would this affect everyday business?"

FYI The Sea of Galilee takes its name from a Hebrew expression meaning "District of the Gentiles." It was called Lake Tiberias by the Romans, and, in Old Testament times, Lake Gennesaret. The Sea of Galilee was the scene of many events in the life of Jesus. One dramatic one was the calming of the storm. Sudden and violent storms are frequent on this sea. They are caused by cold air masses passing over the water from the north. It was along this shore that Jesus called the fishermen to be his disciples. As over twenty species of fish flourish in this sea, fishing is still an active industry. About one thousand tons of fish are netted annually.

Presentation (cont'd)

◆ Direct attention to the 🌣 **thought provoker** on page 76. Have the young people form small groups in which to share their responses.

If time allows, have the young people remain in the same groups for a marketplace interview conducted at the time of Jesus. One person in each group can take the role of a roving reporter who is interviewing the market buyers and sellers. Have the groups present their interviews for all.

◆ Have the young people remain in their same groups to discuss the questions of *Things to Share, Things to Think About,* and *On Line with the Parish.*

Conclusion ___ min.

◆ Distribute the handout *Walking on Water.* Have a volunteer read Matthew 14:22–23. You may want to reread the FYI on page 75.

◆ Direct attention to *Words to Remember* on page 77. The definition for *Aramaic* is on page 76; the description of *Sepphoris* is on page 76.

Assessment: If you administering *Chapter 9 Assessment,* allow ten minutes for its completion.

Many Languages

What language did Jesus learn as he grew up? His everyday language would have been Aramaic. In ancient times *Aramaic* was the common language for business and government throughout the entire area of the Near East, including Israel, Syria, and Mesopotamia. It was the language used by the common people, and this included Jesus and his family. So extensive was the use of Aramaic that it was spoken throughout the region for over a thousand years.

Today when we read the New Testament, we find some Aramaic words. In Mark 5:41, for example, Jesus says to the girl whom he is restoring to life, "'Talitha koum,' which means, 'Little girl, I say to you, arise!'" In Mark 14:36 as well, Jesus addresses God the Father with the word *Abba*, which was a loving way of saying "Father."

Along with Aramaic Jesus knew Hebrew, the language of the ancient Israelites that was used by the Jews for worship. He would have learned Hebrew at the synagogue. Besides this Jesus would have known some Greek so that he could conduct business with foreigners from other parts of the Roman Empire. More than likely, however, he did not know Latin, which was the language of the Roman soldiers who occupied his country.

All in all, Jesus' many languages served him well in his ministry: Aramaic for teaching the common people, Hebrew for speaking about the Scriptures and God's law, and Greek when speaking with others from foreign lands. Even today, knowing many languages is an important skill.

Some people may wonder why Aramaic never became the language of the New Testament, especially because it was the language of Jesus himself. The entire New Testament, in fact, was written in Greek. Why was this so? At the time of Jesus, Greek was the official language of the Roman Empire. Although the Roman language was Latin, the Romans themselves preferred Greek because they liked and imitated the Greek culture. Today we might say that Greek was the "in" language. Most important, the use of Greek by the early Church and the New Testament writers tells us that the message of Christianity quickly spread from Israel to the wider world of the Roman Empire and the world of Greek-speaking Jews and Gentiles.

🌣 *How have you been influenced by your country, your culture, and your language? Give some examples.*

Ancient texts written in Greek, Hebrew, and Latin

76

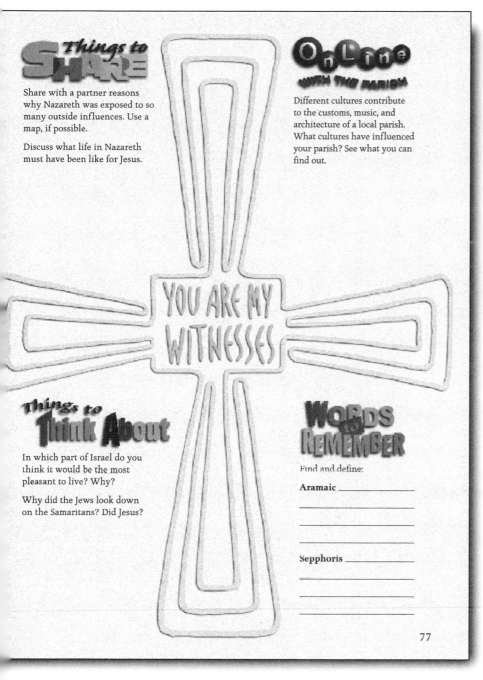

Things to SHARE

Share with a partner reasons why Nazareth was exposed to so many outside influences. Use a map, if possible.

Discuss what life in Nazareth must have been like for Jesus.

OnLine WITH THE PARISH

Different cultures contribute to the customs, music, and architecture of a local parish. What cultures have influenced your parish? See what you can find out.

Things to Think About

In which part of Israel do you think it would be the most pleasant to live? Why?

Why did the Jews look down on the Samaritans? Did Jesus?

WORDS to REMEMBER

Find and define:

Aramaic _____

_____

_____

_____

Sepphoris _____

_____

_____

_____

77

Conclusion (cont'd)

FORUM Assignment

✔ Read pages 78-85. Underline in pencil the statements that express six main ideas.

✔ Complete the handout *Walking on Water*.

Closing Prayer: Explain that the phrase *Kyrie eleison* (Ky-re-ay eh-lay-ee-son) meaning "Lord, have mercy," is Greek. It became part of the liturgy when Greek was still the predominant language in the Mediterranean area.

Ask the group to respond "Lord, have mercy" or "Kyrie eleison" to each of the following petitions. Invite the young people to add their own.

• For the times when we have mocked another's culture, language, or way of doing things. . . .

• For the times when we have refused to communicate with another in a polite and caring way. . . .

• For the times when we have used words as a weapon rather than as a means of healing. . . .

Evaluation: Do the young people understand the reasons Israel was considered the crossroads of the world at the time of Jesus? Have they explored the culture of and languages spoken in Galilee?

FOR CHAPTER 10

• sign "You're grounded"
• props for café setting (optional)
• copies of handout *God We Ask Your Blessing*, page 78C
• copies of *Chapter 10 Assessment*, page 85A
• copies of *Highlights for Home*, page 85B

Assessment

 1 Israel's geography included
a. desert.
b. a river valley.
c. mountains and hills.
d. all of the above

2 Israel was a crossroads between
a. Galilee and Samaria.
b. Judaea and Samaria.
c. Mesopotamia and Egypt.
d. Jerusalem and Cana.

3 Nazareth was located
a. in Samaria.
b. in Galilee.
c. in Judaea.
d. in Sepphoris.

4 Circle the *false* answer. Jesus probably spoke
a. Hebrew.
b. Aramaic.
c. some Greek.
d. Latin.

5 Hebrew was the language
a. of foreign merchants.
b. of the common people.
c. of Jews at worship.
d. of the Roman Empire.

 6 The *Via Maris* was
a. a major city of Judaea.
b. a city near Rome.
c. a major trading route.
d. a large trading ship.

7 The entire New Testament was originally written in
a. Aramaic.
b. Hebrew.
c. Latin.
d. Greek.

8 The main city of Galilee was
a. Sepphoris.
b. Nazareth.
c. Bethlehem.
d. Jerusalem.

 9 The Romans
a. allowed the Jews to worship God publicly.
b. forced the Jews to worship false gods.
c. forbid worship of any type.
d. forced the Jews to worship God privately.

 10 Why was Israel considered a crossroads for people of the ancient world?

_____
_____
_____
_____
_____
_____

Highlights for Home

Focus on Faith

It was said by the ancient Celts that in certain "thin places" (geographical locations) a person might come into direct contact, if only for a moment, with the past or the future. We can only imagine how fascinating it would be to peer through such a "thin place" into the first-century world Jesus occupied.

To see Jesus walking along the shore of the Sea of Galilee or to see him enjoying a wedding feast in Cana would be a memory to cherish.

Lacking these "thin places," we encourage the young people to become familiar with Jesus' world by studying the culture and customs of his homeland. Chapter 9 gives them an introduction to the geography and languages of ancient Israel. It provides us with an idea of what it was like for Jesus to live at the crossroads of the world.

By joining your son or daughter in this "armchair pilgrimage," you will be helping him or her to get ready to hear the good news of Jesus.

Conversation Starters

. . . . a few ideas to talk about together . . . .

◆ Imagine your family is about to make a pilgrimage to the Holy Land. What places do you most want to see? Why?

◆ In what ways does knowing more about Jesus' world help us to hear the gospel with greater understanding?

Feature Focus

The feature *On Line with the Parish* directs our attention to the ways different cultures may contribute to the customs, music, and architecture of a local parish. With your son or daughter, explore the cultures that have influenced your parish community. Some parishes celebrate cultural diversity in liturgy or festivity. Try to participate in your parish's celebration or join others in planning and holding one.

Reflection

The photo on pages 70 and 71 shows outer space, and the photo on pages 72 and 73 shows a vast expanse of desert. Read the following verse from Robert Frost's poem "Desert Places" about traveling alone by night in a snowstorm.

> They cannot scare me with their empty spaces
> Between stars—on stars where no human race is.
> I have it in me so much nearer home
> To scare myself with my own desert places.

Talk with Jesus in prayer about your own "desert places." Are they places of loneliness, confusion, or meaninglessness? Ask Jesus to help you to see time alone in your desert places as time out for prayer and spiritual growth.

JESUS AND HIS TIMES

Adult Focus

The climate, housing, and customs of Israel and its people were the background for the life of Jesus of Nazareth. The more we get to know about the time and place in which Jesus lived, the more we get to know him. This knowledge can never substitute for our faith in Jesus, the Son of God, but it fills out the picture that the gospels provide for us.

When presenting this chapter, help the young people understand that for Jesus and his people, life was exciting. It was a life of work, learning, music and dance, stories and song, games and sports. It was a life to be celebrated in praise of God, both in the family and in the larger community.

Help the young people think about themselves joining their faith ancestors in following Jesus. To do this you may want to share Psalm 138:1–2.

> I thank you, LORD, with all my heart;
>   before the gods to you I sing.
> I bow low toward your holy temple;
>   I praise your name for
>   your fidelity and love.
> For you have exalted over all
>   your name and your promise.

Catechism Focus

The theme of Chapter 10 corresponds to paragraphs 125, 127, and 531–534 of the *Catechism*.

Enrichment Activities

Reaching Out

Record on tape the young people reading the blessing on the handout. Then ask the young people to think about people their age who may need encouragement and support. Then have each person write a note of encouragement to someone in a rehabilitation center, a shelter for runaways, or another type of center that helps young people pull their lives together. While the young people are writing, you may want to play a recording of "Here Is My Life" from *Most Requested Music from the Spirit From Joe Wise* (GIA). Send the tape, the notes, and the blessings to the center.

Guest Speaker

Invite a carpenter to talk to the group about tools, workmanship, and products of the trade.

Teaching Resources

Overview

To recognize that the land and customs of Israel and its people were the background for Jesus' life and teachings.

Opening Prayer Ideas

Reflect on the concept of "being grounded."

or

Pray together Psalm 133 or Psalm 47.

Materials

- Bibles, journals, and highlighters
- sign "You're grounded."
- props for café setting (optional)

New Testament Journal:

For Chapter 10, use pages 22–23.

REPRODUCIBLE MASTERS
- *God, We Ask Your Blessing,* page 78C
- *Chapter 10 Assessment,* page 85A
- *Highlights for Home,* page 85B

Supplemental Resources

VIDEO
The Last Supper
Vision Video
P.O. Box 540
Worcester, PA 19490-0540

BOOK
The Land and People Jesus Knew
J. Robert Teringo (1985)
Bethany House Publishers,
Minneapolis, MN

CHAPTER ten

God, We Ask Your Blessing

Blessings have always been a part of Jewish prayer life. Read the blessing on this page written for contemporary youth. Decorate the border.

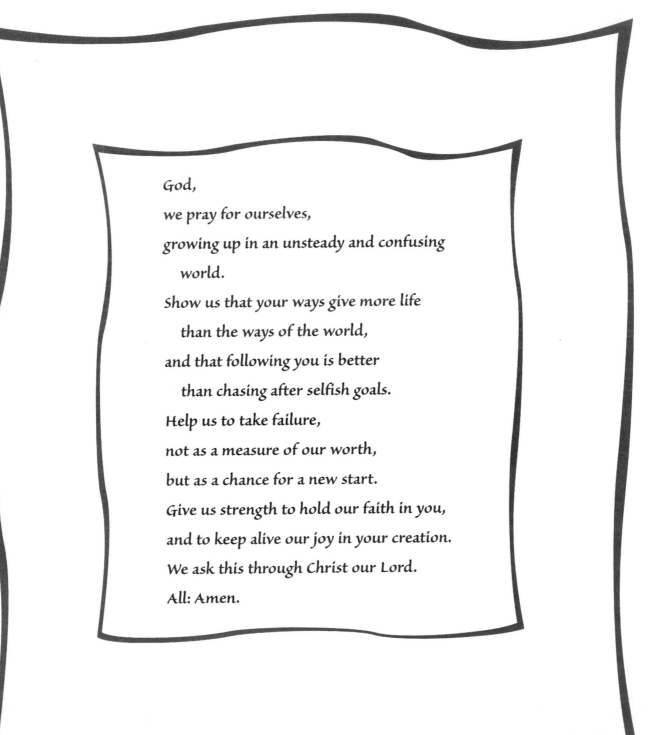

God,

we pray for ourselves,

growing up in an unsteady and confusing
    world.

Show us that your ways give more life
    than the ways of the world,

and that following you is better
    than chasing after selfish goals.

Help us to take failure,

not as a measure of our worth,

but as a chance for a new start.

Give us strength to hold our faith in you,

and to keep alive our joy in your creation.

We ask this through Christ our Lord.

All: Amen.

CHAPTER 10

Jesus and His Times

Where did this man get such
wisdom and mighty deeds?
Is he not the carpenter's son?
Matthew 13:54–55

79

Objective: To recognize that the land and customs of Israel and its people were the background for Jesus' life and teachings.

Introduction ___ min.

Opening Prayer: Before the session begins, prepare a sign with the message "You're grounded." At the beginning of the prayer, hold up the sign and use the following script.

What would you do or what would your reaction be if you went home and found this sign in your room?

Would you consider it a positive greeting? A positive interpretation is a possibility. You could translate "You're grounded" to mean "You're protected." If lightning strikes near your house, you're relatively safe because someone has grounded the electrical outlets in your home.

You could also take the message to mean "You're rooted." Your roots are strong enough to with-stand slight storm winds of arguments with friends, slight setbacks in school, or family dis-agreements.

You could also take the message to mean "You're not to go out. You need some time out to spend time with your family strengthening those roots."

Well, consider yourselves grounded. Through your studies of the truths of faith you're strengthening and nourishing your roots. Think of the people who help you stay grounded, rooted in faith, hope, and love, as you sing together the first verse of "Now Thank We All Our God." Shock these people this week by thanking them for grounding you.

Now thank we all our God,
With heart and hands and voices,
Who wondrous things hath done,
In whom his world rejoices,
Who from our mother's arms
Hath blessed us on our way
With countless gifts of love,
And still is ours today.

Forum: Have volunteers prepare a first-century, open-air café setting. Ask the stagehands to set a small table in front of the room. Glasses or mugs are possible props as pairs of young people enact the meeting between Peter and his friend. Give several young people the opportunity to share Peter's responses to his friend's questions on the handout *Walking on Water*.

Presentation ___ min.

Note: At this time, you may want to show a segment of *Jesus of Nazareth* to illustrate the clothing and housing of Jesus' time. The director consulted biblical scholars to achieve historical accuracy.

◆ Have the young people form three groups to represent acting troupes. Invite each group to write the dialogue and plan the costuming and the props for a reenactment of one of the following gospel accounts:

- John 13:1–4—Jesus washing the disciples' feet
- Mark 2:1–12—Jesus healing the paralytic
- Luke 15:21–32—Planning and acting out the feast for the returned lost son.

The execution of this activity can be as elaborate or simple as you wish. Consider having the reenactments presented in a later session. If reenactments are not feasible, you may have the troupes read the passages and note the cultural aspects described.

What kind of house did Jesus live in? What did he wear? Did he go to school? What did he do for fun? The gospels do not answer any of these questions, but thanks to historians, geographers, and archaeologists we have some answers to these questions.

Life in Nazareth

Everywhere in the world, climate affects the way people live. This was true for Jesus and the people of Nazareth. They lived in a Mediterranean climate. This influenced every aspect of their lives, from the clothes they wore to the houses in which they lived.

Clothing The climate of Israel was hot and dry, and this required the use of loose-fitting clothing. Both men and women wore tunics, long pieces of material sewn up the sides with openings for the head and arms. A belt around the waist secured the tunic and made it look neater. Most people also wore a head covering for protection from the heat of the sun. Jesus would have worn the head covering popular with the men of his day. This consisted of a square piece of cloth that fell back over the neck and was kept in place with a circle of cord. Women wore veils. Such head coverings protected a person's head, face, and neck from the sun.

Clothing typical at the time of Jesus

80

Contemporary folk dancing

Most people wore sandals because tight-fitting shoes would have made their feet hot and sore and would have been unhealthy. However, wearing sandals meant that people's feet got dirty very quickly. As a result people had to stop often and shake the dust from their feet. A sign of hospitality was to wash the feet of those who came to your home for a visit.

Housing The climate also had an influence on the way houses were built. A typical house was square and made of mud, bricks, and stone. It faced north and opened away from the heat of the sun. To keep the house cool, there were few windows. This left the interior dark, but the use of oil lamps made the houses light and comfortable.

The roof of a house was always flat; it could be used as an extra room after the sun had set. Made of branches and rolled clay, the roof could also be broken open easily. We find an example of this in Mark 2:1–12. According to Mark, Jesus was in a house filled with people. So great was the crowd that the roof had to be opened in order that a paralytic could be lowered in to see Jesus.

Most houses had only one story, although rich people sometimes had an upper story or room. It was in one of these upper rooms that Jesus celebrated the Last Supper. Inside, houses had dirt floors and were sparsely furnished. People sat and also slept on mats on the floor. Tables were rare; but when they were used, they were low to the ground, unlike tables today. In comparison with the lives of many modern people, Jesus and the people of his time lived in a very simple way.

Leisure Time Living a simple way of life did not mean that people could not have fun. One of the favorite pastimes of people in Jesus' day was dancing, especially at celebrations such as weddings. This folk dancing was lively and high-spirited. It was usually accompanied with music played on flutes, horns, cymbals, and drums called timbrels. Jesus himself talked about music and dancing in the parable of the prodigal son (Luke 15:25).

Some leisure time was taken up with sports and games of the day. Young children would play games such as hide-and-seek and blindman's bluff. Older children played board games similar to chess. Wrestling matches, archery contests, and footraces were also popular.

Instead of going to the pagan theaters of the Romans and Greeks, the Jews of Jesus' day listened to their own traveling storytellers and teachers. Around campfires in the desert, on rooftops in the towns, or on mountainsides, people gathered to hear the stories about their ancestors in faith and about God's love. Perhaps the best example of this type of traveling teacher was Jesus himself.

81

◆ Have volunteers summarize "Life in Nazareth" on pages 80 and 81. Ask, "What benefits are there to living a simple way of life? How can we do this in our complicated, supertechnological world?" Discuss the ways we can use technology to enable us to spend more quality time with others in celebrating life.

◆ Direct attention to the **thought provoker** on page 82. You may want to have the young people mime their responses. Encourage them to recognize that enjoying prayer and liturgy is one way we can show God that we believe life is to be celebrated.

You may want to plan a prayer service around the theme of celebrating life or a related theme: joy, praise, thanksgiving, or God's gifts. The last five psalms (Psalms 145–150) are often prayed by the Church on festive occasions. You may want to choose one of them for your prayer service.

FYI Before the age of radio and television, involvement in music was very active and personal. Saint Augustine shared this viewpoint. In one sermon he instructed:

You should sing as wayfarers do—sing, but continue your journey. Do not be lazy, but sing to make your journey more enjoyable. Sing, but keep going. What do I mean by keep going? Keep on making progress. This progress, however, must be in virtue. . . .

Presentation (cont'd)

◆ Have the young people look at the art reproduction of the Holy Family on page 82. Ask, "What does this scene say to you about the relationships Jesus, Mary, and Joseph shared?"

Invite the young people to write their responses in their journals.

◆ Discuss with the young people the statements they have underlined. Then have them highlight the key concepts highlighted here.

◆ Have a volunteer summarize the way girls were educated in Jesus' time. Have another volunteer summarize the education of boys by their fathers. You may want to show the video *The Last Supper.* The video shows the preparation of dishes served for the Passover meal. The package includes an eighteen-page recipe book you may want to share with the group. The video is available from:

Vision Video
P.O. Box 540
Worcester, PA 19490-0540

For Jesus and his people, life was exciting. It was not a life of work only but was filled with music and dance, stories and song, games and sports. Far from being dull and gloomy, life was to be celebrated in praise of God, both in the family and in the larger community.

How do you show God that life is to be celebrated?

The Jews of Jesus' day interpreted the first commandment literally. That is why they never carved or painted images and did not encourage the visual arts. Catholics, too, understand that images can never substitute for the one true God or be worshiped. The early Church, however, began to realize that the works of artists are powerful tools that can lead us to the worship of God and the veneration of the saints. That understanding continues today and explains why so much of the world's great art has been encouraged by the Church.

Preparing for Life

Why did Jesus become a carpenter? Why were some of his disciples fishermen? The answer is the same for each question: They received their skills from their families. In fact, the family was the real center for education at the time of Jesus.

The Youth of Our Lord, John Rogers Herbert, 1847–1856

82

At Home For the first few years of life, children were taught by their mothers. Each Jewish mother would teach her children how to pray and would share with them the wonderful stories about their ancestors in faith, beginning with Abraham and Sarah. Because there were no books, all this was done from memory.

After about the age of three, girls continued to be taught by their mothers. They had to learn how to plan meals according to the strict dietary laws of the Jews. They also had to learn how to cook the special dishes used for the Passover celebration and other festivities. Jewish mothers prepared their daughters for the hard task of running a home and bringing up children. This included cleaning, cooking, sewing, weaving, and mending. The girls were taught to grind the grain and make bread. Some girls even had to help with the care of animals and with the harvest. In all aspects of life, the mother of the family prepared her daughters for the future so that eventually they, too, could be good wives and mothers.

Fathers looked after the education of their sons. Naturally a father would want to pass on what he knew to his son, especially his trade. So generally brickmakers' sons became brickmakers; shepherds' sons tended the flocks with their fathers; carpenters' sons learned how to work with wood and how to build things; merchants' sons were taught how to buy and sell goods. A boy's education took place as he worked side by side with his father.

In the New Testament Jesus is known as "the carpenter's son" (Matthew 13:55). Joseph, the foster father of Jesus, taught him the trade of carpentry. No doubt Saint Paul, who was known as a tentmaker (Acts 18:3), learned this trade from his father. Paul used this valuable skill to support himself on his journeys as he spread the good news about Jesus.

At School In addition to the education that boys received at home, it was customary for them to go to the synagogue school in their town or village. They began when they were six or seven years old and completed their studies when they were thirteen. School was not easy. Days were long, and holidays were few. At the synagogue school boys learned to read and write Hebrew, the language of the Scriptures. They would repeat the verses of Scripture until they knew them by heart. The teacher in a synagogue school was a scribe who was called a *rabbi* (teacher). Teachers were respected members of the community.

A young man who wanted to become a rabbi continued his education after age thirteen. He was sent to Jerusalem, where he studied under famous rabbis. In addition to teaching the children, a rabbi at the local synagogue taught the adults on the Sabbath. He interpreted the Scriptures and helped the people to live according to God's law. Although Jesus never studied to be a rabbi, he was given that title (John 3:2) because people, including his enemies, recognized that he was a great teacher.

What similarities do you see between your education and the one Jesus had? Explain.

83

◆ Have a volunteer summarize the education that a young boy received in a synagogue school. Ask, "What did a young man who wanted to become a rabbi do?" (*After the age of thirteen, he went to Jerusalem, where he studied under famous rabbis.*)

◆ Have a volunteer summarize *Catholic ID* on page 82. Ask, "How does religious art help you to pray and to worship? What form of Christian art speaks most powerfully to you?"

Note: You may want to refer to Chapter 7 of *Morality: A Course on Catholic Living,* a text in William H. Sadlier's *Faith and Witness* series. This chapter presents the Church's teaching about the importance of the family in today's society.

Presentation (cont'd)

◆ Ask a volunteer to read *Catholic Teachings* on page 84. List on the board ways the young people show respect for elders, those in authority, and every person.

Have the young people write their responses to the questions in *Things to Share* and *On Line with the Parish* in their journals.

Conclusion ___ min.

◆ Distribute the handout *God, We Ask Your Blessing.* Encourage the young people to display the prayer in a place where they may see it and pray the words often.

◆ Direct attention to *Words to Remember.* The definition for both words are on page 83.

Assessment: If you are going to administer *Chapter 10 Assessment,* allow about ten minutes for its completion.

CATHOLIC TEACHINGS

About Respect for Others

Basing its teaching on the Ten Commandments, the Church wants us to live a life filled with respect for others. This means respect for our elders and all those in authority, whether they are members of our family or not. This respect also extends to those who are different from us, to those who are less fortunate—in fact, to every person. We find this attitude of respect in Jesus, who learned from his family, his community, and his faith. Wise people try to make this attitude part of their lives, too.

Ready to Hear the Good News

The land and customs of Israel and its people were the background for the life of the greatest man who ever walked the face of the earth, Jesus of Nazareth. Knowing about geography and customs is both interesting and helpful. The more we get to know about the place and time in which Jesus lived, the more we get to know him. Such knowledge can never substitute for our faith in Jesus, the Son of God, but it fills out the picture that the gospels provide for us.

Now we are ready to turn to the good news of Jesus Christ and all that he means for us. We will be better able to understand the Jesus who sought out both rich and poor, the Jesus who healed the sick and forgave sinners, the Jesus who taught us of God's overwhelming love for us, the Jesus who saved us from sin by his death and resurrection and who changed the world forever.

84

Answers for Chapter 10 Assessment

| 1. d | 2. d | 3. a | 4. a | 5. b |
| 6. b | 7. c | 8. a | 9. d | 10. Accept reasonable responses. |

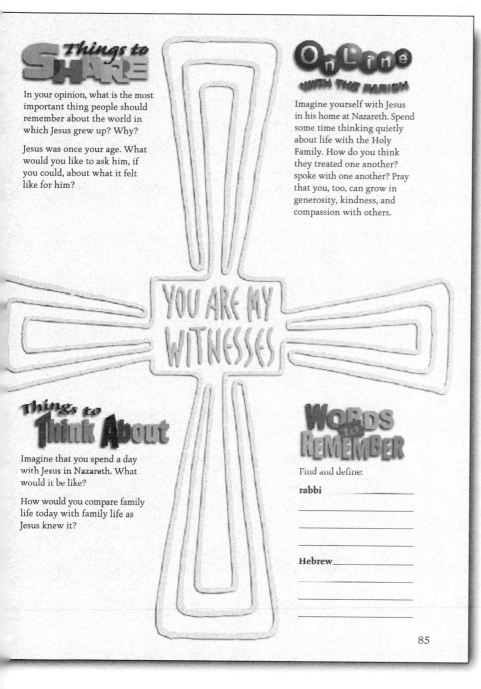

Things to SHARE

In your opinion, what is the most important thing people should remember about the world in which Jesus grew up? Why?

Jesus was once your age. What would you like to ask him, if you could, about what it felt like for him?

OnLine WITH THE PARISH

Imagine yourself with Jesus in his home at Nazareth. Spend some time thinking quietly about life with the Holy Family. How do you think they treated one another? spoke with one another? Pray that you, too, can grow in generosity, kindness, and compassion with others.

YOU ARE MY WITNESSES

Things to Think About

Imagine that you spend a day with Jesus in Nazareth. What would it be like?

How would you compare family life today with family life as Jesus knew it?

Words to Remember

Find and define:

rabbi _____
_____
_____
_____

Hebrew _____
_____
_____
_____

85

Conclusion (cont'd)

FORUM Assignment

✔ Read pages 86–93. Underline in pencil the sentences that express six main ideas.

✔ Have fun decorating the border of the blessing on the handout *God, We Ask Your Blessing*. Also, ask at least two members of your family the questions in *Things to Think About*. Be prepared to share your response and your family members' responses during the next *forum*.

Closing Prayer: Change the last paragraph of "Ready to Hear the Good News" to a prayer. Ask the young people to respond, "Make us ready to hear the good news" each time you pause.

Jesus, help us be better able to understand you who sought out both rich and poor, (*Pause.*) you who healed the sick and forgave sinners, (*Pause.*) you who taught us of God's overwhelming love for us, (*Pause.*) you who saved us from sin by your death and resurrection, (*Pause.*) and you who changed the world forever.

Then read together the blessing on the handout.

FOR CHAPTER 11

- copies of handout *Seeing Three Together*, page 86C
- copies of *Chapter 11 Assessment*, 93A
- copies of *Highlights for Home*, 93B
- battery-operated flashlights or candles (optional)

Evaluation: Do the young people appreciate the importance of preparing to hear the good news by learning more about the culture of Jesus and his disciples?

Assessment

For questions 1–3, circle the one that does *not* belong.

1 Clothing in Jesus' time
- **a.** was loose-fitting.
- **b.** included tunics and sandals.
- **c.** provided protection against the heat.
- **d.** was identical to Roman clothing.

2 In Jesus' time Jewish girls
- **a.** helped with the harvest.
- **b.** were taught by mothers.
- **c.** learned homemaking skills.
- **d.** learned Greek in school.

3 People gathered to hear stories about ancestors in faith
- **a.** in Roman theaters.
- **b.** around campfires.
- **c.** on rooftops.
- **d.** on mountainsides.

4 A house in Jesus' time
- **a.** was flat and simple.
- **b.** was made of plywood.
- **c.** had three or more floors.
- **d.** had solid roofing.

5 To keep a house cool
- **a.** there were many windows.
- **b.** there were few windows.
- **c.** the house faced south.
- **d.** none of the above

6 Jesus was given the title *rabbi* because
- **a.** he studied to be one.
- **b.** he was considered a great teacher by all.
- **c.** he never went to the Temple.
- **d.** none of the above

7 The _____ was the real center for education.
- **a.** Temple
- **b.** village synagogue
- **c.** family
- **d.** marketplace

8 In Jesus' time Jewish boys
- **a.** learned a father's trade.
- **b.** went to Roman schools.
- **c.** went to public school.
- **d.** were uneducated.

9 At the synagogue school, boys learned to read and write ___ , the language of the Scriptures.
- **a.** Greek
- **b.** Roman
- **c.** Aramaic
- **d.** Hebrew

10 Tell one thing about Jesus and his world that you did not know before this chapter. In what way does it help you know him better?

_____

_____

_____

_____

Highlights for Home

Focus on Faith

The climate, housing, and customs of Israel and its people were the background for the life of Jesus of Nazareth. The more we get to know about the time and place in which Jesus lived, the more we get to know him. This knowledge can never substitute for our faith in Jesus, the Son of God, but it fills out the picture that the gospels provide for us.

Help your son or daughter understand that, even though daily life was simple and "totally unplugged" for Jesus and his people, it was exciting. Jesus and his people engaged in everyday living in work, learning, music and dance, stories and song, games and sports.

With your son or daughter, reflect on the following words of Pope Paul VI on his visit to Nazareth on the feast of the Holy Family:

> May Nazareth teach us what family life is, its communion of love, it austere and simple beauty, and its sacred and inviolable character.

Conversation Starters

. . . . a few ideas to talk about together . . . .

◆ Jesus, his friends, and his family celebrated life. How might we follow their example?

◆ What stories about our ancestors in faith do I wish to remember and to share with others?

Feature Focus

Catholic Teachings on page 84 reminds us that we are called to reflect in our own lives the respect Jesus extended to others. We do so when we show respect for elders, teachers, priests, and others in authority. Likewise, the poor and those who are different from us are to be treated with kindness and courtesy.

Reflection

Jesus himself was aware of the various aspects of weather and climate (see Luke 12:54-56). He urged his followers to be similarly aware of "the present time." Being aware of our family climate is one way to renew love for one another.

On any given day, the climate of your family may affect every member's thoughts, acts, and relationships with family members, friends, and fellow workers. Ask yourself the following questions:

• What's the current family climate? Has a whirlwind of activity caused people to exchange angry, heated words?

• Have you frozen each other out so there's no or very little communication? How can you help the thawing, melting process?

• Are you in a relatively mellow, temperate mode? What can you do to maintain or regain this balmy atmosphere?

THE GOOD NEWS ABOUT JESUS

Adult Focus

In Proverbs 25:25 we read:

> *Like cool water to one faint from thirst
> is good news . . .*

The gospels are that refreshing water; the gospels are the good news of Jesus. The gospels announce the incarnation and birth of God's only Son, the bursting in of God's kingdom in its fullness in Jesus, and the arrival of the Savior bringing forgiveness of sins and salvation for the whole world.

In this chapter the young people learn that the four gospel writers are like painters who use the same subject. Each gives us a different way of approaching Jesus, but each gives us the same truth about Jesus in the end.

This chapter focuses on the synoptic Gospels of Matthew, Mark, and Luke. The writers of these gospels were especially interested in writing about the parables and miracles of Jesus. In presenting this chapter, help the young people appreciate the similarities and differences among the synoptic gospels. Help the young people to show their gratitude for "the good news," the refreshing water of Jesus' message that quenches our thirst for the truth and the life.

Catechism Focus

The theme of Chapter 11 corresponds to paragraphs 125–127, 139, 141, and 515 of the *Catechism.*

Enrichment Activities

Being Heralds of the Good News

Have the young people form small groups to write a slogan or good advice about the importance of young people listening to and living according to the good news of Jesus Christ. Have the young people design a billboard that announces the group's message to the general public.

Food for Thought

To celebrate the good news you may want to order Scripture cookies (made like fortune cookies) from the Catholic Catalog Company (1–800–435–0225). As an alternative, make gospel muffins or cupcakes. Ask a volunteer team to help you prepare strips of paper on which are printed gospel verses. Put one strip at the bottom of each cake to be discovered during the celebration.

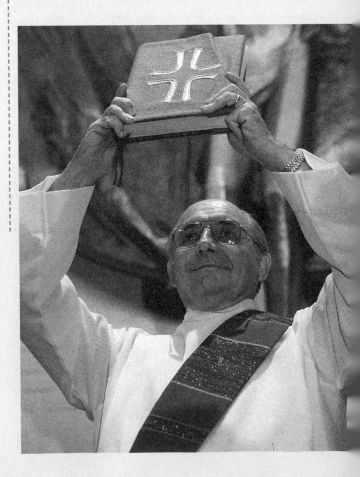

Teaching Resources

Overview

To discover the meaning and the importance of the gospel; to explore the similarities and differences among the synoptic gospels.

Opening Prayer Ideas

Celebrate the good news about Jesus.

or

Read and reflect on Mark 1:14–15.

Materials

- Bibles, highlighters, journals
- battery-operated flashlights or candles

New Testament Journal:

For Chapter 11, use pages 24–25.

REPRODUCIBLE MASTERS
- *Seeing Three Together,* page 86C
- *Chapter 11 Assessment,* page 93A
- *Highlights for Home,* page 93B

Supplemental Resources

VIDEO
Journey to the Mountaintop
Liguori Publications
One Liguori Drive
Liguori, MO 63057–9999

CHAPTER eleven

Seeing Three Together

Compare the parallel passages of the synoptic gospels.

Title of the gospel account: _____

	Matthew	Mark	Luke
Similarities			
Differences			

The Good News About Jesus

Praise to you, Lord Jesus Christ

Objectives: To discover the meaning and the importance of the gospel; to explore the similarities and differences among the synoptic gospels.

Introduction ___ min.

Opening Prayer: Set the stage for a prayer experience by having the group first imagine that the young people of your town have been in the news headlines many times this month. Ask, "Is it all bad news?" Explain that it is unfortunate that the news agencies do such a good job of telling us bad news. Ask, "What are some good things the young people in your town are doing that you would like to read about or hear about in news reports?" Discuss this point for a brief period. Then give each person a strip of newsprint and have him or her write a "good news" headline about the actions of young people.

If possible, darken the room and have the young people "light" several battery-operated flashlights or candles. Have the young people bring their headlines and gather in a circle. Have them imagine that they have gathered for a candlelight vigil to share good news about young people.

Ask the young people to listen as you read aloud the following message Pope John Paul II gave to the young people of Cuba in January 1998.

> I have come . . . as a messenger of truth and life, to bring you good news, to proclaim to you "the love of God made known in Christ Jesus our Lord" (Romans 8:39). This love alone can light up the night of human loneliness; this love alone can strengthen the hope of all who search for happiness.
>
> Open the doors of your heart and your life to Jesus, "the true hero, humble and wise, the prophet of truth and love, the companion and friend of young people" (Vatican Council II, Message to Young People). (*Origins*, February 5, 1998)

Then have the young people take turns sharing their "good news" headlines. Offer together a prayer or song of praise.

Forum: Read the first question for *Things to Think About* on page 85. On the board, draw a circle. Divide the circle into three sections. In one section write *morning*. Ask the young people to share their thoughts about a morning spent with Jesus. Write descriptive words or phrases in the morning section on the board. Follow the same procedure for an afternoon and evening spent with Jesus in Nazareth.

Then have the young people form two groups. Give each group a sheet of posterboard to chart the similarities and differences between family life today and family life as Jesus knew it.

Presentation ___ min.

◆ Have a volunteer read the questions at the top of page 88. List the young people's responses on the board.

◆ Have volunteers summarize pages 88 and 89. Then write the word *evangelist* on the board and have the group define. (*gospel writer*)

◆ First review the three stages of the development of the gospels:

• Jesus himself

• the Church with its oral tradition and the apostolic preaching about Jesus

• the gospels themselves.

*W*hy do Catholics stand at Mass for the proclamation of the gospel? Why are the words of the gospel so important? What do you think?

Observing, Diana Ong, 1997

Gospel and Gospel

Most people know that the word *gospel* means "good news." However, many people are surprised when they find out that the word originally referred to political good news. What type of political news would be good in ancient times? News about three events in particular was cause for special celebration:

• the birth of an heir to the throne, which meant that the ruling family would continue in power

• the beginning of the reign of a new king

• the visit of a king to one of his cities.

Ancient peoples would be excited upon hearing such good news. On these happy occasions the king might pardon those accused of crimes, or he might promise that new buildings or facilities would be built for the people.

Knowing this, we can understand why the writers of the New Testament chose the word *gospel* to describe the good news of Jesus Christ. This good news was also cause for celebration:

• the incarnation and birth of God's only Son

• the bursting in of God's kingdom in its fullness in Jesus

• the arrival of the Savior bringing forgiveness of sins and salvation for the whole world.

88

The gospel of Jesus Christ, then, announces astonishing news. For this reason it is easy to see why Catholics stand whenever the gospel is proclaimed in the liturgy. Among all the Scriptures the gospels are our principal source for the life and teaching of Jesus. We acclaim the reading of the gospel in song, we stand when it is read, and the priest or deacon kisses the page on which the sacred words are printed. No other part of Scripture is treated in the same way.

In the New Testament the good news about Jesus is told from four different points of view: according to the views of Matthew, Mark, Luke, and John. No one should be confused by this, however. There is only one good news about Jesus, but it is told in four unique ways.

Where did the inspired words of the four gospels come from? What were their origins? Who wrote them down? We already know that the gospels came about in three stages. First there was Jesus himself; then came the Church with its oral tradition and the apostolic preaching about Jesus; and finally there came the gospels themselves, written between the late 60s and the early 90s of the first century A.D.

Because these gospels were written so many years after the time of Jesus, the writers were probably not eyewitnesses to his life and ministry. They were what we might call second-generation Christians. Guided by the Holy Spirit, they took what they had received and organized what they knew and believed about Jesus in four different ways. They did this to serve the spiritual needs of the communities for which they wrote.

One way to look at the four gospels is to consider them as four different portraits of the same Person. The four *evangelists*, or gospel writers, are like painters who used the same subject. Each gives us a different way of approaching Jesus, but each gives us the same truth about Jesus in the end.

This truth about Jesus is so important that the four gospels are placed first in the New Testament. But that does not mean they were written first. In fact the gospels were among the last books of the New Testament to be written. Most of the epistles, or letters, had been written long before the gospels. When Paul used the word *gospel* in his letters, he was referring simply to the good news of Jesus, not to the works of Matthew, Mark, Luke, or John.

A reminder of the four different visions of the evangelists

◆ Then ask the following questions to check the young people's understanding of "Gospel and Gospel":

• Why did the writers of the New Testament choose the word *gospel* to describe the good news of Jesus Christ?

• How do Catholics show at Mass that we consider the gospels our principal source for the life and teaching of Jesus? (*We acclaim the reading of the gospel in song, we stand for the reading, the priest or deacon kisses the page on which the sacred words are printed.*)

• When were the gospels written? (*after the epistles, between the late 60s and the early 90s of the first century A.D.*)

Then have the young people highlight the key concepts highlighted on reduced pupil pages 88 and 89.

◆ Write on the board in large letters the following headline: One Gospel—Four Gospels. Have the young people explain. (*There is only one good news about Jesus, but it is told in four unique ways.*)

Presentation (cont'd)

◆ Have a volunteer read the *thought provoker* on page 90. Discuss the young people's responses.

◆ Ask a volunteer to define *synoptic*. (*looking at together*) Then ask, "Why are the Gospels of Matthew, Mark, and Luke called the *synoptic gospels*?" (*When we look at them together, we see many similarities.*)

◆ Direct attention to the 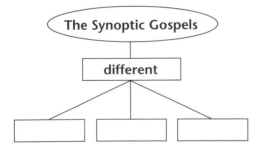 **thought provoker** on page 91. Distribute the handout *Seeing Three Together*. Have the young people work in pairs to complete the chart on the handout. To each pair, assign one set of readings listed on page 91.

◆ On the board or on newsprint draw the chart below. Involve the young people in completing it.

Ask the young people to reread the first paragraph of "A Closer Look at the Synoptics" on page 91 to find the "three differences" left blank in the chart. Fill them in. (*point of view, audience, emphasis*)

Then ask, "How did these differences come about? Name one way." (*The writers rearranged events in order to bring out their significance.*)

```
        ┌─────────────────────────┐
        │  The Synoptic Gospels   │
        └───────────┬─────────────┘
              ┌──────┴──────┐
              │  different  │
              └──────┬──────┘
         ┌───────────┼───────────┐
      ┌──┴──┐     ┌──┴──┐     ┌──┴──┐
      │     │     │     │     │     │
      └─────┘     └─────┘     └─────┘
```

In discussing the gospels, we should be clear about one other point. When the gospels were first written, they did not contain the names of the men who wrote them. It was only many years later that people tried to identify the evangelists by name. As we look at each gospel, we will discuss the question of its authorship. But the most important thing to remember is that each gospel account is the good news about Jesus, not the good news about Matthew, Mark, Luke, or John.

> *Why do you think the gospels are so important in the life of the Church?*

Similar but Different

The more time we spend with the gospels, the more we discover about their unique features. What strikes us first is that the Gospels of Matthew, Mark, and Luke are very similar to one another. The Gospel of John is quite different from the other three. Why is this so?

It is obvious that the writers of the Gospels of Matthew, Mark, and Luke were especially interested in writing about the parables and miracles of Jesus. But the writer of John's Gospel put his gospel together from a different point of view. Rather than emphasizing the details of Jesus' life and ministry, he wanted to give a deeper reflection on Jesus and what he meant for the world. That is why John's writing is so much more symbolic than that of Matthew, Mark, or Luke. Put simply, John was a great thinker; Matthew, Mark, and Luke were great narrators.

If we put the Gospels of Matthew, Mark, and Luke side by side in parallel columns and look at them together, we see many similarities. That is why they are called the *synoptic gospels*. *Synoptic* is a word that means "looking at together." It is easy to remember the meaning of this word by recalling its Greek roots: *optic*, meaning "to see," and *syn*, meaning "together."

90

We can appreciate the similarities found in the synoptic gospels by comparing a few of the many parallel passages. In doing so, it is easy to see that there are many more similarities than differences. Here are several examples that are contained in all three of the synoptic gospels:

- the baptism of Jesus: Matthew 3:13–17, Mark 1:9–11, and Luke 3:21–22
- the temptation of Jesus: Matthew 4:1–11, Mark 1:12–13, and Luke 4:1–13
- the cure of Peter's mother-in-law: Matthew 8:14–15, Mark 1:29–31, and Luke 4:38–39
- the parable of the mustard seed: Matthew 13:31–32, Mark 4:30–32, and Luke 13:18–19.

Choose one of the examples given above, and compare the parallel passages. What similarities do you find? Name any differences you detect.

A Closer Look at the Synoptics

The fact that the synoptic gospels have similarities does not mean that they are exactly the same. Each writer presented a different point of view, each was directing his gospel to a different audience, and each had a different emphasis in relating the good news of Jesus.

This means that, like all ancient writers, they felt free to adapt what they knew about Jesus to their narratives. They were not worried about the exact sequence of events in Jesus' life, for example. The writers rearranged the events in order to bring out their significance more clearly. They did not change the truth; they simply put it in a different order.

Several passages illustrate the freedom that the synoptic writers exercised in relating the truth of the gospel. Look, for example, at the different versions of the Beatitudes in Matthew 5:3–11 and Luke 6:20–26. Matthew lists eight beatitudes, whereas Luke has only four and tells them from a completely different point of view. Which is correct? Both are correct. Both give the teaching of Jesus, but with different emphases.

In what ways do you think the four gospel accounts can be compared to four different fingerprints?

91

◆ Have a volunteer read Matthew 5:3–11 and another volunteer read Luke 6:20–26. Ask the young people to summarize the differences between the two accounts.

◆ Have the young people look at the comparison chart at the top of page 92. Ask, "What does Matthew include in the Lord's Prayer that Luke does not?" (*Our Father; Your will be done, on earth as it is in heaven; but deliver us from the evil one.*)

Have a volunteer explain what details are different in these two accounts. (*In Matthew, Jesus is teaching the crowds during the Sermon on the Mount; in Luke, Jesus is teaching only the disciples while he himself is at prayer.*) Ask, "Which of these versions of the Beatitudes and the Lord's Prayer is correct?" (*Both are. Both give the teaching of Jesus, but with different emphases.*)

◆ Discuss the statements the young people have underlined on pages 90 through 92. Have them highlight the key concepts highlighted on the reduced pages.

Presentation (cont'd)

◆ If time allows, have partners look up and compare the two versions of Jesus walking on the water in Mark 6:45–51 and Matthew 14:22–33. Encourage them to consider why the versions are different. Ask, "What was Matthew trying to say about Jesus?" (*that Jesus was the Son of God*)

◆ After a volunteer summarizes *Scripture Insight* on page 92, explain that we will be learning more about the differences between the synoptic gospels and the Gospel of John in Chapter 12.

◆ Have a volunteer summarize *On Line with the Parish.* If possible, display a Book of the Gospels or show photos of decoratively covered gospel books. Discuss ways the parish shows love and respect for the gospels. (*One of these ways is by providing religious education about the four gospels.*)

You may want to have the young people make covers for their Bibles. Explain that their designs should reflect respect and gratitude for God's word.

Conclusion ___ min.

◆ Have the young people form small groups to discuss the questions in *Things to Think About* and *Things to Share.*

◆ Direct attention to *Words to Remember* on page 93. The definition for *evangelists* is on page 89; the definition for *synoptic gospels* is on page 90.

Assessment: If you plan to administer *Chapter 11 Assessment,* allow about ten minutes for its completion.

The Lord's Prayer: A Synoptic Comparison

Matthew 6:9–13

Our Father in heaven,
 hallowed be your name,
 your kingdom come,
 your will be done,
 on earth as in heaven.
 Give us today our daily bread;
 and forgive us our debts,
 as we forgive our debtors;
 and do not subject us to the final test,
 but deliver us from the evil one.

Luke 11:2–4

Father, hallowed be your name,
 your kingdom come.
 Give us each day our daily bread
 and forgive us our sins
 for we ourselves forgive everyone
 in debt to us,
 and do not subject us to the
 final test.

In much the same way, the Lord's Prayer is different in Matthew 6:9–13 and Luke 11:2–4. The Our Father has seven petitions in Matthew and five in Luke. In Matthew's Gospel Jesus teaches the prayer in an extended version during his Sermon on the Mount. In Luke's Gospel Jesus gives the Our Father to his disciples while he himself is at prayer. These two synoptic evangelists have used the same teachings of Jesus but summarized them in their own ways; each had a different emphasis in relating the good news. (See the comparison chart).

In telling the same stories, the synoptics sometimes change certain details. By doing so, they give us new insights into Jesus and our faith in him. In telling of the time when Jesus walked on the water, for example, the writers of Matthew and Mark end their accounts with different conclusions. In Mark the disciples remained astonished and confused about Jesus (Mark 6:45–51). Matthew, however, concludes his account with the disciples professing their faith in Jesus as the Son of God (Matthew 14:22–33).

Matthew does this in other places as well. He frequently introduces professions of faith that are not part of other gospel accounts.

You may wish to read and compare these two accounts of Jesus walking on the water.

Now that we know the difference between the synoptic gospels and the Gospel of John, we can turn our attention to each gospel individually.

Scripture Insight

Do all the synoptic gospels—Matthew, Mark, and Luke—tell the same stories? The answer is no. Sometimes only two tell the same story; sometimes a story appears in only one gospel. Does the fact that John's Gospel occasionally has the same story as the synoptics make it a synoptic gospel, too? No. It is just too different from the other three gospels.

92

Answers for Chapter 11 Assessment

1. d	2. b	3. c	4. a	5. c
6. b	7. a	8. c	9. d	10. Accept reasonable responses.

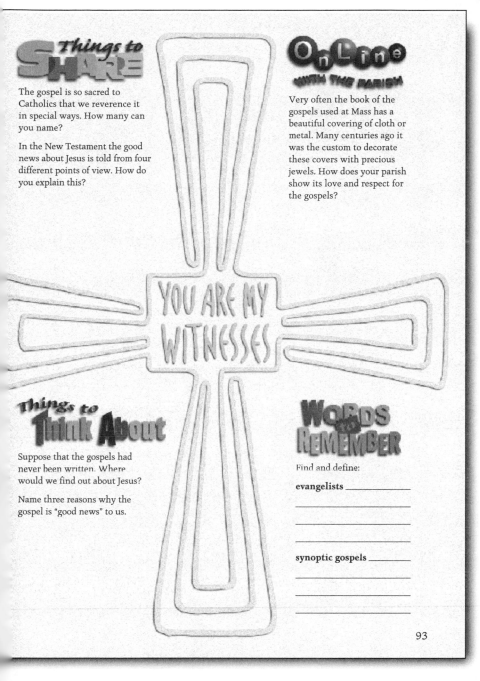

Things to SHARE

The gospel is so sacred to Catholics that we reverence it in special ways. How many can you name?

In the New Testament the good news about Jesus is told from four different points of view. How do you explain this?

OnLine WITH THE PARISH

Very often the book of the gospels used at Mass has a beautiful covering of cloth or metal. Many centuries ago it was the custom to decorate these covers with precious jewels. How does your parish show its love and respect for the gospels?

Things to Think About

Suppose that the gospels had never been written. Where would we find out about Jesus?

Name three reasons why the gospel is "good news" to us.

WORDS to REMEMBER

Find and define:

evangelists _____

_____

_____

synoptic gospels _____

_____

_____

_____

93

Conclusion (cont'd)

FORUM Assignment

✔ Read pages 94–101. Underline in pencil the statements that express six key ideas.

✔ Present a short, five-minute interview between yourself and Mark, Matthew, Luke, or John that may be used for a documentary film. Your task is to find out as much as you can about the evangelist and his gospel. In your script, the evangelist is to communicate as clearly as possible both his identity and his purpose in writing his gospel.

◆ Encourage the young people to share *Highlights for Home*, page 93A, with their families.

Closing Prayer: Invite the young people to look again at the photo on pages 86 and 87. Pray together a verse from the traditional hymn "Thou, Whose Almighty Word."

> Hear us, we humbly pray,
> And where the gospel day
> Sheds not its glorious ray,
> Let there be light!

Evaluation: Have the young people discovered the meaning and the importance of the gospel; Have they explored the similarities and differences among the synoptic gospels?

FOR CHAPTER 12

- bell for games (optional)
- index cards for games (optional)
- copies of handout *An Evangelizer's Plan*, page 94C
- copies of *Chapter 12 Assessment*, page 101A
- copies of *Highlights for Home*, page 101B

Assessment

1. Love and respect is shown for the gospels when
   a. we stand for the gospel reading.
   b. we acclaim the gospel in song.
   c. the priest or deacon kisses the page on which the sacred words are printed.
   d. all of the above

2. The gospel writers were
   a. definitely eyewitnesses of Jesus.
   b. probably not eyewitnesses.
   c. all Jews.
   d. none of the above

3. The synoptic gospels
   a. were written by John.
   b. are filled with poetic images.
   c. are similar but different.
   d. are all read on Easter Sunday.

4. *Synoptic* means
   a. "looking at together."
   b. "seeing things separately."
   c. "full of sin."
   d. none of the above

5. The Gospels of Matthew, Mark, and Luke
   a. have the same points of view.
   b. speak to the same audiences.
   c. have different emphases.
   d. were written in the same year.

6. The gospels were ___ of the New Testament to be written.
   a. the first books
   b. among the last books
   c. the in-between books
   d. none of the above

7. John's writing ___ than that of Matthew, Mark, or Luke.
   a. is more symbolic
   b. includes more miracle accounts
   c. includes more parables
   d. includes more narrative

8. The word *gospel* originally referred to
   a. the announcement of Jesus' birth.
   b. Jesus' parables.
   c. political good news.
   d. accounts of Jesus' miracles.

9. The gospels were written
   a. immediately after Pentecost.
   b. five centuries after Jesus died.
   c. before Saint Paul's letters.
   d. in the second half of the first century A.D.

10. Explain the similarities among the synoptic accounts from the list in the left column on page 91.

   _____
   _____
   _____
   _____

Highlights for Home

Focus on Faith

"A reading from the holy gospel according to. . . ." Matthew or Mark or Luke or John. We have heard these words countless times, and have responded, "Glory to you, Lord." This chapter helps our young people explore the meaning of these words: that the gospel, the good news, is handed down to us not in rote form but in four complementary accounts. We hear the gospel *according to* four complementary but different voices reflecting the faith tradition of the Church.

In this chapter the young people learned that the gospel writers, the evangelists, probably were not eye-witnesses to the life of Jesus, but were what we might call second-generation Christians. Guided by the Holy Spirit, they took what they had received and organized what they knew and believed about Jesus in four different ways.

This chapter focused on the similarities and differences of the three synoptic gospels. It also described the differences between the synoptic gospels and the Gospel of John. Chapter 12 will focus on each gospel and evangelist individually.

Conversation Starters

. . . . a few ideas to talk about together . . . .

◆ How can you, personally or as a family, show your love and respect for the gospel?

◆ Which of the synoptic gospels—Matthew, Mark, or Luke—are you most familiar with? Which would you like to learn more about?

Feature Focus

Scripture Insight on page 92 explains that not all the synoptic gospels include the same stories. Sometimes the story is in only two of the gospels; sometimes a story is in only one of these gospels.

Reflection

Then every scribe who has been instructed in the kingdom of heaven is like the head of a household who brings from his storeroom both the new and the old.

Matthew 13:52

In many ways, each of the four evangelists could be compared to this wise head of a household who knows well what his family needs, and each of the gospels could be seen as a storeroom: a place of provision, of nurturing, of treasures new and old.

These abundant storerooms are always open to us, especially at the Sunday Eucharist. When our provisions—our faith, our hope, our love—are running low, we need only open one of these storerooms to find what we need for life.

FOUR POINTS OF VIEW

Adult Focus

In his book *Celtic Meditations*, Father Edward Farrell wrote, "Each person who knows my name has a unique way of saying it, calling me, seeing me, mirroring me. . . ." In this chapter, we can see that each evangelist certainly had a unique way of saying Jesus' name and of sharing who Jesus is. They did this by using specific titles for him, and by proclaiming the good news of Jesus for their own and future generations.

When presenting this chapter, help the young people realize that the more time we spend with the gospels, the more we discover their unique features. Each evangelist was directing his gospel to a different audience, and each had a different emphasis in proclaiming the good news of Jesus. For example, Mark emphasizes that Jesus is the suffering Messiah; Matthew stresses that Jesus is the great lawgiver and teacher, the new Moses. John calls Jesus Lamb of God (John 1:29), Bread of Life (John 6:35), and the Good Shepherd (John 10:11). Luke portrays Jesus as merciful and compassionate, especially embracing sinners, the poor, and the outcasts. Luke wanted us to know that Jesus was the Savior of the whole world.

Catechism Focus

The theme of Chapter 12 corresponds to paragraph 515 of the *Catechism*.

Enrichment Activities

Celebrate the Evangelists

Have the young people form four groups. Each group is to make a mask to symbolize one of the four evangelists that you will assign to them. (See a description of the symbol for each gospel writer on pages 72 through 75.) They may use paper bags, old pillowcases, plaster of Paris, or other available materials.

Have each person in each group write one statement that explains a characteristic of the group's evangelist or his portrayal of Jesus. Set up a "spotlight space" as a focal point. Ask the groups to stand in it to show their masks and to read their statements.

Conclude by having the group process as they sing a hymn about the good news of Jesus. Choose one with an upbeat tempo. "And the Father Will Dance," "We Walk by Faith," or "Gospel Acclamations" by Marty Haugen, and "You Are the Voice" by David Haas are appropriate. The lyrics and music for these hymns are found in the *Glory & Praise* hymnal.

Teaching Resources

Overview

To discover the characteristics of each of the four gospels; to appreciate the ways Matthew, Mark, Luke, and John proclaim the good news of Jesus.

Opening Prayer Ideas

Read and reflect on Matthew 5:14–16.

or

Sing or listen to a recording about the good news of Jesus.

Materials

- Bibles, journals, and high-lighters
- bell for games (optional)
- index cards for games (optional)

REPRODUCIBLE MASTERS
- *An Evangelizer's Plan,* page 94C
- *Chapter 12 Assessment,* page 101A
- *Highlights for Home,* page 101B

New Testament Journal:
For Chapter 12, use pages 26–27.

Supplemental Resources

VIDEO
- *St. Mark's Gospel*
- *The Gospel According to St. Matthew*
Palisades Home Video
P.O. Box 2794
Virginia Beach, VA 23450

An Evangelizer's Plan

We are called today to be evangelizers. We must proclaim in our day the words and actions of Jesus of Nazareth.

We must take up the gospels again and reread the word of God. In this way we can be evangelizers, sharers of the good news for all the world to hear.

Evangelizers engage in real communication of faith. They accept the invitation to change their lives and turn to the Lord. In order to do this well, consider yourself as an evangelizer-in-training. Follow a Scripture-exercise program that you plan each week. Choose a theme for each week and a reading from one of the four gospels (gospel read at Mass on Sunday) that is in keeping with the theme. Then plan prayerful exercises to do each day. Write your first weekly plan below.

Hope

Weekly Theme: _____   **Scripture:** _____

Sunday
Monday
Tuesday
Wednesday
Thursday
Friday
Saturday

Four Points of View

What I say to you in the darkness, speak in the light; what you hear whispered, proclaim on the housetops.
Matthew 10:27

Objectives: To discover the characteristics of each of the four gospels; to appreciate the ways Matthew, Mark, Luke, and John proclaim the good news of Jesus.

Introduction ___ min.

Before the session begins, set up a prayer table. Open a Bible to Matthew 5:14–16. Place it and a battery-operated candle or lamp and small candles (one for each person) on the table.

Opening Prayer: Invite the young people to look at the photo on pages 94 and 95. Read together Matthew 10:27. Then have a volunteer read Matthew 5:14–16. Ask the young people to reflect on the following points and to write their reflections in their journals.

God has given you certain gifts to use to proclaim his message of love. List these gifts in your journal. Write one way you will use each gift to build up the kingdom of God.

Then invite the young people to approach the table one by one. Address each person by name, give him or her a small candle as you say, "(Person's name), Jesus has asked you to speak his message in the light and to use your gifts to proclaim the good news."

Then conclude by singing or listening to a recording about the good news of Jesus. "Gospel Acclamations" by Marty Haugen or "You Are the Voice" by David Haas are appropriate. The lyrics and music for these hymns are found in the *Glory & Praise* hymnal.

Forum: Have the young people form two groups. One group should be composed of those who prepared an interview with Matthew or Mark, the other group with Luke or John. Ask the group members to share the questions they prepared for an interview with one of the evangelists. Then have each group formulate one set of questions and answers for each of their assigned evangelists. Have volunteers from each group take the roles of the interviewer and the evangelist to present the documentary interview to the entire group.

Presentation ___ min.

Note: At this time, you may want to show segments from the videos *St. Mark's Gospel* and *The Gospel According to St. Matthew*. (See *Supplemental Resources*.)

◆ Call attention to the illustrations on pages 97 and 98 as aids to recalling the symbols of the first two evangelists. (the winged lion for Mark and the winged human for Matthew) Ask, "Why were these symbols chosen?" (*Mark's Gospel begins with John the Baptist crying in the desert, so a lion—considered a desert animal—was chosen; Matthew's Gospel begins with a genealogy of the human ancestors of Jesus.*)

◆ Have the young people share the key concepts they underlined for "Mark: A Winged Lion" and "Matthew: A Winged Human." Then have them highlight the statements highlighted here.

◆ Use *Catholic Teachings* on page 96 as a reminder that the gospels are the key to understanding Jesus for all ages to come.

96

The gospel writers were content to remain almost unknown. They knew that the good news they were telling was about Jesus—and that was all that mattered to them. But there are things we can discover about the four evangelists. What do you think we can find out about them?

Christ Pantocrator
(Lord of the Universe), mosaic,
Cefalu, Italy

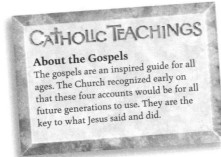

CATHOLIC TEACHINGS

About the Gospels
The gospels are an inspired guide for all ages. The Church recognized early on that these four accounts would be for all future generations to use. They are the key to what Jesus said and did.

96

Mark: A Winged Lion

By comparing the gospels over the centuries, Scripture scholars have concluded that Mark's Gospel was the first to be written. The placing of Matthew as the first gospel in the New Testament is a custom that came from the early Church and that continues today. But Mark was written first.

The author of the Gospel of Mark is not mentioned in the gospel itself; however, he is generally considered to be John Mark, who is mentioned in Acts 12:12. We know that Mark was the cousin of Barnabas, the traveling companion of Saint Paul. Mark was at Paul's side during his imprisonment by the Romans (Colossians 4:10). Later Mark was also with Peter in Rome (1 Peter 5:13).

Mark's association with Peter and Paul helps scholars to assign a date to his writing. They have concluded that the Gospel of Mark was written somewhere between A.D. 65 and 70. As a disciple of Peter, Mark may have written his gospel in Rome. In any case it seems clear that he was a Jewish Christian who wrote for a Gentile audience. One clue to this is that he takes the time to translate Aramaic words and expressions and to explain Jewish customs.

Because his gospel was the first to be written, Mark is credited with inventing the gospel literary form. Even though Mark's Gospel is the shortest of the four, it still tells the good news with excitement, using lively and vivid words. It almost seems that Mark is bringing us along to walk side by side with Jesus. Some people say that his portrait of Jesus was influenced by Peter the apostle, who was Jesus' constant companion on his travels through Palestine. Reading Mark is like seeing Jesus through the eyes of Peter.

Mark, painting by Tissot 19th century

What do we learn about Jesus from Mark? Mark wants us to know that Jesus is the suffering Messiah. We also learn that Jesus asks his disciples for a radical change in their lives. That would not always be easy, and it could even involve suffering. How should Jesus' disciples bear this hardship? Mark's answer is that they should look to the cross and their crucified Lord. Jesus, who suffered and died for us, shows us that we, too, must be faithful, even during suffering.

The traditional symbol for the writer of Mark's Gospel is a winged desert lion. It was chosen because this gospel opens with the voice of John the Baptist crying out in the desert wilderness.

Matthew: A Winged Human

Scholars think that the author of Matthew's Gospel was also a Jewish Christian. He probably was a scribe, a teacher familiar with Jewish customs and everything that had to do with the Jewish religion. In his gospel he taught as a true rabbi, directing his writing to a Jewish audience. That is why his writing is filled with typical Jewish expressions. For example, Matthew was the only one of the synoptic gospel writers to speak of the kingdom of heaven, rather than the kingdom of God. The reason for this is that out of reverence the Jews did not pronounce the divine name.

So familiar was the writer with his Jewish roots that he placed more than 130 references to the Old Testament in his gospel. A clue to the writer's identity as a Jewish scribe may come from Matthew 13:52, where Matthew writes, "Every scribe who has been instructed in the kingdom of heaven is like the head of a household who brings from his storeroom both the new and the old."

97

◆ Challenge the group to a game of "M or M." Have the young people form two teams and have each team choose a captain. Give a bell to each team captain. Appoint a scorekeeper who is to remain neutral. Call out each of the phrases below. The team that rings first and gives the correct evangelist's name receives ten points.

You may want to decide whether the teams may use their books or not before you begin.

- Gospel written first (*Mark*)
- a scribe (*Matthew*)
- taught as a true rabbi (*Matthew*)
- cousin of Barnabas (*Mark*)
- used typical Jewish expressions (*Matthew*)
- associated with Peter and Paul (*Mark*)
- only one to speak of the kingdom of heaven (*Matthew*)
- winged desert lion (*Mark*)
- invented the gospel literary form (*Mark*)
- used more than 130 references to the Old Testament (*Matthew*)
- familiar with Mark's Gospel (*Matthew*)
- Gospel written between A.D. 65 and 70 (*Mark*)
- winged human (*Matthew*)
- shortest of the four gospels (*Mark*)
- portrait of Jesus influenced by Peter (*Mark*)
- wrote for Gentile audience (*Mark*)
- only Gospel to use the word *church* (*Matthew*)
- begins with listing of Jesus' ancestors (*Matthew*)

Presentation (cont'd)

◆ Invite partners to share responses to the ☀ **thought provoker** on page 98. Then elicit the understanding that reading Mark's Gospel is like seeing Jesus through the eyes of Peter, and that Mark shows us that we must be faithful even during suffering, as Jesus was. Matthew relies heavily on Old Testament references and shows that Jesus is the new teacher of Israel, the "new Moses." Matthew is the only evangelist to use the word *church*.

◆ Have volunteers explain the symbols used for the writers of Luke's Gospel and John's Gospel.

◆ Have the young people form two groups. Give each group a set of ten index cards. Ask one group to write a characteristic of Luke's Gospel or a description of Luke on one side of a card. They should write *Luke* on the back of each card. Ask the other group to follow the same directions to pre-pare a set of cards for John's Gospel. Collect the cards and shuffle them.

Then challenge the group to a game of "L or J." Follow the same directions given for playing "M or M" on guide page 97.

◆ Discuss with the young people the statements they underlined. Have them highlight or underline in color the key concepts highlighted on pages 98 through 100.

◆ Direct attention to the ☀ **thought provoker** on page 100. Have the young people write their responses in the space provided.

From all that we know, this gospel was written between A.D. 70 and 90. A careful reading of Matthew tells us that he was familiar with Mark's Gospel. He also knew that the Temple of Jerusalem no longer existed; the Temple had been destroyed in A.D. 70. Matthew's Gospel is later and comes from a community that had more time to reflect on Jesus and what he meant for the Church. Matthew is the only one of the four gospels in which the word *church* is actually used; it is also the only gospel concerned with the Church's organization (Matthew 16:18; 18:17).

Matthew's Gospel contains more of Jesus' sayings than the other gospels. That is why some people have compared it with a type of catechism, useful for teaching. For these and other reasons, this gospel has for centuries been called the Church's gospel. It has always been held in high esteem and was the most frequently quoted of the gospels.

Who is Jesus for Matthew? Jesus is the fulfillment of all God's promises that came down through Moses and the prophets. Jesus is now the great lawgiver and teacher. He is the new Moses, described as giving the famous Sermon on the Mount (Matthew 5–7). Jesus did this just as Moses taught God's law from Mount Sinai.

The traditional symbol for the writer of Matthew's Gospel is a winged human figure. It was chosen because this gospel begins with the genealogy, or listing, of Jesus' human ancestors.

> ☀ *What is the most surprising thing you have learned about the Gospels of Mark and Matthew? Explain.*

Matthew, painting by Tisso[t] 19th centur[y]

Luke: The Winged Ox

The Gospel of Luke is unusual among the four gospel accounts because it is probably the only one written by a Gentile rather than by a Jew. Eve[r] since the second century, the author of Luke has been identified with the "beloved physician" of Colossians 4:14. Because this gospel is written in somewhat polished Greek, we know that the write[r] must have been well educated. His home was probably Antioch in Syria, the third-largest city of the Roman Empire in the first century.

Why did Luke write his gospel? For one thing, we know that he was an early companion of Saint Paul. This meant that he knew a great deal about Jesus and his teachings. But more important, he was involved in missionary work to the Gentiles and became sensitive to the needs of converts from paganism. With his writing ability and his missionary experiences, he was well suited to share his understanding of the gospel message with other Gentiles. He wanted them to know that Jesus was the Savior of the whole world, including both Jews and Gentiles.

One of the most interesting facts about Luke is that his gospel is the first book of a two-volume work: the gospel itself and the Acts of the Apostles. When we look at the beginning of each of these books (Luke 1:3; Acts 1:1), we see that Luke addresses both of them to the same person, Theophilus, whose name means "lover of God." Luke wanted Theophilus and every other lover of God to "realize the certainty of the teachings" they had received (Luke 1:4).

Luke probably wrote his gospel between A.D. 80 and 85. What portrait of Jesus does he give us? Luke's Jesus is filled with mercy and compassion. He cares for everyone but shows a special tenderness for the afflicted and oppressed. This includes sinners, the poor, and outcasts. Think of the parable of the Good Samaritan, which is found only in this gospel (Luke 10:29–37). Jesus' identification with the lowly goes even further. He respects everyone and defends the dignity of all. He is especially sensitive to women. In fact Luke presents many stories of women not found in the other gospels.

The traditional symbol for the writer of Luke's Gospel is a winged ox. Oxen were sacrificial animals. This symbol was chosen because Luke's Gospel begins with Zechariah, the father of John the Baptist, offering a sacrifice in the Temple.

John: A Soaring Eagle

When the Church wants to express its deepest belief in Jesus, it turns to one gospel only: the Gospel of John. This is made clear when we look at the major celebrations of the liturgical year. At Christmas Mass During the Day, we hear the beginning of John's Gospel. At the Holy Thursday Evening Mass of the Lord's Supper, John's account of the washing of the feet is read each year. On Good Friday we join in proclaiming the account of Jesus' passion and death according to John. On Easter Sunday we sing alleluia before hearing John's Gospel. Selections from this gospel are heard during most of the Easter season and always on Pentecost Sunday. Truly the Church must see something tremendously important for us in John's Gospel to have chosen it so often.

Luke, painting by Tissot, 19th century

99

◆ Help the young people summarize the characteristics of the four gospels. Ask them to chart the portrait of Jesus given by each gospel writer. The following is an example.

Mark

• walking side by side with Jesus

• suffering Messiah

• portrait of Jesus influenced by Peter the apostle

Matthew

• the fulfillment of God's promises

• new Moses

• lawgiver and teacher

Luke

• merciful and compassionate

• respects everyone and defends everyone's dignity

• especially sensitive to women

John

• Lamb of God

• Bread of Life

• Good Shepherd

Presentation (cont'd)

◆ Have a volunteer read *Catholic ID*. Ask the young people if they have ever seen these symbols used in Church art and architecture.

◆ Have the young people form small groups to discuss the questions in *Things to Share*.

◆ Direct attention to *On Line with the Parish* on page 101. Refer to the *Enrichment Activity* on page 94A.

Conclusion ___ min.

◆ Have the young people identify the evangelists by their symbols. (*Matthew, Mark, Luke, John*)

◆ Distribute the handout *An Evangelizer's Plan*. Have a volunteer read the introduction and a second volunteer read the directions. Write the following plan on the board as an example.

Weekly theme: Friendship
Gospel passage: John 15:11–17

Monday: While walking, I will examine what kind of friend I am to others.

Assessment: If you are going to administer *Chapter 12 Assessment*, allow about ten minutes for its completion.

Does the Church's choice indicate that John's Gospel is better than that of Matthew, Mark, or Luke? Of course not. All four are part of God's inspired word. What it does tell us, however, is that John is different from the synoptics. This gospel soars to the heights of reflection. As mentioned before, John is not interested in simply giving us the narrative of Jesus' life and ministry. His primary interest is to give us a deeper insight into the meaning of Jesus' words and deeds. That is why he uses so many symbols and writes in such a beautiful and poetic way.

This picturesque language is evident very early on in the gospel when Jesus is called the Lamb of God (John 1:29). Other examples include the time when Jesus is named the Bread of Life (John 6:35) and the Good Shepherd (John 10:11). Language such as this has also led scholars to date this gospel as the last one, written between A.D. 90 and 100.

Who wrote this magnificent gospel? Many people have thought it was the apostle John. However, because it was written so many years after the death and resurrection of Jesus, its author was most likely a Jewish disciple or disciples of some eyewitness to Jesus. That eyewitness could very well have been the apostle John.

The traditional symbol for the writer of John's Gospel is a soaring eagle. It was chosen because of the sublime and majestic content of this gospel. Readers of this gospel often feel as if they, too, are eagles soaring high into the sky.

John, painting by Tissot, 19th century

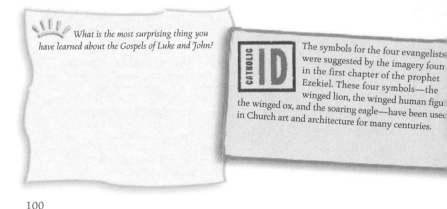

What is the most surprising thing you have learned about the Gospels of Luke and John?

CATHOLIC ID
The symbols for the four evangelists were suggested by the imagery found in the first chapter of the prophet Ezekiel. These four symbols—the winged lion, the winged human figure, the winged ox, and the soaring eagle—have been used in Church art and architecture for many centuries.

100

Answers for Chapter 12 Assessment
1. a   2. c   3. b   4. a   5. c
6. b   7. a   8. d   9. c   10. Accept reasonable responses.

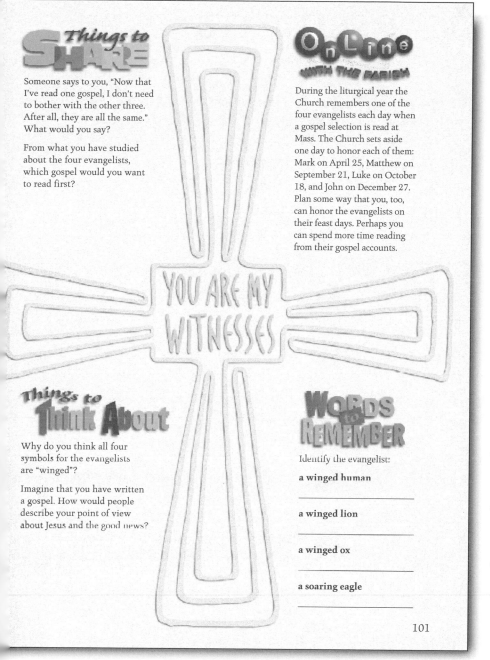

Things to SHARE

Someone says to you, "Now that I've read one gospel, I don't need to bother with the other three. After all, they are all the same." What would you say?

From what you have studied about the four evangelists, which gospel would you want to read first?

OnLine WITH THE PARISH

During the liturgical year the Church remembers one of the four evangelists each day when a gospel selection is read at Mass. The Church sets aside one day to honor each of them: Mark on April 25, Matthew on September 21, Luke on October 18, and John on December 27. Plan some way that you, too, can honor the evangelists on their feast days. Perhaps you can spend more time reading from their gospel accounts.

Things to Think About

Why do you think all four symbols for the evangelists are "winged"?

Imagine that you have written a gospel. How would people describe your point of view about Jesus and the good news?

WORDS to REMEMBER

Identify the evangelist:

a winged human
_____

a winged lion
_____

a winged ox
_____

a soaring eagle
_____

101

Conclusion (cont'd)

FORUM Assignment

✔ Read pages 102–109. Underline in pencil the statements that express six key ideas.

✔ Complete the handout *An Evangelizer's Plan*.

Closing Prayer: Invite the young people to look again at the photo on pages 94 and 95. Explain that the response to each of the prayers below is "Father, we thank you." Each prayer is taken from the Liturgy of the Hours on the evangelist's feast day.

- Father, you gave Saint Mark the privilege of preaching your gospel.
- God of mercy, you chose a tax collector, Saint Matthew, to share the dignity of the apostles.
- Father, you chose Luke the evangelist to reveal by preaching and writing the mystery of your love for the poor.
- God our Father, you have revealed the mysteries of your Word through John the apostle.

Evaluation: Do the young people appreciate that the four gospels tell the good news of Jesus through the unique perspectives of Mark, Matthew, Luke, and John?

FOR CHAPTER 13

- preparations for opening prayer
- copies of handout *Praying to Jesus*, page 102C
- copies of *Chapter 13 Assessment*, page 109A
- copies of *Highlights for Home*, page 109B
- construction paper: orange, yellow, red, and gold
- banner of praise

Assessment

1 Matthew's Gospel is the only one
a. concerned with the Church's organization.
b. read at Mass on Holy Thursday.
c. that does not include parables.
d. that portrays Jesus as the suffering Messiah.

2 The Gospel of Mark
a. copied Matthew's Gospel.
b. was written in A.D. 100.
c. was written first.
d. is placed first in the Bible.

3 The Gospel of Luke
a. was written by a Jew.
b. portrays a compassionate Jesus.
c. is used for major liturgical celebrations.
d. is not a synoptic gospel.

4 The Gospel of John
a. has many poetic images.
b. was written immediately after Jesus' resurrection.
c. is a synoptic gospel.
d. was the first written.

5 The parable of the Good Samaritan is found only in the Gospel of
a. Matthew.
b. Mark.
c. Luke.
d. John.

Use the following code to match the evangelist with the picture he gave of Jesus in his gospel.
a. Matthew
b. Mark
c. Luke
d. John

6 ___ the suffering Messiah

7 ___ the new Moses

8 ___ Lamb of God

9 ___ defender of the dignity of all

10 Explain the symbols used to identify two of the four gospel writers.

_____
_____
_____
_____
_____
_____
_____
_____
_____
_____
_____

Highlights for Home

Focus on Faith

In this chapter your son or daughter learned that each of the four evangelists was directing his gospel to a different audience. Each had a different emphasis in proclaiming the good news of Jesus. The following is a summary.

Mark was a Jewish Christian who wrote for a Gentile audience. Reading Mark is like seeing Jesus through the eyes of Peter. Mark wants us to know Jesus is the suffering Messiah and that Jesus asks his disciples for a radical change in their lives.

Matthew was a Jewish Christian writing for a Jewish audience. For Matthew Jesus is the fulfillment of all God's promises, new great lawgiver and teacher, the new Moses.

Luke was a Gentile writing for the Gentiles. Luke's Jesus is filled with mercy and compassion. He respects and defends the dignity of all.

John's Gospel was written by a Jewish disciple or disciple of an eyewitness of Jesus. In symbolic language Jesus is called the Lamb of God (John 1:29), the Bread of Life (John 6:35), and the Good Shepherd.

Conversation Starters

. . . . a few ideas to talk about together . . . .

◆ In what ways will you become more familiar with the one gospel that appeals to you most?

Feature Focus

In the *Catholic ID* feature on page 100 the young people are encouraged to recognize the symbols for the four evangelists. These symbols (winged desert lion for Mark; winged human figure for Matthew; winged ox for Luke; soaring eagle for John) were suggested in the first chapter of the prophet Ezekiel. The symbols for the three synoptic gospel writers were chosen in reference to the beginnings of these gospels. The symbol for the writer of John's Gospel was chosen because of the sublime and majestic content of this gospel.

Reflection

How many times during the course of the year do you feel weighted down by troubles? Have you said to yourself, "If only I could take on wings! If I could soar among eagles!"?

Saint Thérèse of Lisieux, who is known for the spirit of her "little way," had a strong love for the Scriptures and meditated on the four gospels. Spend some time reflecting on her prayer. Add your own words.

Lord Jesus, I am not an eagle.
All I have are the eyes and the heart
  of one.
In spite of my littleness, I dare to gaze
    at the sun of love
    and long to fly toward it.
I want to imitate the eagles,
    but all I can do is flap my small wings.
    What shall I do?

Human and Divine

Adult Focus

When the Word became flesh, the invisible God became visible. To those who encountered him, Jesus revealed that "whoever has seen me has seen the Father" (John 14:9). He promised that his followers would be counseled and comforted by the Holy Spirit.

Chapter 8 focuses on the divinity of Jesus. He is both human and divine. He is Son of God, Savior, Messiah, and Lord. His "I AM" statements and descriptions, with their echoes of the Old Testament language of Yahweh, are a deliberate identification with God and reveal the Father in a unique way.

When presenting this chapter, help the young people understand that the truth about God that Jesus revealed cannot be changed. The three Persons of the Trinity are Father, Son, and Holy Spirit. They are the three Persons in the one God. That is why we are baptized in the *name* of the Father, and of the Son, and of the Holy Spirit—and in no other name.

Catechism Focus

The theme of Chapter 14 corresponds to paragraphs 209 and 485–486 of the *Catechism*.

Enrichment Activities

Making a Mini-Retreat

Set aside time for a mini-retreat. If possible, find a setting different from your usual place of meeting. Use the descriptions of Jesus on the chart on page 108 for prayer-session themes. An excellent resource to use is:

Time with Jesus: Twenty Guided Meditations for Youth
by Thomas F. Catucci
Ave Maria Press, 1993
Notre Dame, IN
800-282-1865

Computer Connection

Have the young people use a multimedia software program, such as *Hyperstudio®*, to create a multimedia Faith Journal. The young people should include the time and date of each entry they make in their journals.

Those using the *Hyperstudio®* program can set up the journal as a stack of cards by creating buttons that allow them to manipulate the stack and progress from card to card. Have the journalists add a button for each date. Inform them that any word or icon can be used as a button.

Journal entries may take the form of questions to God, prayers, and thoughtful reflections on New Testament readings. The young people might also wish to include scanned-in pictures, digitized photographs, imported sounds, and clip art. Encourage them to be creative by using different borders, backdrops, and features such as fading to black or white from card to card. Journals should be updated periodically throughout the year.

Teaching Resources

Overview

To reaffirm that Jesus is a divine Person with two natures: a human nature and a divine nature; to explore Jesus' statements about and descriptions of himself.

Opening Prayer Ideas

Praise procession and praise mosaic

or

Read and reflect on John 12:12–16.

Materials

New Testament Journal:

For Chapter 13, use pages 26–27.

- Bibles, journals, and highlighters
- large paper banner
- construction paper: orange, yellow, red, gold

REPRODUCIBLE MASTERS

- *Praying to Jesus*, page 102C
- *Chapter 13 Assessment*, page 101A
- *Highlights for Home*, page 101B

Supplemental Resources

VIDEO
Jesus of Nazareth
Videos with Values
1509 Washington Ave.
St. Louis, MO 63103

Praying to Jesus

The following titles of Jesus are part of a prayer of the Church. The response to each special title is "Have mercy on us." Choose four of the titles. Write the titles and cite a passage from the gospels that will help you reflect on Jesus. An example follows:

Title: Jesus, model of obedience

Gospel reading: Luke 22:39–44
Jesus' agony in the garden

GOD OUR FATHER IN HEAVEN,

God the Son, Redeemer of the world,

God the Holy Spirit,
Holy Trinity, one God,

Jesus, Son of the living God,
Jesus, dawn of justice,
Jesus, Son of the Virgin Mary,
Jesus worthy of our love,
Jesus worthy of our wonder,
Jesus, prince of peace,
Jesus, pattern of patience,
Jesus, model of obedience,
Jesus, father of the poor,

Jesus, God of peace,
Jesus, author of life,
Jesus, good shepherd,
Jesus, the true light,
Jesus, eternal wisdom,
Jesus, infinite goodness,
Jesus, our way and our life,
Jesus, teacher of the evangelists,
Let us pray.

Lord,
may we honor the holy name of Jesus
enjoy his friendship in this life
and be filled with eternal joy in the kingdom
where he lives and reigns for ever and ever.
Amen.

Selections from the Litany of the Holy Name

CHAPTER 13

Human and Divine

Rabbi, you are the Son of God;
you are the King of Israel.
John 1:49

Objectives: To reaffirm that Jesus is a divine Person with two natures: a human nature and a divine nature; to explore Jesus' statements about and descriptions of himself.

Introduction ___ min.

Opening Prayer: Before the session begins, prepare a large paper banner with a prayer of praise to Jesus, Son of God. Have available sheets of orange, yellow, red, and gold construction paper.

At the beginning of the prayer, give each person a sheet of construction paper. Have them draw a rectangular shape on the paper and cut out the shape. On this shaped paper, invite each person to write a prayer of praise.

Then invite the young people to look at the art work on pages 102 and 103. Proclaim together John 1:49. Then have a volunteer read aloud the story of Jesus' entry into Jerusalem (John 12:12–16).

Invite the young people to carry the praise prayer in procession to the banner you have prepared. Then each person should tape or paste their prayer to the banner to make a praise mosaic. During the procession have the young people sing a familiar hymn of praise. The words and music to "All Glory Laud and Honor," "Crown Him with Many Crowns," or "The King of Glory" are found in the *Worship* hymnal. As an alternative, you may want to play a recording of the "Hallelujah Chorus" from *Handel's Messiah.*

Forum: Have the young people share their evangelizer's plans with the people who are seated near them. Remind the young people that they should put these prayers in action.

Presentation ___ min.

◆ Have a volunteer read the introductory paragraph at the top of page 104. Discuss responses to the question.

◆ Ask volunteers to summarize pages 104 and 105. Then have the young people form small groups. Ask the members of the groups to imagine that they are in a group of Jesus' disciples discussing his teaching about his Father. Have the group members discuss their responses to each of the passages listed on page 105.

Note: The following activity is optional.

◆ Give each person a lump of modeling clay and newspapers to cover his or her workplace. Have the young people make the symbol of the Trinity shown on page 105. Ask them to try not to show the spots where they have begun or ended. Have all set aside the symbols to dry.

◆ Have a volunteer read the first paragraph on page 106. Explain that after a child has been baptized in the name of the Father, Son, and Holy Spirit, the priest or deacon may pray the following final blessing:

My brothers and sisters, we entrust you all to the mercy and help of God the almighty Father, his only Son, and the Holy Spirit. May he watch over your life, and may we all walk by the light of faith, and attain the good things he has promised us.

Two thousand years ago many wandering preachers walked the hills of Israel and visited its villages and towns. What made Jesus of Nazareth different from them?

Human God and Divine Human

What made Jesus different was that he was both human and divine. At the incarnation the second Person of the Blessed Trinity became Man. He took on our human nature in every way except one: sin. John's Gospel speaks about the incarnation by saying that the Word of God, who had existed from all eternity, became flesh:

In the beginning was the Word,
and the Word was with God,
and the Word was God....
And the Word became flesh
and made his dwelling among us.
John 1:1, 14

104

Jesus was the Word made flesh. Could people tell that Jesus was a divine Person simply by looking at him? No. Jesus looked and lived just like everyone else. The gospels remind us that he had to eat and sleep. He knew what it was to experience joy and suffering. He had to work and pray. That is because Jesus was both human and divine. The Church proclaims this truth by teaching that he is a divine Person with two natures: a human nature and a divine nature. For this reason we can describe Jesus as the human God and the divine human.

When the Word of God, the second Person of the Blessed Trinity, became one of us at the incarnation, something truly wonderful happened: The invisible God became visible. In Jesus we would begin to see who God really is because Jesus would reveal this to us. And what did Jesus reveal? He revealed that God is a Trinity of Persons. God is Father, Son, and Holy Spirit. Jesus is the Father's Son, the Son of God. It is very important for us to understand this relationship of Jesus to the Father. Let's take a closer look at the way it is described in the New Testament.

The author of John's Gospel made it clear that Jesus revealed his Father to us in a completely new and unique way. He let us know that God is not just the creator of the universe, who is worshiped by many people in many religions. God is uniquely Jesus' Father. This is what we learn from John's Gospel:

- Only the Son has seen the Father: "Everyone who listens to my Father and learns from him comes to me. Not that anyone has seen the Father except the one who is from God; he has seen the Father" (6:45–46).

- The Son came from the Father: "I came from God and am here; I did not come on my own, but he sent me" (8:42).

- The Son returns to the Father: "Now I am leaving the world and going back to the Father" (16:28).

- The Father is glorified in the Son and always hears the Son: "Whatever you ask in my name, I will do, so that the Father may be glorified in the Son. If you ask anything of me in my name, I will do it" (14:13–14).

- The Son has made known what he heard from the Father: "I have called you friends, because I have told you everything I have heard from my Father" (15:15).

Imagine what it was like for Jesus' disciples and others to hear God spoken about in this way! They must have been shocked to hear someone identify himself so closely with God. After all, these were Jews who had struggled for many centuries to maintain their belief in the one true God.

Of course, Jesus was not talking about many gods. He was speaking about himself and his Father, two Persons of the Blessed Trinity. At other times Jesus also spoke about the third Person of the Blessed Trinity: "The Advocate, the holy Spirit that the Father will send in my name—he will teach you everything and remind you of all that [I] told you" (John 14:26).

◆ Have the young people highlight the statements that are highlighted on reduced pupil pages 104 and 105.

Note: The following activity is optional.

◆ Write the following prayer on the board:

I walk this day with the Father,
I walk this day with the Son,
I walk this day with the Spirit,
The threefold all-kindly.

Explain that this prayer is based on one that has been passed on by the people of the Outer Hebrides, islands off the coast of Scotland. The people intoned this prayer on their way to work in the fields or on the sea. Invite the young people to pray these words and to be confident that God is with them throughout the day. Ask those who are musically inclined to make up a chant or rap beat for the prayer.

105

Presentation (cont'd)

◆ Have the young people respond to the  thought provoker on page 106.

◆ Have volunteers summarize "Meeting Jesus." Have the young people highlight the key concepts highlighted on reduced pupil pages 106 and 107.

◆ Have a volunteer read *Catholic ID* on page 107. If time permits, distribute sheets of light-colored construction paper. On their sheets have the young people draw overlapping circles. While they are drawing, have them repeat in chant the following prayer:

> Jesus, you are the Alpha and the Omega, the first and the last, the beginning and the end.

◆ Explain that every year, at the Easter Vigil, the paschal candle is lit in the darkened church as a sign of Christ's resurrection. The celebrant first prepares the candle by cutting a cross in the wax. Then he traces the Greek letter *alpha* above the cross, the letter *omega* below and the numerals of the current year between the arms of the cross.

Father, Son, and Holy Spirit is the language that Jesus used in revealing his own identity and that of the other Persons of the Blessed Trinity. This is the language we find in the New Testament. The truth about God that Jesus revealed cannot be changed. The three Persons of the Trinity are Father, Son, and Holy Spirit. They are the three Persons in the one God. That is why we are baptized in the *name* of the Father, and of the Son, and of the Holy Spirit— and in no other name.

In what way is your attitude toward Jesus different from your attitude toward other great heroes of history?

Laughing Jesus
Nuñez Segura, 1988

Meeting Jesus

If we are willing to spend time with the New Testament, especially the gospels, we have the opportunity to really meet Jesus. Not only can we find his teachings and the challenges he offers his disciples, but we are also introduced to Jesus himself. We can discover what Jesus wants us to know about him.

One day Jesus was in the Temple, and a group of people gathered around him. They were wondering who he was and wanted to know more about him. Jesus replied to their questions and told them, "The Father and I are one" (John 10:30). Another time he said, "The Father is in me and I am in the Father" (John 10:38). Through these astonishing words we learn more than the fact that Jesus is the Son of God. We learn that Jesus shared the same divinity as God the Father.

Jesus made this even clearer at other times when he spoke about himself. Some of his most memorable statements contain the words *I am*.

106

In Catholic churches we often see the alpha and omega, A and Ω, which are symbols for Christ. Alpha and omega are the names of the first and last letters of the Greek alphabet. In the last book of the Bible, Jesus says, "I am the Alpha and the Omega, the first and the last, the beginning and the end" (Revelation 22:12). These same words were the words God had spoken of himself in Isaiah 41:4. Jesus is truly the first and the last, the beginning and the end. He is the only Son of the Father. He is divine.

◆ If possible, have the young people visit the church, and share with them the following prayer of the celebrant as he traces the letters on the paschal candle:

> Christ yesterday and today
> the beginning and the end
> Alpha
> and Omega
> all time belongs to him
> and all the ages
> to him be glory and power
> through every age forever. Amen.

◆ Ask the young people to work in pairs. Assign each set of partners one or more of the passages listed for "Old Testament Background" in the chart on page 108. Have the partners locate the reference in the Old Testament and write the way God identifies himself. Then have the partners write what connection they see with Jesus' statements and descriptions listed on the chart.

When Jesus spoke these words, his listeners could make an immediate connection to words of the Old Testament. In the Book of Exodus, for example, God revealed himself to Moses by saying, "This is what you shall tell the Israelites: I AM sent me to you" (Exodus 3:14). In Hebrew, the language of the Old Testament, Yahweh was God's name. *Yahweh* means "I AM."

The people around Jesus would also know from the Old Testament that God identified himself in other ways, saying such things as, "It is I," "Fear not," and "Do not be afraid." Jesus used these same expressions to comfort his disciples. By using the language of Yahweh from the Old Testament, Jesus was revealing his relationship to the Father, who loved and cared for his people.

Study the chart on page 108. Notice how often Jesus used the same language that Yahweh (God) used in the Old Testament.

One day Jesus was preaching in the Temple. The people asked him whether he was greater than their father, Abraham, or the prophets. Jesus surprised them by saying, "Amen, amen, I say to you, before Abraham came to be, I AM" (John 8:58). This was a startling statement. At the time of Jesus, Abraham would have been dead almost two thousand years! Jesus was saying that he existed before Abraham. Because he used the divine name, I AM, the people picked up stones to throw at him. They thought Jesus was blaspheming by identifying himself with God.

As the chart makes clear, there are several types of "I am" statements that were spoken by Jesus. When we see an "I am" statement in capital letters, we know that it refers to the divine name. The other "I am" statements in the chart are descriptions Jesus gave of himself and his divine mission. Jesus, who is one with the Father, was able to reveal the Father in a unique way.

107

Presentation (cont'd)

◆ Play or sing together "Be Not Afraid." Words and music can be found in the *Glory & Praise* hymnal. Ask, "What lyrics relate to Jesus' statements and descriptions listed on the chart?"

◆ Have the young people form small groups to discuss the questions in *Things to Think About* and *Things to Share*.

◆ Have a volunteer read *On Line with Parish*. If possible, ask one of the priests of your parish to show the young people the alpha and omega on chalices, sacred vessels, vestments, or altar cloths in your parish.

Conclusion ___ min.

◆ Have the young people define the *Words to Remember*. The definition for *Blessed Trinity* is on page 106. The meaning of *Yahweh* is on page 107.

Assessment: If you are going to administer *Chapter 13 Assessment*, allow about ten minutes for its completion.

Jesus Speaks About Himself

Statements About Himself		Old Testament Background
John 6:20	"It is I. Do not be afraid."	Exodus 3:14; 6:6–8; Isaiah 41:4–10; 43:1–3, 10–13, 25; 45:18; 46:4; 48:12
John 8:24	"If you do not believe that I AM, you will die in your sins."	
John 8:28	"When you lift up the Son of Man, then you will realize that I AM."	
John 8:58	"Amen, amen, I say to you, before Abraham came to be, I AM."	
John 13:19	"From now on I am telling you before it happens, so that when it happens you may believe that I AM."	

Descriptions of Himself		Old Testament Background
John 6:35	"I am the bread of life."	Exodus 13:21; 16:4; Deuteronomy 32:39; Psalm 24:7–10; Isaiah 5:1–7; 40:11, 27–29; 41:4
John 8:12	"I am the light of the world."	
John 10:9	"I am the gate."	
John 10:11	"I am the good shepherd."	
John 11:25	"I am the resurrection and the life."	
John 14:6	"I am the way and the truth and the life."	
John 15:1	"I am the true vine."	
Revelation 22:12	"I am the Alpha and the Omega, the first and the last, the beginning and the end."	

108

Answers for Chapter 13 Assessment

1. b   **2.** a   **3.** c   **4.** c   **5.** b
6. c   **7.** b   **8.** d   **9.** a   **10.** See page 104.

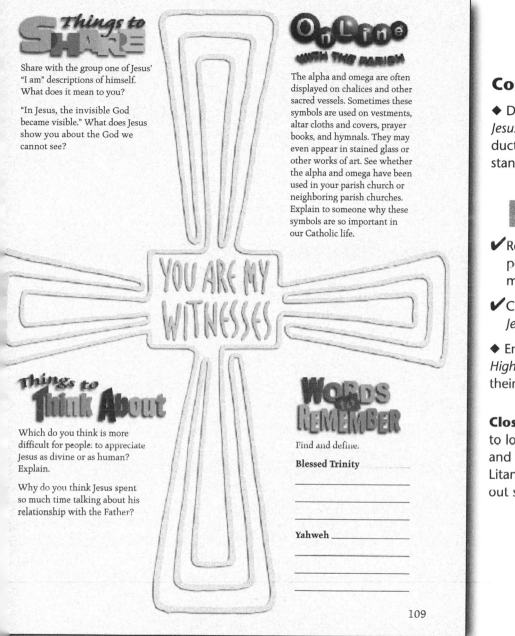

Things to SHARE

Share with the group one of Jesus' "I am" descriptions of himself. What does it mean to you?

"In Jesus, the invisible God became visible." What does Jesus show you about the God we cannot see?

OnLine WITH THE PARISH

The alpha and omega are often displayed on chalices and other sacred vessels. Sometimes these symbols are used on vestments, altar cloths and covers, prayer books, and hymnals. They may even appear in stained glass or other works of art. See whether the alpha and omega have been used in your parish church or neighboring parish churches. Explain to someone why these symbols are so important in our Catholic life.

Things to Think About

Which do you think is more difficult for people: to appreciate Jesus as divine or as human? Explain.

Why do you think Jesus spent so much time talking about his relationship with the Father?

WORDS to REMEMBER

Find and define:

Blessed Trinity _____

_____

_____

_____

Yahweh _____

_____

_____

_____

109

Conclusion (cont'd)

◆ Distribute the handout *Praying to Jesus.* Have a volunteer read the introduction. Make sure everyone understands the directions.

FORUM Assignment

✔ Read pages 110–117. Underline in pencil the statements that express six main ideas.

✔ Complete the handout *Praying to Jesus.*

◆ Encourage the young people to share *Highlights for Home,* page 109B, with their families.

Closing Prayer: Ask the young people to look at the art work on pages 102 and 103. Pray the selections from the Litany of the Holy Name on the handout sheet.

Evaluation: Do the young people understand that Jesus is a divine Person with two natures: a human nature and a divine nature? Have the young people explored Jesus' statements about and descriptions of himself?

FOR CHAPTER 14

• preparations for opening prayer
• screen prop (optional)
• "Abba! Father!" in *Glory & Praise* hymnal
• copies of handout *Through the Roof,* page 110C
• *Final Assessment,* page 126
• *Chapter 14 Assessment,* page 117A

Assessment

1 In his "I AM" statements, Jesus
a. identified himself with his disciples.
b. identified himself with God.
c. tried to confuse his followers.
d. compared himself to Moses.

2 Jesus took on our human nature in every way except
a. sin.
b. experiencing joy.
c. experiencing suffering.
d. human needs of hunger and thirst.

3 In Hebrew *Yahweh* means
a. "light."
b. "shepherd."
c. "I AM."
d. "Father."

Circle the one that does *not* belong.

4 Jesus said, "I am
a. the bread of life."
b. the resurrection and the life."
c. Abraham."
d. the first and the last."

5 We are baptized in the name of God
a. the Father only.
b. the Father, Son, and Holy Spirit.
c. the Son only.
d. the Holy Spirit only.

6 In the Temple when Jesus used the divine name, I AM, many people
a. praised him.
b. felt sorry for him.
c. picked up stones to throw at him.
d. professed their belief in him.

7 The Church teaches that Jesus
a. had only a human nature.
b. had a human nature and a divine nature.
c. had only a divine nature.
d. none of the above

8 ___ Gospel speaks about the incarnation by saying that the "Word became flesh."
a. Matthew's
b. Mark's
c. Luke's
d. John's

9 When we see "I am" statements in capital letters, it refers to
a. the divine name.
b. Jesus' description of himself.
c. Jesus' divine mission.
d. none of the above

10 What made Jesus different than the preachers of two thousand years ago?

© William H. Sadlier, Inc. Permission to duplicate is granted to the users of the *Faith and Witness* Program.

Highlights for Home

Focus on Faith

When the Word became flesh, the invisible God became visible. To those who encountered him, Jesus revealed that "whoever has seen me has seen the Father" (John 14:9). He promised that his followers would be counseled and comforted by the Holy Spirit.

Chapter 13 focuses on the divinity of Jesus. He is both human and divine. He is Son of God, Savior, Messiah, and Lord. His "I AM" statements and descriptions, with their echoes of the Old Testament language of Yahweh, are a deliberate identification with God and reveal the Father in a unique way.

Help your son or daughter understand that the truth about God that Jesus revealed cannot be changed. The three Persons of the Trinity are Father, Son, and Holy Spirit. They are the three Persons in the one God. That is why we are baptized in the *name* of the Father, and of the Son, and of the Holy Spirit—and in no other name.

Conversation Starters

. . . . a few ideas to talk about together . . . .

◆ What image comes to mind when you make the sign of the cross?

◆ What do Jesus' words "Fear not" or "Do not be afraid" mean to you? What can you do to profess your belief in Jesus' words?

Feature Focus

In the *Catholic ID* on page 107 the young people learn that the alpha and omega, A and Ω, are symbols for Christ. Alpha and omega are the names of the first and last letters of the Greek alphabet. These letters symbolize Christ in Catholic church architecture, stained glass, altar cloths, and sacred vessels. In the last book of the Bible, Jesus says, "I am the Alpha and the Omega, the first and the last, the beginning and the end" (Revelation 22:12).

Reflection

Reflect on the meaning of the lyrics of one of the hymns we sing to commemorate and celebrate Jesus' entry into Jerusalem.

All glory, laud, and honor
To thee, Redeemer King!
To whom the lips of children
Made sweet hosannas ring.
Thou art the king of Israel,
Thou David's royal Son,
Who in the Lord's Name comest,
The King and Blessed One.

CHRIST THE LORD

Adult Focus

Jesus not only told us about his divinity. He showed us by his actions that he was divine. His divine power not only extended to the forgiveness of sins but to the working of miracles as well. In this chapter this truth is shown by using the example of Jesus forgiving and curing the paralytic who was lowered through the roof to see Jesus (Mark 2:1–12).

Jesus wanted people to know that God had come into the world in a new and dramatic way. Jesus brought God's mercy and forgiveness to all people. And in doing so, Jesus let everyone know that he was the Messiah and Lord.

Emphasize with the young people that Jesus taught us that God is our Father. Together as a Church community we proclaim God holy and work for the coming of the kingdom. Together we ask for bread, the bread we need to live and the Bread of Life. Together we ask for forgiveness and the strength to do God's will, whatever temptations we face. Baptized in the name of the Father, and of the Son, and of the Holy Spirit, we pray as sons and daughters of God, "Our Father."

Catechism Focus

The theme of Chapter 14 corresponds to paragraphs 436–455, 2599–2602, 2761–2854 of the *Catechism*.

Enrichment Activities

Our Father Booklets

Invite the young people to illustrate their favorite verses of the Lord's Prayer. Then have the young people use the illustrations they prepared to make Our Father booklets. Organize "booklet groups," each beginning with a person who illustrated the petition "Our Father, who are in heaven." Continue forming each group with the people who chose the remaining petitions. Ask volunteers to hand-print any petitions that may be missing from a group's booklet. (You can also use a computer with a variety of type fonts to do this.) Then direct the groups to staple their illustrated petitions together in order. Display the booklets for the school or parish to see, or use them as the basis for a prayer session with younger children.

Daily Bread

Invite a representative of a group that works to combat hunger to speak to the young people. Ask the guest speaker to inform the young people about ways they can participate in the process of seeking justice for those who yearn for daily bread.

Teaching Resources

Overview

To learn that in bringing God's mercy and forgiveness to all people, Jesus let everyone know he was Messiah and Lord; to explore the meaning of the verses of the Our Father.

Opening Prayer Ideas

Look at the photo on pages 110 and 111. Pray together John 6:68.

or

Pray together: "Jesus, teach us to pray."

Materials

- Bibles, highlighters, journals
- screen prop (optional)
- recording "I Know the Father Loves Me," *Beginning Today* (GIA)
- "Abba! Father!" in *Glory & Praise* hymnal

REPRODUCIBLE MASTERS
- *Through the Roof,* page 110C
- *Chapter 14 Assessment,* page 117A
- *Final Assessment,* pages 126–127
- *Highlights for Home,* page 117B

New Testament Journal:
For Chapter 14, use pages 34–35.

Supplemental Resources

VIDEOS
Jesus of Nazareth
Videos with Values
1509 Washington Ave.
St. Louis, MO 63103

Yeshua: "The Land, the Promise, The Messiah"
Gateway Films/Vision Video
Post Office Box 540
Worcester, PA 19490-0540

Through the Roof

Read the story of Jesus' cure of the paralytic (Mark 2:1–12).
Imagine you are the paralyzed man or a person in the house
listening to Jesus. Write a script. In your dialogue, include
reactions to Jesus when he said, "Your sins are forgiven."

_____ : _____
_____

_____ : _____
_____

_____ : _____
_____

_____ : _____
_____

Christ the Lord

To whom shall we go?
You have the words of eternal life!
John 6:68

Objectives: To learn that in bringing God's mercy and forgiveness to all people, Jesus let everyone know he was Messiah and Lord; to explore the meaning of the verses of the Our Father.

Introduction ___ min.

Opening Prayer: Invite the young people to look at the photo on pages 110 and 111. Read together the verse from the Gospel of John on page 111. Have the young people imagine that all the people in the buildings pictured are asking this question at precisely the same moment that they are. Ask, "Is such a moment difficult for you to imagine? Why or why not?"

Explain that moments like these were not so difficult to imagine a few hundred years ago. When the town clocks would strike the hour, many people would stop and say a short prayer to acknowledge God's presence. And, more recently during Advent, many people prayed the following words several times a day:

> Hail and blessed be the hour and
>   the moment
> In which the Son of God became Man.

Ask the young people to do the following:

> Think of the words that you could pray a few times each day to help you remember that Jesus is with you always. Take time to pray them now. Write the words in your journals, taking note of each word after you have written it.

Then play an instrumental recording. *Reflections I or II* by the Dameans (GIA) would be appropriate. Invite volunteers to share their original prayers.

Forum: Have the young people share in small groups the titles and Scripture passages they have written on the handout *Praying to Jesus*.

Presentation ___ min.

◆ Have a volunteer read Mark 2:1–12. Ask the following questions:

- Why were the scribes upset by Jesus' words and actions?
- In what ways did the reactions of other eyewitnesses differ from those of the scribes?

Then have the young people highlight the statements for "Authority to Forgive Sins."

◆ Distribute the handout *Through the Roof.* Allow about five minutes for the young people to write individual scripts.

Then have the young people share their scripts about Jesus curing the paralyzed man. Ask each group to use the members' scripts to write one script for radio listeners. When each group performs the script, place a screen in front of the actors to hide them from view. Have the other groups' members imagine that they are living in the age before television. They are gathered around the radio, listening to the weekly program *Jesus' Life and Mission*.

Note: You may want to show a ten-minute segment of the video *Jesus of Nazareth.* The story of the healing of the paralytic is on the first tape.

People did not always accept Jesus' message. Sometimes they turned away and left him. Once when this happened, he looked at the Twelve and asked them whether they also wanted to leave him. Simon Peter responded, "Master, to whom shall we go? You have the words of eternal life" (John 6: 68).

Are there things in Jesus' teaching that you find hard to accept? Do you walk away from him? Or, like Peter, do you recognize him as the Son of God?

112

Paralyzed Man Lowered Through the Roof, Tissot, 19th century

Authority to Forgive Sins

Jesus not only told us about his divinity; he also showed us by his actions that he was divine. One very important way he did this was by forgiving sins. An example can be seen in Mark 2:1–12. One day a crowd gathered in the house where Jesus was staying. There were so many people that no one else could come through the door. When a paralytic, a paralyzed man, was brought to see Jesus, the man's friends could not get him into the house. Instead they opened up the roof and slowly lowered the man down on a mat to see Jesus.

When Jesus saw the faith of the people, he said to the paralyzed man, "Your sins are forgiven." Some of those present were scandalized and accused Jesus of blasphemy. They said, "Who but God alone can forgive sins?"

Jesus knew what they were thinking. In order to show that he had authority to forgive sins, he said to the paralyzed man, "I say to you, rise, pick up your mat, and go home." Immediately the man got up. As he walked away, the crowd exclaimed, "We have never seen anything like this." They knew that only God could forgive sins. By his actions Jesus was letting them know that he had authority to forgive sins and was, therefore, divine. His divine power extended not only to the forgiveness of sins but to the working of miracles as well.

By showing his divinity in these ways, Jesus was not denying his humanity. But he did want to let people know that God had come into the world in a new and dramatic way. Jesus brought God's mercy and forgiveness to all people. And in doing so, Jesus let everyone know that he was the Messiah and Lord.

113

Presentation (cont'd)

◆ Ask volunteers to explain why so many did not recognize Jesus as the Messiah. Ask, "What had the prophets told God's people about the Messiah?" List the following on the board:

• He would come to set God's people free from oppression.

• He would bring them into a whole new relationship with God.

• He would guide them in the ways of justice.

◆ Ask, "What does the word *messiah* mean?" (*It is a Hebrew word that means "the anointed one."*)

Then write the word *christos* on the board. Ask the young people to explain the word's use in the New Testament. (*The New Testament used the Greek word christos to translate the word messiah.*) Emphasize with the young people that when we say Jesus Christ, we are not using *Christ* as Jesus' family name.

◆ Have a volunteer explain why we use the title *Lord* for Jesus.

Presentation (cont'd)

◆ Ask the young people to respond to the ⚜ thought provoker on page 114 in the space provided. While they are writing, you may want to play a recording of "The Hallelujah Chorus" from Handel's *Messiah*.

◆ Direct the young people's attention to the *Scripture Update*. Ask, "Who first organized the Bible into chapters and verses?" Have volunteers explain the history of the divisions used within the books of the Old Testament and the New Testament.

◆ If possible, play a recording of a thematic song. "I Know the Father Loves Me" by the Dameans (*Beginning Today*, GIA) would be appropriate.

Then have volunteers roleplay Jesus and two of his disciples in a conversation. The disciples are questioning Jesus, asking him when, where, why and how he prays. The responses for Jesus are found on page 115.

Invite other sets of three to take a turn in the same roleplay until all the possible responses are given.

◆ Write *Abba* on the board. Ask a volunteer to explain the meaning. (*an Aramaic name for "father" that expressed deep respect and affection for one's father*)

Scripture Update

The biblical authors did not divide their books into chapters and verses. They wrote a continuous manuscript without any divisions whatsoever. When, then, did we get chapters and verses in the Bible? It happened in A.D. 1226 when Stephen Langton, the archbishop of Canterbury in England, decided to divide each book into numbered chapters. Later, in 1551, a French printer named Robert Estienne divided these chapters into smaller segments called verses. These divisions made it easier to find one's way around the Bible.

The division into chapters and verses is universally followed today. It is very practical because everyone now knows where to find a passage, or section, of the Bible when the proper reference is given. For example, Mark 2:4 means the Gospel of Mark, chapter 2, verse 4. It can mean nothing else. And the use of numbered references makes it unnecessary for people to print out entire sections of the Bible.

Bible references can offer even more details. For example, Mark 2:1–12 means the Gospel of Mark, chapter 2, verses 1 through 12. This is the way we indicate the whole of Mark's account of the healing of the paralytic. Mark 2—4 is a different reference. The longer dash indicates that we move not just from verse to verse but from chapter to chapter. So Mark 2—4 means the Gospel of Mark, chapters 2 through 4.

Messiah and Lord

God's people had been waiting a long time for the promised Savior. He would come to set them free from oppression and bring them into a whole new relationship with God. Over the centuries some people began to think of the Savior, or Messiah, as a warrior or political leader. They forgot the words of the prophets, who spoke of the Messiah as the one who would lead the people to God and guide them in the ways of justice. That is one reason why so many did not recognize Jesus as the Messiah.

114

What does the word *messiah* mean? It is a Hebrew word that means "the anointed one." In ancient times kings, priests, and prophets were anointed with oil as a sign of their special roles in the world. Just think of David, who was anointed by Samuel and became the greatest king of Israel. The Savior, however, was to be greater than David. The Savior would be the most important person ever to come into the world. One day a Samaritan woman said to Jesus, "I know that the Messiah is coming, the one called the Anointed; when he comes, he will tell us everything." After she said this, Jesus replied, "I am he, the one who is speaking with you" (John 4:25, 26).

Jesus is the promised Messiah. The New Testament, written in Greek, used the word *christos*, or Christ, to translate the word *messiah*. When we say Jesus Christ, therefore, we are not using *Christ* as Jesus' family name. It is his title. When we say Jesus Christ, we are really saying Jesus the Christ, or Jesus the Messiah, or Jesus the Anointed One. All three mean the same thing.

There is one more title of Jesus that we must understand clearly. Jesus is the Lord. Why do we call him Lord? In the Old Testament Yahweh was God's name. To show reverence for this name, the word *Lord* was generally used in place of *Yahweh*. Lord, therefore, is a divine title reserved for God. And because Jesus is a divine Person and the Son of God, he, too, is called Lord. We see this often in the gospels, as in Luke 11:1, where Jesus' disciples said to him, "Lord, teach us to pray." Then he taught them the Lord's Prayer.

⚜ *Which of these titles of Jesus is especially meaningful to you? Tell why.*

◆ Have the young people highlight the main ideas highlighted in this chapter.

◆ Have the young people form small groups. Give each group leader a copy of the following questions the group should discuss:

• Why do we pray "Our Father" not "My Father"?

• What are we expressing when we say "hallowed be thy name"?

• For what are we praying when we say, "Thy kingdom come"?

• What does it mean to do God's will?

• How does the "daily-bread" petition guide our actions?

• What does the "forgive-us" petition require us to do?

• For what do we ask when we pray "deliver us from evil"?

Allow ten minutes for discussion. Then have a spokesperson from each group share its responses with all the young people.

The Lord's Prayer

In the gospels Jesus is frequently described as being at prayer, especially at important moments in his life. After his baptism by John the Baptist, Jesus went out to the desert to pray. Later he prayed before he called the twelve apostles to follow him. He prayed at his transfiguration and again in the garden of Gethsemane before his passion. He prayed alone; he prayed with others in the synagogue; he even prayed on the cross.

As Jesus went about his preaching, crowds of people pressed in upon him. That is one reason why he sometimes needed to go off by himself to a quiet place for prayer. On these occasions he would often pray throughout the whole night. What would Jesus do during these long times of prayer? He would be in silent communion with his Father, whom he often addressed as Abba.

Abba was an Aramaic word that expressed deep respect and affection for one's father. It was similar to our word *Dad* and showed how intimate Jesus was with the Father.

One time, Luke reports, the disciples saw Jesus at prayer; they realized how deeply he was in communion with the Father. They were so impressed that they wanted to be able to pray as Jesus was praying. So after he had finished his prayer, they said to Jesus, "Lord, teach us to pray" (Luke 11:1). Then Jesus taught them the prayer that we know today as the Our Father, or the Lord's Prayer. A short version of the prayer is found in Luke 11:2–4 and a long version in Matthew 6:9–13. The Church's liturgical tradition has followed Matthew's long version, which has seven petitions. Let's take a look at the prayer as we recite it today.

115

FYI In her book *The Way of Perfection,* Saint Teresa of Avila teaches us to pray the Our Father with sincere hearts. She reminds us that Jesus is right there praying with us as our brother. When we pray together, our Father "must bear with us, however great our offenses," Teresa says. And however good an earthly father is, God surpasses all in goodness. "He must cherish us; he must sustain us," Teresa assures us.

Presentation (cont'd)

◆ Read together *Catholic Teachings* on page 116. Discuss the ways the Our Father is a summary of the whole gospel.

◆ Allow a few minutes for the young people to write their prayers in the space provided for the ⚡**thought provoker** on page 116.

◆ Have the young people form small groups to discuss *Things to Share*.

Have the young people respond to the first question in *Things to Think About* by writing in their journals.

Conclusion ___ min.

Assessment: You may want to administer a cumulative review test by having the young people work with partners to complete the *Final Assessment*, pages 126 and 127. If you are administering *Chapter 14 Assessment*, page 117A, allow five to ten minutes for its completion.

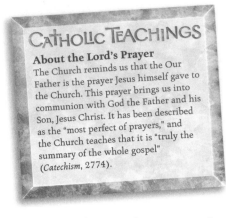

CATHOLIC TEACHINGS

About the Lord's Prayer

The Church reminds us that the Our Father is the prayer Jesus himself gave to the Church. This prayer brings us into communion with God the Father and his Son, Jesus Christ. It has been described as the "most perfect of prayers," and the Church teaches that it is "truly the summary of the whole gospel" (*Catechism*, 2774).

Our Father, who art in heaven We open the prayer by calling God our Father. We dare to do this because by Baptism into the death and resurrection of Jesus Christ, we are the adopted sons and daughters of God. Baptism makes us children of God. Jesus invited us to say, not *my* Father, but *our* Father, reminding us that we pray as baptized members of the Church community.

Hallowed be thy name In this first petition we proclaim that God alone is holy. Standing before the awesome mystery of God, we cry out using the words that come from the prophet Isaiah: "Holy, holy, holy" (Isaiah 6:3). This is what the word *hallowed* means: "holy." God, who is so completely different from anyone or anything that we know, always remains a mystery. But he has revealed himself to us and has done this most fully in Jesus.

Thy kingdom come To be part of God's kingdom means to be loved and protected by God. The kingdom of God is a symbol reminding everyone that God is the Lord of the universe, who takes care of his people and brings them salvation. The kingdom of God is God's rule and reign over people's lives. In this petition we pray that the kingdom will become a reality for all people.

Thy will be done on earth as it is in heaven This petition is connected to the first two. It reminds us that Jesus said, "Not everyone who says to me, 'Lord, Lord,' will enter the kingdom of heaven, but only the one who does the will of my Father in heaven" (Matthew 7:21). As children of God we have to be people who actively proclaim God's holiness and work for his kingdom.

Give us this day our daily bread Trusting in God as his children, we pray for our nourishment, both physical and spiritual. Only God can truly satisfy the hungers of the world. This petition reminds us that so many in the world go to bed hungry each night for lack of bread. So we must realize our responsibility to care for those less fortunate, who are victims of poverty and oppression. Because we are followers of Jesus, we pledge to work at changing any situation that supports injustice. This petition also reminds us of the Eucharist, the Bread of Life.

And forgive us our trespasses as we forgive those who trespass against us In this fifth petition we admit that we must forgive others if we hope to receive God's forgiveness. It's as simple as that.

And lead us not into temptation God does not tempt us, nor will God let us be tempted beyond our strength. We pray that we may always choose to do God's will, as the Holy Spirit guides and strengthens us.

But deliver us from evil Everyone has to struggle against evil. But we know that Jesus has saved us from sin. He sends the Holy Spirit, who brings us the grace to live in hope.

Choose one petition of the Our Father. Then write a prayer of your own, using that petition as your focus or theme. Share it with others.

116

Answers for Chapter 14 Assessment

1. c 2. a 3. b 4. c 5. a

6. c 7. a 8. c 9. d 10. Accept reasonable responses.

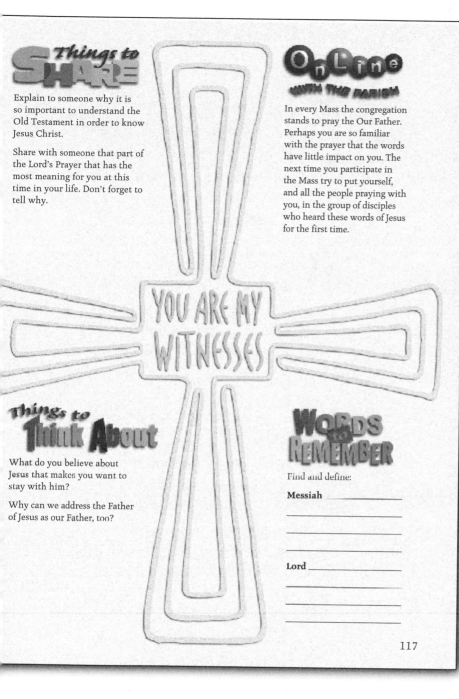

Things to SHARE

Explain to someone why it is so important to understand the Old Testament in order to know Jesus Christ.

Share with someone that part of the Lord's Prayer that has the most meaning for you at this time in your life. Don't forget to tell why.

On Line WITH THE PARISH

In every Mass the congregation stands to pray the Our Father. Perhaps you are so familiar with the prayer that the words have little impact on you. The next time you participate in the Mass try to put yourself, and all the people praying with you, in the group of disciples who heard these words of Jesus for the first time.

YOU ARE MY WITNESSES

Things to Think About

What do you believe about Jesus that makes you want to stay with him?

Why can we address the Father of Jesus as our Father, too?

Words to REMEMBER

Find and define:

Messiah _____
_____
_____
_____

Lord _____
_____
_____
_____

117

Conclusion (cont'd)

◆ Read together *On Line with the Parish*. Remind the young people that we also proclaim the Our Father at Baptism and Confirmation.

◆ Direct attention to *Words to Remember*. The explanation of *Messiah* and *Lord* is on page 114.

◆ Encourage the young people to share *Highlights for Home*, page 117B, with their families.

Closing Prayer: Listen to a recording of or sing "Abba! Father!" by Carey Landry. The lyrics and music can be found in the *Glory & Praise* hymnal. Then pray together the Our Father. Encourage the young people to share the prayers they have written for the *thought provoker*.

Evaluation: Do the young people understand that in bringing God's forgiveness to all people, Jesus let everyone know that he was the Messiah and Lord? Have they explored the meaning of the verses of the Our Father.

Assessment

1 The biblical authors
 a. divided their books into chapters.
 b. divided their books into verses.
 c. did not divide their books into chapters and verses.
 d. none of the above

2 Jesus showed his divinity by
 a. forgiving sins and working miracles.
 b. calling disciples to follow him.
 c. preaching to crowds.
 d. being baptized by John.

3 The word *messiah* means
 a. "a great prophet."
 b. "the anointed one."
 c. "one who has authority."
 d. "descendant of David."

4 Circle the one that does *not* belong.
When we say Jesus Christ, we are really saying
 a. Jesus, Son of God.
 b. Jesus the Messiah.
 c. Jesus' last name.
 d. Jesus the Anointed One.

5 In the gospels, Jesus is described as
 a. being frequently at prayer.
 b. only praying after his baptism.
 c. never addressing God as Father.
 d. only praying with others.

6 The verse "our daily bread" in the Our Father refers to
 a. only physical nourishment.
 b. only spiritual nourishment.
 c. physical and spiritual nourishment.
 d. none of the above

7 Circle the *false* statement about Jesus.
 a. He denied his humanity.
 b. He prayed on the cross.
 c. He had the authority to forgive sins.
 d. Jesus is the Lord.

8 *Abba* was used
 a. to mean "anointed one."
 b. to mean "first and last."
 c. to express affection for one's father.
 d. to refer to the Blessed Trinity.

9 Matthew's version of the Our Father
 a. is not used in the liturgy.
 b. has no petitions.
 c. is shorter than Luke's version.
 d. has seven petitions.

10 Choose one petition of the Our Father and explain its meaning.

_____

_____

_____

_____

_____

© William H. Sadlier, Inc. Permission to duplicate is granted to the users of the *Faith and Witness* Program.

Highlights for Home

Focus on Faith

It is the perfect prayer. Most of us learned it at our mother's or father's knee. Saint Augustine said it contained everything in all of the other Scripture prayers put together. Saint Thomas Aquinas observed that it united all the things we could "rightly desire." The Lord's Prayer, given to us by Jesus, expresses our unity as the sons and daughters of God.

"Lord, teach us to pray," asked the disciples, recognizing their need to become more like the one they followed. And Jesus responded, "This is how you are to pray: Our Father in heaven . . ." (Matthew 6:9). In Aramaic he may have prayed "Abba" or "Dad," expressing his astounding intimacy with the God of Abraham and Moses. Whoever heard Jesus pray in these words knew that a totally new revelation had come. The Son of God, who could forgive sins and heal the sick, shared with his friends the privilege of praying "Abba."

As parents, you have the privilege of sharing the meaning of the Our Father with your sons and daughters. May we find ways to let our young people know that we treasure this prayer.

Conversation Starters

. . . . a few ideas to talk about together . . . .

◆ What can we as a family do to give the needy their "daily bread"?

◆ Is there anyone we (or I) have not yet forgiven? How might praying the Our Father help?

◆ What will I do to avoid those persons, places, or things that might tempt me beyond my strength?

Feature Focus

The *Catholic Teachings* feature on page 116 reminds us that the Our Father has been called a summary of the whole gospel. This prayer brings us into communion with God the Father and his Son, Jesus Christ. When we live by these seven petitions, we ourselves become living gospels, evangelizers of the good news.

Reflection

In a quiet place where you can be alone, relax in the presence of the Lord. Ask yourself, "Whom do I need to forgive?" Ask Jesus to help you to understand why this person or these persons may have offended you. Ask yourself, "Is the person fearful? intimidated? jealous? insecure? swayed by peer pressure? stressed out? Have I offended this person or these persons?"

Then pray slowly and mindfully:

Forgive us our sins as we forgive those who trespass against us.

JESUS IN ART

Adult Focus

This section celebrates multiple reflections of Jesus Christ in art evoked by Scripture. It invites the young people to contemplate the beauty, the mystery, and the universality of Jesus, who belongs to the world in every age. The Church reminds us:

> Sacred art is true and beautiful when its form corresponds to its particular vocation: evoking and glorifying, in faith and adoration, the transcendent mystery of God—the surpassing invisible beauty of truth and love visible in Christ. . .
>
> *Catechism*, 2502

Through the works of great masters like Rembrant and Velasquez, the text draws the young people into prayerful reflection on Jesus. Scriptural themes are explored in each session as the young people focus on gospel passages harmonized with selected paintings and Scripture.

Poet and artist William Blake once observed, "I myself do nothing. The Holy Spirit accomplishes all through me." In that sense, this section is a celebration of the Holy Spirit who empowered the artists and who guides the beholders.

Catechism Focus

The theme of this section corresponds to paragraphs 525, 533–534, 547, 604–607, 643–644 and 2501–2502 of the *Catechism*.

Enrichment Activities

Touring a Museum

If possible, plan a field trip to a museum where sacred art is exhibited. If necessary, seek a knowledgeable guide who can make connections between the art and the scriptural accounts. Or, plan a "virtual" tour by selecting segments from videos like *Vatican City: Art and Glory, Christ in Art* (both from Ignatius Press), and *In the Footsteps of Peter* (Wellspring Media, 1-800-722-6705).

Sharing the Riches

Plan a visit to a Catholic senior residence where the young people can share the artwork in this section with the sick and elderly. They might invite the seniors to choose their favorite paintings and Scripture passages from the text. They might also read aloud from the gospels to those who are visually-impaired. Conclude with a sing-a-long of familiar hymns and share refreshments.

Teaching Resources

Overview

To celebrate multiple reflections of Jesus Christ in art evoked by Scripture.

Materials—Session 1

- Bibles and journals
- group assignments on index cards
- art supplies

- recording of "He Came Down," *Many & Great* (GIA)
- lyrics and/or recording of Christmas carol

Materials—Session 2

- Bibles and journals
- parish hymnals
- "Your Words Are Spirit and "Life" by Bernadette Farrell (OCP)

Materials—Session 3

- Bibles and journals
- *Glory Day* video or album

St. Anthony Messenger/
Franciscan Communications
1615 Republic Street
Cincinnati, OH 45210

New Testament Journal:
Use pages 60–63.

Objective: To explore the ways some artists have depicted the infancy and childhood of Jesus.

Introduction ___ min.

Opening Prayer: Proclaim together Luke 2:11 at the top of page 178. You may want to sing a traditional or contemporary Christmas carol.

Presentation ___ min.

◆ Explain that today's art, Scripture, and music reflection explores how various artists have depicted the infancy and childhood of Jesus. Call on volunteers to respond to the question on this page.

◆ Divide into small groups of "Art Amplifiers." Distribute Bibles and art supplies. Have these paintings and gospel citations listed on the board:
- *Madonna and Child* (Luke 2:1–14)
- *Adoration of the Shepherds* (Luke 2:15–18)
- *The Passover in the Holy Family* (Matthew 26:17–19)
- *Hopi Virgin and Child* (Luke 2:25–35)
- *The Holy Family* (Luke 2:41–52).

For each of the five works of art, a group member reads aloud the assigned gospel passage. The group then shares insights on the following questions (on index cards for group leaders).

- How does the African *Madonna and Child* reflect the message of the gospel passage? What material does the artist use? What does this piece of art express about the artist's vision of who Jesus is for him?

- How does De LaTour's painting communicate the message of Luke's "The Visit of the Shepherds"? What feelings does it convey to you? Does it bother you that the artist puts the birth of Christ in seventeenth-century France? Why or why not?

- What possible connections do you see between Rossetti's painting and Matthew's "Preparations for the Passover"? (Clues: Joseph is marking the doorframe with the blood of a Passover lamb; Mary is collecting bitter herbs for the Passover supper; John the Baptist is fixing the sandal of Jesus.) What do you think the artist is trying to communicate about the Holy Family?

Jesus in Art

A savior has been born for you who is Messiah and Lord.

Luke 2:11

On these pages we will see some of the ways artists of different ages and cultures have expressed who Jesus is for them. As you reflect on the images and the words of Scripture, you should try to answer Jesus' question: "Who do you say that I am?"

Artists have always been fascinated with the least-known period of Jesus' life: his infancy and childhood. Perhaps because so much is left to the imagination and to faith, the interpretations of the child Jesus seem unlimited and highly personal. Artists often depict him as a member of their own race.

Now listen as a member of your group reads Luke 2:1–14. How do you feel the different pieces of art on these pages reflect the gospel account?

✝ Do you have a favorite image or picture of the Christ child? Describe it.

Madonna and Child
African, 20th century

In this wooden carving an African artist gives Jesus and Mary African features and dresses them in traditional clothing.

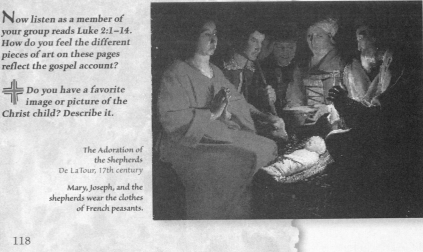

The Adoration of the Shepherds
De LaTour, 17th century

Mary, Joseph, and the shepherds wear the clothes of French peasants.

118

The Passover in the Holy Family
Rossetti, 1856

The artist paints the Holy Family preparing, as religious Jews, for the feast of Passover. He even includes Jesus' cousin, the young John the Baptist.

Hopi Virgin and Child 2
Giuliani, 20th century

The artist portrays a Native American Mary and Jesus wearing traditional Hopi clothes.

Read Luke 2:41–52.
Christ Returning from the Temple with His Parents
Rembrandt, 1654

In this etching the artist depicts Jesus, Mary, and Joseph returning to Nazareth from Jerusalem.

✝ *If you were able to paint or carve an image of the child Jesus, what would you want to show?*

119

Allow about fifteen minutes before sharing key insights from each group.

• Invite the young people to use art materials to respond to the closing question at the bottom of page 119. (At this time they might do a rough sketch of a painting, a wood carving, or a clay model to work on.)

Conclusion ___ min.

◆ At this time you may want to show a segment of Lucien Deiss' musical video *Mary of Nazareth* (OCP) to amplify the impact of today's reflection. Consider "Part Two: A Journey into the Heart of the Holy Family." The video is available from:

Oregon Catholic Press
5536 NE Hassalo
Portland, OR 97213

Closing Prayer: Invite the young people to sing and move to the lively song "He Came Down" from the Iona Community album of world music *Many & Great* (GIA). As an alternative, they might sing a carol like "Go Tell It On the Mountain."

• How does Father Guiliani's *Hopi Virgin and Child* reflect the message of "The Presentation in the Temple" from Luke's Gospel? What do both mother and son seem to know? What is the main impression this Native American art conveys to you about Mary and Jesus?

• What connections do you see between Rembrandt's painting and "The Boy Jesus in the Temple" (Luke 2:41–52)? How would you describe the relationship of the boy Jesus and his parents?

FOR SESSION 2

• preparations for opening prayer
• parish hymnals
• "Your Words Are Spirit and Life" by Bernadette Farrell (OCP) (optional)

Objective: To explore some artists' interpretations of Jesus in his teaching ministry.

Introduction ___ min.

Opening Prayer: Proclaim together John 6:63.

Invite the young people to write in their journals the words of Jesus that give them "spirit and life."

Presentation ___ min.

◆ Invite the young people to imagine themselves as a Rembrandt, a Michelangelo, or a Vermeer. What teaching of Jesus would they most like to portray? Why? How would they want Jesus to look?

◆ Explain that today's reflection will follow this pattern: Scripture reading aloud, commentary on the art, sung response. Practice the sung response. Suggested: "Your Words Are Spirit and Life" by Bernadette Farrell (*Christ, Be Our Light* album, OCP). The lyrics are in most parish hymnals. Or, choose another refrain familiar to the young people.

• *The First Word:* John 10:14–16
Discuss: Why is this third-century Good Shepherd so appealing? How does he reflect the Jesus whose words we have just heard? What words from this reading do you most want to remember? After the sharing all join in the sung response.

• *The Second Word:* John 4:4–30
Discuss: What feelings about Jesus and the woman of Samaria does the artist William Dyce convey? How does Jesus' living water change her life? Why do you think this one-on-one teaching encounter between Jesus and the woman worked so well? What words from this reading do you most want to remember? (Sung response.)

The words I have spoken to you are spirit and life.

John 6:63

The pictures on these pages show artists' interpretations of Jesus in his ministry of teaching, the main work of his public life. See how each artist depicts Jesus from his own vantage point, artistic style, religious understanding, and culture. Take time to look up and read aloud the Scripture account that each artist portrays.

✝ What words of Jesus give you "spirit and life"? If you were an artist, what teaching of Jesus would you wish to portray? Explain your choice.

Read John 10:14–16.
The Good Shepherd
late 3rd century

This ivory carving is the earliest figure of Jesus we have. The artist depicts him as a young, gentle, Good Shepherd.

The image of Jesus as the Good Shepherd has appealed to artists of every age. Why do you think this is so?

Read John 4:4–30.
The Woman of Samaria
William Dyce, 1806–1864

A weary Jesus asks a Samaritan woman for a drink. In return he offers her "living water." The artist captures the moment just before Jesus changes her life forever.

What "living water" does Jesus offer us?

120

• *The Third Word:* Mark 10:13–16
Discuss: If you were a child in this scene painted by Fritz von Uhde, how would you feel? How does the artist capture the heart of the gospel reading? If an artist were to place Jesus in a contemporary situation with children, what might the painting look like? What words from this reading do you most want to remember? (Sung response.)

Read Mark 10:13–16.
Let the Children Come to Me
Fritz von Uhde, 1884

Uhde, a Dutch artist, places Jesus in a Dutch schoolroom. The artist wanted the children of his time to understand Jesus' love for them.

Imagine that you are an artist. You want to paint this same theme, but in a contemporary setting. What would your painting be like?

Read Luke 10:38–42.
Christ in the House of Martha and Mary
Jan Vermeer, c. 1654–1656

Vermeer pictures Jesus at the home of Martha and Mary. Mary sits listening to Jesus, totally absorbed in him, while Martha complains that she is doing all the work. What do you think Jesus is saying to her?

Read John 13:31–35.
Detail from a Byzantine mosaic in Hagia Sophia 12th century

This Byzantine mosaic shows a serious, thoughtful Jesus in the act of teaching.

• *The Fifth Word:* John 13:31–35
Discuss: How does this ancient Byzantine mosaic fit the Jesus who just spoke to us in the gospel? Why might Jesus have been so serious and thoughtful when teaching the new commandment in John's Gospel? What words from this reading do you most want to remember?

Note: A mosaic is made by placing small stones or tiles into a pattern. Mosaics are usually on walls or floors.

Conclusion ___ min.

Closing Prayer: Have a prayer leader offer these petitions followed by the response: Your words, Lord, are spirit and life.

• Help us to hear you in a world filled with TVs, CDs, VCRs and video games,

• Help us to stay tuned to the Bible when we feel confused, alone, or down on ourselves,

• Help us to remember how much you love us and are counting on us to be lights for the world,

In the name of the Father. . . .

• *The Fourth Word:* Luke 10:38–42
Discuss: What does Vermeer's painting tell us about the relationships among Jesus, Martha, and Mary? How does the artist clarify what our response to Jesus the Teacher should be? What words from this reading do you most want to remember? (Sung response.)

FOR SESSION 3

• preparations for opening prayer
• camcorder (optional)
• *Glory Day* video or album (St. Anthony Messenger Press, or OCP)
• *Christ in Art* video (Ignatius Press) (optional)

Objective: To explore the ways some artists have depicted the crucified and risen Jesus.

Introduction ___ min.

Opening Prayer: If possible, play from the *Glory Day* video or recording "Blest Are They." Read together John 20:29 at the top of page 122.

Have a volunteer read the prayerful activity suggested in the right column at the bottom of page 122.

Presentation ___ min.

◆ Review the opening paragraphs on page 122. Have the young people write or sketch the image of Jesus most needed by our world today. Share on a voluntary basis.

◆ Explain that today's reflection includes: gospel reading aloud, text commentary reading, and response in the form of a prayer written in journals. (If you choose, add these reflection questions.)

• *Christ on the Cross*
  How might looking at this painting every day change you? Why?

• *Donatello's Crucifix*
  The crucifixion is probably the most frequently depicted image in art. Why might this be so?

• *Jesus with Thomas*
  How are we sometimes like Thomas in his doubting? Why?

• *The Supper at Emmaus*
  How do we recognize Jesus in our midst?

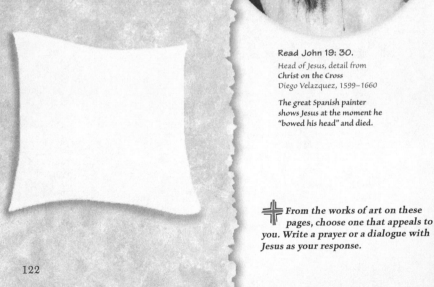

Blessed are those who have not seen and have believed.

John 20:29

The early Christians did not have many images of Christ. Perhaps that is because in times of persecution it would have placed them in danger. The religious images used in the early Church were symbols such as a fish or a lamb or a laurel wreath. The earliest image we have of Christ is the Good Shepherd carving from the third century (see page 120).

It was not until the fourth century that the cross began to appear in Christian art. After that we begin to see many other events of Christ's life depicted.

What images of Jesus do you feel our world needs to see today? Write or sketch your response here.

Read John 19: 30.
Head of Jesus, detail from
Christ on the Cross
Diego Velazquez, 1599–1660

The great Spanish painter shows Jesus at the moment he "bowed his head" and died.

✠ From the works of art on these pages, choose one that appeals to you. Write a prayer or a dialogue with Jesus as your response.

122

Conclusion ___ min.

◆ Have the young people prepare a prayer space to their liking. Display three texts open to the various works of art in this section. Enthrone the Bible. Light battery-operated candles or prayer lamps.

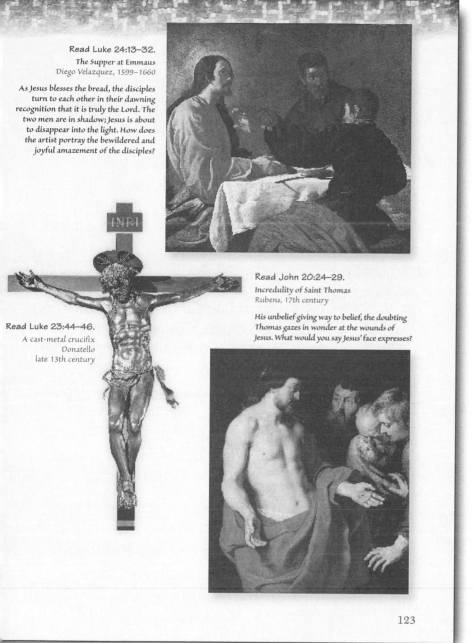

Read Luke 24:13–32.

The Supper at Emmaus
Diego Velazquez, 1599–1660

As Jesus blesses the bread, the disciples turn to each other in their dawning recognition that it is truly the Lord. The two men are in shadow; Jesus is about to disappear into the light. How does the artist portray the bewildered and joyful amazement of the disciples?

Read Luke 23:44–46.

A cast-metal crucifix
Donatello
late 13th century

Read John 20:24–29.

Incredulity of Saint Thomas
Rubens, 17th century

His unbelief giving way to belief, the doubting Thomas gazes in wonder at the wounds of Jesus. What would you say Jesus' face expresses?

123

R2: "A savior has been born for you who is
Messiah and Lord."

All: Save us, Lord, from every evil. You who were once young like us, guide us through our rocky teen years.

R3: "The words I have spoken to you are spirit and life."

All: Lord, help us to hear and understand and be filled with energy and joy.

R4: "Who is this whom even wind and sea obey?"

All: You are Jesus, worker of saving signs and wonders.

R5: "Blessed are those who have not seen and have believed."

All: Lord, we do believe. Help our unbelief!

Stand, link arms over shoulders, sway and sing to one of the *Glory Day* songs like "Song of the Body of Christ." Close with a sign of peace.

Closing Prayer: Choose two volunteers to proclaim the following gospel verses. Group responses as follows:

R1: "Who do you say that I am?"

All: You are Son of God, Savior, Brother, Friend.
You belong to all the world's people.

Name _____

Circle the letter beside the **best** answer.

1 To understand Jesus and the Church fully, we must know
  a. only the Old Testament.
  b. only the letters of Paul.
  c. both the Old and the New Testaments.
  d. only the New Testament.

2 The word *testament* in reference to the Bible means
  a. a covenant with God.
  b. a "last will and testament."
  c. testifying or giving witness.
  d. a book.

3 The Holy Spirit inspired the human authors of the Bible by
  a. dictating each word.
  b. guiding them in choosing the truth God wanted taught.
  c. having nothing to do with the writing until the Church approved it.
  d. appearing to them.

4 The literary form known as gospel is
  a. a letter.
  b. poetry.
  c. an announcement of good news.
  d. a listing of ancestors.

5 _____, a Jewish historian, mentioned Jesus and the early Christians in his history of the Jewish people.
  a. Pilate
  b. Josephus
  c. Nero
  d. Saint Paul

6 According to the _____ theory of inspiration, God alone is the author of the Bible.
  a. Church's theory
  b. God-as-assistant
  c. dictation theory
  d. later-approval

7 The seventy-three books of the Bible are called
  a. the canon of Sacred Scripture.
  b. the Old Testament.
  c. the New Testament.
  d. none of the above

8-10 Put the three stages of the process of the formation of the gospels in the New Testament in the correct sequence.
  a. stage 1   **b.** stage 2   **c.** stage 3
  ___ oral tradition
  ___ written gospels
  ___ life and teachings of Jesus

Define the following terms.

11 Bible _____

_____

_____

_____

_____

12 divine inspiration _____

_____

_____

_____

_____

13 biblical covenant _____

_____

_____

_____

_____

14 apocalyptic writings _____

_____

_____

_____

_____

15 oral tradition _____

_____

_____

_____

_____

16 midrash _____

_____

_____

_____

_____

17 parable _____

_____

_____

_____

_____

18 Explain why the earliest members of the Church relied on oral tradition to share the message of Jesus.

_____

_____

_____

_____

_____

19 Why is it important to know and understand the Jewish people whose heritage Jesus shared?

_____

_____

_____

_____

_____

20 Give one reason we say that the Bible is the Church's book.

_____

_____

_____

_____

_____

For extra credit

Why did the biblical writers make use of many literary forms?

ASSESSMENT

Chapters 8-14

Circle the letter beside the **best** answer.

1 The _____ was the center of Jewish life and worship.
a. Day of Atonement
b. Sabbath
c. Temple
d. struggle

2 The gospels were written
a. while Jesus was alive.
b. immediately following Jesus' resurrection.
c. the mid to latter part of the first century A.D.
d. on Pentecost.

3 The Gospels of Matthew, Mark, and Luke are called synoptic because
a. they have more similarities than differences.
b. they were written by the same author.
c. they were all very different in content.
d. they were all written at the same time.

4 The Gospel of _____ portrays Jesus as the suffering Messiah.
a. Matthew
b. Mark
c. Luke
d. John

5 The Gospel of _____ portrays Jesus as the Savior of the world filled with compassion and mercy.
a. Matthew
b. Mark
c. Luke
d. John

6 The Gospel of _____ portrays Jesus as the great lawgiver and teacher.
a. Matthew
b. Mark
c. Luke
d. John

7 Jesus revealed his divinity by
a. his words about himself.
b. performing miracles.
c. forgiving sins.
d. all of the above

8 When we say "Jesus Christ," we are saying
a. Jesus the Messiah.
b. Jesus' last name is Christ.
c. Jesus the Anointed One.
d. both **a** and **c**

9 The prayer that Jesus taught the apostles is known today as
a. the Apostles' Creed.
b. the Our Father or Lord's Prayer.
c. the Glory to the Father.
d. the Hail Mary.

FINAL

10 At the time of Christ, Israel was part of the _____ Empire.
- **a.** Egyptian
- **b.** Greek
- **c.** Chinese
- **d.** Roman

Define the following terms.

11 sacrifice _____
_____
_____

12 evangelists _____
_____
_____
_____

13 Yahweh _____
_____
_____
_____

14 new commandment _____
_____
_____
_____

15 the Shema _____
_____
_____
_____

16 synagogue _____
_____
_____
_____

17 Explain briefly why Israel was considered the crossroads of the ancient world.
_____
_____
_____

18 Why did the writers of the New Testament choose the word *gospel* to describe the good news of Jesus Christ?
_____
_____
_____

19 Why was the soaring eagle chosen as the symbol for the writer of John's Gospel?
_____
_____
_____

20 Explain the meaning of one of the seven petitions of the Our Father.
_____
_____
_____

For extra credit

Why are the Gospels of Matthew, Mark, and Luke called the synoptic gospels?

Answer Sheet for Semester Tests

Midsemester Test

1. c **2.** a **3.** b **4.** c **5.** b

6. c **7.** a **8.** b **9.** c **10.** a

11. a collection of seventy-three books that were written over a period of many centuries to hand on a message about faith in God

12. the special influence of the Holy Spirit on the human authors of the Bible

13. a solemn agreement between God and his people, legally binding on both sides and confirmed by offering a sacrifice to God or by a solemn ritual

14. This literary form is highly symbolic and often uses images describing future times and the end of the world.

15. what the apostles experienced about Jesus and what they learned from him, passed on by word of mouth

16. a style of writing that the New Testament authors used to apply Old Testament accounts to people in the New Testament

17. a fictitious short story that uses ordinary experiences of life to teach a deeper spiritual lesson

18. See page 17.

19. See page 56.

20. See page 36.

For extra credit: See page 52.

Final Test

1. c **2.** c **3.** a **4.** b **5.** c

6. a **7.** d **8.** d **9.** b **10.** d

11. a gift offered to God by a priest and destroyed in some way to show that it belonged to God alone

12. gospel writers: Matthew, Mark, Luke, and John

13. In Hebrew, the language of the Old Testament, Yahweh was God's name. Yahweh means "'I AM."

14. At the Last Supper, Jesus summarized all his teaching on love and gave his disciples a new commandment.

15. Jesus prayed the Shema each day. The words of the prayer tell us that because there is only one God, we must love him with our whole being.

16. The synagogue was a place of prayer and study in every village and town.

17. See page 73.

18. See page 88.

19. See page 100.

20. See page 116.

For extra credit: See page 90.